Reprogramming the World

Cyberspace and the Geography of Global Order

P.J. BLOUNT

E-INTERNATIONAL RELATIONS PUBLISHING

E-International Relations
www.E-IR.info
Bristol, England
2019

ISBN 978-1-910814-52-9

Production: Michael Tang
Cover Image: spainter_vfx via Shutterstock

A catalogue record for this book is available from the British Library.

E-IR Open Access

Series Editors: Stephen McGlinchey
Books Editor: Cameran Clayton
Editorial assistance: Kaiqing Su, Adeleke Olumide Ogunnoiki, Daniele Irandoost, Sana Salman, Xolisile Ntuli.

E-IR Open Access is a series of scholarly books presented in a format that preferences brevity and accessibility while retaining academic conventions. Each book is available in print and digital versions, and is published under a Creative Commons license. Free versions of all of our books, including this one, are available on the E-International Relations website.

Find out more at: http://www.e-ir.info/publications

About the E-International Relations website

E-International Relations (www.E-IR.info) is the world's leading open access website for students and scholars of international politics, reaching over 3 million unique readers annually. E-IR's daily publications feature expert articles, blogs, reviews and interviews – as well as student learning resources. The website is run by a registered non-profit organisation based in Bristol, UK and staffed with an all-volunteer team of students and scholars.

Acknowledgements

This research has been supported throughout by a number of individuals. Scholarly support came from Prof. Jean-Marc Coicaud, Prof. Yale Ferguson, Prof. Ellen Goodman, and Prof. David Post. Each of these individuals gave valuable feedback during the drafting process. In addition to their support, the scholarship of each of these individuals played an important role in the final product. I would also like to thank Prof. Joanne Gabrynowicz who asked me to develop an International Telecommunications Law class at the University of Mississippi School of Law. The material gathered for that course was the bedrock on which this research is built. Additionally, I would like to thank T.J. Koger who helped me gather the materials that made up the initial syllabi in this class. Numerous friends who, though not subject matter experts, engaged repeatedly with me in discussions of my topic and posed challenging questions that shaped my thinking. In particular, I would like to thank: Wil Cook, David Molina, Christopher Hearsey, Jeff Benvenuto, Matthew Holly, and James Woods. My family for their support. My parents, Percy and Sandra Blount, provided me with a computer well before they were household items (a Commodore 64 is the first computer I remember), but also succumbed to my requests to get an Internet connection in 1994. One might argue that I've been thinking about this book ever since. Finally, I'd like to thank my wife, Kelly Blount, for tolerating this project and its associated stacks of papers and books. I could not have done it without you, my love.

Contents

Table of Abbreviations

AOL	America Online
CB	Citizen Band Radio
DBS	Direct Broadcasting Satellite
DMCA	Digital Millennium Copyright Act
DNS	Domain Name System
FTP	File Transfer Protocol
HTML	Hypertext Markup Language
HTTP	Hypertext Transfer Protocol
HTTPS	Hypertext Transfer Protocol Secure
IANA	Internet Assigned Numbers Authority
ICANN	Internet Corporation for Assigned Names and Numbers
ICP	Internet Content Provider
IETF	Internet Engineering Task Force
IGC	Internet Governance Communities
IO	International Organization
IoT	Internet of Things
IRC	Internet Relay Chat
ISOC	Internet Society
ISP	Internet Service Provider
ITAR	International Traffic in Arms Regulations
ITU	International Telecommunication Union
NGO	Nongovernmental Organization
NSA	National Security Agency
NSF	National Science Foundation
MNC	Multinational Corporation
PCLOB	Privacy and Civil Liberties Oversight Board
PGP	Pretty Good Privacy
PP-14	ITU Plenipotentiary Conference 2014
PSP	President's Surveillance Program
R2P	Responsibility to Protect
TCP/IP	Transfer Control Protocol/Internet Protocol
TV	Television
UDHR	Universal Declaration of Human Rights
UDRP	Universal Dispute Resolution Policy
UK	United Kingdom
UN	United Nations
UNCOPUOS	UN Committee on the Peaceful Uses of Outer Space
UNGA	General Assembly
URI	Uniform Resource Identifier
URL	Uniform Resource Locater
US	United States
USML	United States Munitions List

| W3C | World Wide Web Consortium |
| WWW | World Wide Web |

Introduction

"Sir, line your borders with soldiers, arm them with bayonets to keep out all the dangerous books which may appear, and these books, excuse the expression, will pass between their legs and fly over their heads and reach us."

Denis Diderot

1

The Problem of New Spaces

In June of 2013, Edward Snowden ignited a global debate about the nature of government surveillance in the electronic sphere. The government documents leaked by the former National Security Agency (NSA) contractor revealed mass electronic surveillance by the United States and a number of partner governments such as the United Kingdom.[1] These leaks raised serious legal, political, and ethical questions about the nature of individual privacy in the face of secret government surveillance programs. The dominant narrative of the Snowden affair, as it unfolded in the media, was one of expanding government power impinging on individual rights in the electronic sphere. There was also a counter narrative involved in this incident that exhibits a complementary ebbing of the state's power to control information.

Perhaps the best illustration of this counter narrative is the farcical vignette that takes place in the basement of *The Guardian*'s building in London. In July of 2013, "a senior editor and a Guardian computer expert used angle grinders and other tools to pulverize the hard drives and memory chips on which the encrypted" leaks from Snowden were stored.[2] These two men were overseen by note-taking government officials who had ordered the destruction of the equipment.[3] This scene functions as a tableau that illustrates the core issue that Snowden exposed: the increasing dissonance Cyberspace causes in the application of state power. In *The Guardian*'s basement, the state appears in physical form and asserts a right to control information based on physical realities. It uses legal and physical coercion to destroy a machine that contains information.

---

[1]   Greenwald & Ball, "The Top Secret Rules That Allow NSA to Use US Data without a Warrant," (2014); Hopkins & Borger, "Exclusive: NSA Pays £100m in Secret Funding for GCHQ," (2013); and Dorling, "Snowden Reveals Australia's Links to US Spy Web," (2013).
[2]   Borger, "NSA Files: Why The Guardian in London Destroyed Hard Drives of Leaked Files," (2014).
[3]   *Id.*

In the pre-digital era, the same tableau might have been one of police destroying a printing press; the destruction of a printing press being an efficient means of containing information and destroying a message. In the digital age, the UK government remained insistent on this same method of control. It physically destroyed the machinery of the newspaper, despite the fact "that other copies of the files existed outside the country and that *The Guardian* was neither the sole recipient nor steward of the files leaked by Snowden."[4] The effectiveness of the state's power to coerce is limited within a specific space and time, because the object of its control existed outside the space of the state. More *specifically*, not only was this information outside of the space of the UK, it existed outside the space of any state. The leaks themselves existed in a global space. In the past, the rationale for destroying the printing press was linked to its locality and its central position in the distribution network for its messages. Now, the message is no longer linked to the locality of the machine, and in McLuhan's word "the medium" has been transfused with "the message."[5] As a result, the state's ability to control information is bounded, and *The Guardian* "preferred to destroy [its] copy rather than hand it back to them or allow the courts to freeze [its] reporting."[6] While the individuals using the angle grinders are helpless in the face of the state, the state is helpless in the face of technology: reporting on the leaks continued. Interestingly, the very leaks being destroyed exposed how states are attempting to shift this proposition and reassert power to control information.

New spaces create unique governance issues. This theme can be traced through the historical development of the international system of governance, which is tied to the conceptualization and division of space. From empires to Westphalian states to the modern state, the way in which global space is conceptualized, divided, and compartmentalized is a critical component in understanding the distribution of governance across the globe. This research takes up this thread and argues that Cyberspace creates an alternative geography that is facilitating a respatialization of the world. This respatial- ization, from an international space to a global space, is directly tied to the networkization of real space that creates new abutments and intersections with Cyberspace.

Specifically, the argument herein is that Cyberspace recodes international borders in such a way that international governance has been unable to effectively regulate Cyberspace. The traditional understanding of international space is centered on the state-centric system that developed post-

---

[4]   *Id.*

[5]   Brate, *Technomanifestos* (2002) 195-200.

[6]   Borger, "NSA Files" (2014).

Westphalia, and it entrenches itself in the post-1945 settlement. International space is thus defined by the sovereign equality of nation states that are defined by specific territorial borders. The international geography in this spatial order is an articulation of national spaces and an expression of sovereignty. This geographical shift in borders is not a matter of shifts in physical terrain. Instead, this study understands territory as "a political and legal concept, and not merely a geographical term."[7] Changes in geography require that both the practice and theory of international law and international relations be reevaluated in light of the opening up of a global digital information space that exists external to international space.

As is evident in the episode in the London basement from above, this project does not claim that the state is devoid of power, and certainly not that the state is breathing its last gasps. The state still maintains the primary authority and legitimacy to compel the individuals located within its borders to comply with regulatory mechanisms, and this power is reified through the system of international governance. Instead, the claim here is that the geography of Cyberspace dramatically changes state power in ways that both strengthen and weaken the state. In a global geography the state becomes only one subject among many in global space. While this bifurcation of the international from the global may seem like an exercise in semantics, it represents deeper questions about the notion of governance system at a world-scale. The international system is premised on the state as a primary actor, but the idea of globality acknowledges other actors and thus other participants in the construction of governance mechanisms. Globality in this sense is a spatial geography that encompasses the state system, but is not defined in terms of the borders of that system. It is a geography that serves as an alternative to geography defined by the borders of states and the political-legal content of those borders.

Technology and the Global

It is no coincidence that "ages" of human time are often named after the dominant technology: stone age, iron age, bronze age, machine age, atomic age, space age. These references to technology carry the implication that the named technology was instrumental in shifting social relations and power structures in human society within the span of a temporal bracket. The contemporary Information Age is no different. The Information Age moniker suggests that world power structures are being shaped by Information Communication Technologies (ICT). As such, it is a natural place for inquiry into how governance systems that operate globally are being reshaped by digitized information.

---

[7]   Arendt, *Eichmann in Jerusalem* (1963) 262.

This brings us to the central problem taken up by this research. International law has historically been capable of governing technologies that have transnational effects.[8] The primary example being the law of the sea, which since the historic debate between *mare liberum* and *mare clausum* in the 1600s, has been able to adapt to changes in technology that have increased the state's ability to extend claims over the sea abutting their borders.[9] This trend can be traced throughout the history of international law: the telegraph emerged in the 1830s and in 1865 the International Telegraph Union was formed to govern transnational telegraphy and it absorbed telephone and broadcast technologies in due course;[10] Little Boy was dropped on Hiroshima in 1945 and the Partial Test Ban Treaty entered into force in 1963 followed by the Non-proliferation Treaty (NPT) in 1970; and Sputnik was launched in 1957 and the Outer Space Treaty entered into force in 1967.

The first Internet connection was established in 1968, and the network quickly grew after that with a successful public demonstration in 1972.[11] Today, it goes without saying that Cyberspace has become ubiquitous in everyday life and that it facilitates new types of transnational exchanges. Unlike past transnational technologies, though, international law has been slow to react to Cyberspace. To date only one multilateral treaty dealing directly with Cyberspace has been negotiated. The Budapest Convention on Cybercrime was promulgated though the Council of Europe and has few state parties from outside of Europe. [12] Additionally, the Treaty's requirements are limited to creating regulatory harmony on Cybercrime, and it vests this power into the states themselves in the form of obligations for state parties to adopt legislation. Indeed, much of the problem behind negotiating a treaty is that states are skeptical about trade-offs, meaning that topics such as cyberwar, cyber intelligence gathering, content restrictions, privacy and other human rights, and national security are likely to be excluded from any international agreement on Cyberspace.[13]

International law scholars have struggled with this exact issue, and the scholarship is marked by attempts to identify international norms that govern Cyberspace. Power and Tobin argue for "soft law" principles to govern the Internet in the face of the dearth of international law, and the soft law sources

---

[8]   *See generally* Lyall, "Reaction of International Law to Technical Developments" (2018).

[9]   Shaw, *International Law* (1997) 390–392.

[10]   Codding Jr, "The International Telecommunications Union" (1994) 502.

[11]   Leiner *et al.*, "A Brief History of the Internet" (2012).

[12]   *Convention on Cybercrime* (2004).

[13]   Sofaer, Clark & Diffie, "Cyber Security and International Agreements" (2010) 191. *See also* Dunlap, "Perspectives for Cyberstrategists on Cyberlaw for Cyberwar" (2013) 273.

they identify are often external to international governance meaning that they have to argue for a new understanding of international legal processes.[14] Similarly, Zalnieriute argues for the existence of a customary international norm on data privacy, but she has to advocate for a "modernist" understanding of customary international law, a formulation likely to be found unacceptable by a majority of states.[15] A final example is Kulesza's volume titled *International Internet Law*, which argues that some international mechanisms can be extended into Cyberspace, but spends substantial time discussing other systems of regulation including an entire chapter on domestic law.[16]

The question of why international governance has been unable to extend its reach effectively to Cyberspace as a technology, despite its ability to regulate other transnational technologies, is the primary jumping off point for this research. This broad question has several specific questions that must be answered in order to draw conclusions. The first of these questions is fundamental in international law: where is Cyberspace? In the territorial oriented body of international governance, the location of actions and actors is a threshold question for determining applicable law. Next, we must ask whether the location that is identified for Cyberspace fits into any of the categories understood by international law. If so, then baseline international norms can be established for Cyberspace. If it does not, then we must ask how this new category of Cyberspace interacts with international space. Such interactions will reveal the specific sites at which international governance runs out and is unable to extend its reach.

Similar questions have been addressed in the literature on globalization, which at its core is about the changing of the spatial terms of the world.[17] This research, though closely connected, does not intend to situate itself within this body of scholarship. Globalization is often conceived of as a "respatialization" that "has geographical scope, volume, and density of transactions."[18] Some theorists view globalization as a process, while others consider the term to indicate a theory, and still others use it to indicate a

---

[14] Power & Tobin, "Soft Law for the Internet, Lessons from International Law" (2011) 39–44.

[15] Zalnieriute, "An International Constitutional Moment for Data Privacy in the Times of Mass-Surveillance" (2015) 99–133.

[16] Kulesza, *International Internet Law* (2013).

[17] Cooper, "What Is the Concept of Globalization Good For?" (2001) 196; Jayakar, "Globalization and the Legitimacy of International Telecommunications Standard-Setting Organizations" (1998) 713; Goodhart, "Human Rights and Global Democracy" (2008) 396–97.

[18] Ferguson & Mansbach, *Globalization* (2012) 41–42.

specific temporal era.[19] Others reject it as a "fad."[20] The literature on the whole, though, places into question the "constellation" of international space.[21] Reference to ICT is almost obligatory in these works as it is associated with shortening space and time and facilitating global flows, but globalization theory has "economic roots."[22] In this context, technology is not ignored, but it often is given a supporting role in the shaping of world-scale governance,[23] thereby pushing technology to the edges of the inquiry.[24] For instance, Jayakar analyzes globalization in terms of commercial interests in ICT standard setting bodies, but never addresses how the technology itself is shaping the space in which those decisions unfold.[25] Thus, despite globalization literature's preoccupation with flows and interconnections of all types, there is little scholarship that tries to understand how technology itself serves as an endogenous factor that shapes the space in which flows and interconnections unfold.[26] The scholarship most often presents technology as an external factor best understood in terms of disciplinarily accepted points of inquiry such as conflict or the global political economy. While globalization implies "expanding integration, and integration on a planetary scale," global space itself has been ill-defined.[27] Indeed, one of the deep problems with the definition of global space is that it is often presented as a counterfactual to international space, and not as an independent spatial structure existing autonomously from international space.[28]

To some extent this makes sense. International governance scholarship has often addressed technology as an externality because it was controlled by the state and therefore a function of blood and treasure. The state was the arbiter of technology both through law and policy, and as a result, systems of governance that were established to stabilize states were well suited to establishing frameworks for governing those technologies at the world scale.

---

[19]   *Id. See also* Habermas, *The Postnational Constellation* (2001) 65 and Geyer & Bright, "World History in a Global Age" (1995) 1034–60.

[20]   Cooper, "What is the Concept of Globalization Good For?" (2001) 189–190.

[21]   Habermas, *Postnational Constellation* (2001) 60.

[22]   Jayakar, "Globalization and the Legitimacy" (1998) 714; Cooper, "What is the Concept of Globalization Good For?" (2001) 196; Sassen, *Territory, Authority, Rights* (2006) 168; and Featherstone & Venn, "Problematizing Global Knowledge and the New Encyclopaedia Project" (2006) 1.

[23]   The concept of "world scale" is borrowed from Sassen, *Territory, Authority, Rights* (2006) 14.

[24]   *But see* Sy, "Global Communications for a More Equitable World" (1999) 333.

[25]   Jayakar, "Globalization and the Legitimacy" (1998) 711–38.

[26]   Fritsch, "Technology and Global Affairs" (2011) 28. *See also* Brate, *Technomanifestos* (2002) 195–200.

[27]   Cooper, "What is the Concept of Globalization Good For?" (2001) 196, 200–201.

[28]   *For example, see,* Jayakar, "Globalization and the Legitimacy" (1998) 737 and Betz & Stevens, *Cyberspace and the State* (2011) 55–56.

This is why the International Telegraph Union was established in 1865 and continues to govern international telecommunications as the International Telecommunication Union (ITU).[29] When the state is addressed as the sole arbiter of power, it means that *international* understandings are applied, which place the state at the center of the inquiry. Such a perspective is functional when the state controls technologies of power. For instance, during the Cold War nuclear weapons were controlled by states, and nuclear politics and power unfolded within the context of the state. Cyberspace is different. The state does not control this technology absolutely, despite the fact that state power often unfolds within the space of Cyberspace. This indicates that Cyberspace has a different scope and meaning than previous technologies that function at a global scale, such as nuclear and space technologies. This leaves theory somewhat in the lurch, as a transnational phenomenon seemingly without international control maintains and propagates itself throughout society worldwide.

Instead of a state-oriented perspective, this research investigates Cyberspace as an "endogenous and political factor deeply embedded in the global system."[30] Where earlier technologies existed as the subject of state power, state power is often addressed here as a subject of Cyberspace. This distinction is important, because it indicates that Cyberspace shapes the space in which governance at all scales unfolds. That is not to say that the state does not shape the space in which Cyberspace unfolds, quite the contrary, states still hold significant power over parts of Cyberspace and social life in general.[31] This is the problem with addressing global space as a counterfactual to the international: it presupposes a zero-sum relationship best understood in terms of either/or. Cyberspace, instead, presents a global space best understood as a co-factual to the national and international. It is a new space that is emerging in addition to international space, and its emergence is central to contemporary structuring of world-scale governance. It is not necessarily a space that is always in a contestation with the national as states maintain interests in Cyberspace and often pursue their interests through Cyberspace. The dynamic interaction at the border of the state and Cyberspace is the focal point of this research, because it is in this dynamic that the reprogramming of international space into global space can be observed.

This research asserts that the key to understanding the unfolding of law and politics at the world scale is through an understanding of how Cyberspace shapes social experience of world space through a key value of

---

[29] *See generally* Codding, "The International Telecommunications Union" (1994) 501.

[30] Fritsch, "Technology and Global Affairs" (2011) 28.

[31] Donnelly, "Human Rights" (1998) 16.

interoperability. Interoperability is the core organizing logic for Cyberspace and it has strong sway over the social construction of Cyberspace as a global space. This value puts a primary focus on facilitating cross-platform, cross-network communications. This study's focus is on the technological landscape of communication flows and how the medium structures and facilitates transnational and global information exchange. This cyber-landscape – addressed below in terms of spatial, legal, and political geography – creates a global space that pushes against international borders challenging the concept of the international. This research asserts that Cyberspace imposes an alternate geography that results in redistribution of governance capabilities from international space to global space. It will trace this redistribution through the examination of interactions often used as focal points in international studies as a way to illustrate how key assumptions based on the territory of the state are being challenged within a new geography.

Layers of Geography

The core goal of this research is to articulate a coherent understanding of whether, how, and why Cyberspace changes international governance space. To do this, it must evaluate the three sub questions identified in the preceding section, namely: where is Cyberspace, does it fit into an existing international spatial category, and finally, how does Cyberspace interact with the international system. In order to accomplish this, this research adopts a two-step analytic methodology. In Part I, it articulates a geography of Cyberspace, and in Part II, it layers cyber-geography onto international geography in order to observe how the two spaces interact.

The first task will be to articulate a holistic geography of Cyberspace in both practical and theoretical terms. Using geography as an heuristic for understanding Cyberspace necessitates an interdisciplinary approach, since scholarship on Cyberspace is dispersed across a number of disciplines. A primary focus will be on works that directly address legal and political theory, but themes from sociology, history, and computer science will be evident in the description of the complex interconnections between technical and social processes. This interdisciplinary approach will be used to conceptualize a geography of Cyberspace by describing its borders and boundaries through its spatial, legal, and political characteristics.

This alternate geography will then be used to facilitate observation of points at which Cyberspace interacts with international geography. These two geographies will be layered in order to observe points of interaction and analyze the content of those interactions in terms of spheres of governance.

This analysis will be executed using terms of international governance, which is understood to contain both international law and international relations. Despite the disciplinary divide between international law and politics, they are clearly entangled. Thus, they are presented here as integrated parts of the international governance system. For ease of application the international will be understood to consist of the system in which the traditional state is the primary subject and object of governance.

It will be argued that cybergeography changes the nature of international geography by giving new meaning to state borders. This argument will employ prominently the work of Carl Schmitt and Saskia Sassen. These two, very different, theorists both work with ideas on how governance systems are deployed across space. In his *Nomos of the Earth*, Schmitt argues that international law springs directly from shifting notions of how political legitimacy is tied to geography. Similarly, in *Territory, Authority, Rights,* Sassen argues that world-scale governance systems are the result of different assemblages of territory, authority, and rights. The posited cybergeography of the first section of this book is argued to cause shifts in our understanding of geography and as a result challenge the assemblage of territory, authority, and rights currently deployed by the international system.

This argument will be supported by thematically grouped case studies that exhibit interactions of Cyberspace with international space, or, in other words, where Cyberspace borders international space. To accomplish this conceptual layering of geographies, a hermeneutic approach that seeks to construct meaning through analysis of media narratives and primary legal and political documents will be used. The methodology will be somewhat similar to Reisman's international incident approach. This approach argues that the epistemic unit in international law is the international incident, which is marked by a conflict among states that leads to clarifications in the content and meaning of international law through the negotiated resolution of incidents.[32] Similarly, the case studies will investigate transnational incidents that would traditionally fall within the realm of international governance and examine how Cyberspace changes the content and meaning of those incidents. The cases chosen are grouped thematically, and these themes have been selected for their salience in revealing the shifting nature of the international. Specifically, the themes are built around the territorial, legal, and political geography of international space in order to match the geography adopted in the first part of the research. This will allow the identification and analysis of encounters where cyber and international geographies come into proximity. As a result these themes reach directly to

---

[32] *See generally* Reisman, "International Incidents" (1984) 1 and Blount, "Renovating Space" (2012) 515–686.

critical issues addressed by the international system: the nature and limitation of interstate conflict; the state's central position in the making of international governance; and the nature and limits of individual human rights.   The selected cases or incidents themselves are archetypical of types often examined in international studies, but the specific incidents should not be taken as archetypical of the interactions they represent.   Instead, they are intended to show trends, as more research would be required to chart these trends across a diverse range of interactions.

The examples used in this research were chosen to reveal a common narrative of governance redistribution. While individual cases may have alternative readings in light of traditional international relations or international law theory, it is submitted that if these theories are maintained across the narrative as a whole, then they become dissonant.   Nor is this research an attempt to disprove more traditional theories. Instead, the goal is to illustrate the multidimensional nature of global space and show the limits of such theories in light of the complex nature of networked world of Cyberspace. Just as this research argues that Cyberspace is separate from international space, so too do traditional theories run separately from the alternative geography presented herein.

This study will limit its scope to understanding how spatial redistribution occurs and how this changes power structures at the world-scale. It will not seek to normalize or naturalize these processes. Though the conclusion will argue that cyber-technologies can act as a facilitator of developing govern-ance at the global level, it does not embrace technological determinism. Indeed, it is well documented that technology is dual use and can be turned from liberation to oppression with ease.[33] Technology itself has no ethical content until it is transfused with the politics of human interaction. It is this political content that will be investigated in this research and not necessarily the virtue or vice of that content.

Definitional Issues

In order to avoid confusion, the usage of a number of terms should be clarified at the outset.   First, Cyberspace should be defined.   Unfortunately, this is trickier than it seems.   Indeed, Chapters 2–4 attempt to give a long-form definition of Cyberspace.   Herein, Cyberspace is understood to be a combination of communications technology, specifically the Internet, and the social sphere that has developed within the communicative space created by these technologies.

---

[33]   Morozov, "Political Repression 2.0" (2011).

Additionally, there are a number of spatial terms that are adopted in this research and the author has attempted to be consistent in their usage throughout. 'Space' is used to designate an area or region in both a physical sense (i.e. the space of a room) and a metaphorical sense (i.e. a safe space for discussion). Implicit in the idea of space is that it has contours, boundaries, and borders that demarcate the extent and nature of that space. This means that the term 'space' is often used with qualifiers that designate the limits of a space: physical space, digital space, legal space, political space. Of note are two spaces that are central to the analysis: 'international space' and 'global space.' 'International space' designates a space that is demarcated by borders that construct sovereign territorial states and thus is constituted by the national borders deployed by international governance mechanisms. It should be noted that in this conception, though highly entangled 'national space' constitutes a separate category from 'international space.' 'International space' is a construct of international governance, and the condition of 'international governance' and 'international space' is often referred to in short hand as 'the international.' 'Global space,' on the other hand, designates a space of world-scale that is not marked by national borders. This type of space exists independent of the state system. It should be noted that while, for the purposes of simplifying this analysis, these two spaces are juxtaposed, they are not always easily severable. Central to this argument is that these spaces overlap and intersect, and that global space, and specifically Cyberspace, is often marked by the borders of international space and vice versa. It is this interaction that is at issue, and juxtaposition serves as a useful tool for examining the interaction between the two spaces.

The idea that spaces have boundaries that demarcate them means that spaces, both physical and metaphorical, can be said to have 'geography.' 'Geography' is used herein as a heuristic to describe the particular structure of a space. In real space, this means a description of the physical attributes of that space. In metaphorical spaces, this means a description of the various limitations that mark the contours of that space. For instance, below 'legal geography' is deployed as a way of understanding jurisdiction, which demarcates the limits of the law's application. The term 'alternative geography' is used to designate the new understanding of geography that Cyberspace creates by juxtaposing it to the accepted geography of the international.

In addition to the spatial terminology, there are a variety of governance terms in use that should be clarified. The core concern of this research is that of governance at the world-scale – and 'governance' is used to designate the network of mechanisms that distribute rights, obligations, and limitations within a society, whether legal, political, economic, or of another nature. In this research, 'law' is most often used to designate formal legal systems exercised by organized government; however, law is occasionally used to designate less formal systems that have high regulatory ability, such as in the 'code is law' principle found in Chapter 3. 'Regulation' on the other hand is used in a very broad sense to designate a variety of mechanisms that serve to exert control over actors in a given system. Regulatory processes, in this sense, do not need to flow from formal processes of law, and may come from informal or non-binding processes external to government action. 'Politics' is part of 'governance,' since politics helps to define the content of law and regulation giving further contours to the space that regulatory mechanisms inhabit.

A Reprogrammed World

The world is being reprogrammed. This statement might seem like a quippy metaphor, but this research argues that it means something much more concrete. The central claim of this book is that digital technologies are rewiring the way that society understands and thinks about global order as Cyberspace changes the content of international borders.

Specifically, this work claims that the techno-social assemblage of Cyberspace is creating new connections across the world, and that these connections are difficult to characterize as purely 'transnational' in scope. This research investigates how these changes are literally affecting geography as understood in the modern international governance system. Cyberspace is argued to present an alternative geography that comes into proximity with international borders. These proximities present instances where we can observe a shift in the landscape in which global affairs unfold.

The idea of a reprogrammed world, then, is one that does double duty. First, it performs a metaphorical function and maps the language of computer science and technology onto the system of global order. Throughout this work, the reader will find the use of these metaphors as a way to explain how digital technologies affect governance. Second, it describes a real and actual process that requires evaluation of the design of the international governance system. While international governance has never been a static process, the reprogramming being described herein is extraordinarily different from previous shifts in international governance. It is not the result of a war or of a contingent of sovereigns negotiating rules; it is a technologically driven process that redistributes power within that system and challenges the core concept of territorial sovereignty.

Understanding the importance of this is as easy as turning on the news, or more accurately connecting to the news. We live in a world of "fake news", data breaches, election hacking, and cyberwarfare. We live in a world in which 280 characters can change everything. Our analog past has been replaced with digital realities. The world itself is being reprogrammed and understanding that phenomenon is critical to understanding the future of global society.

Part I

Networked Geography

"The objective space of a house – its corners, corridors, cellar, rooms – is far less important than what poetically it is endowed with, which is usually a quality with an imaginative or figurative value we can name and feel: thus a house may be haunted, or homelike, or prison like or magical. So space acquires emotion and even rational sense by a kind of poetic process, whereby the vacant or anonymous reaches of distance are converted into meaning for us here."

Edward Said

2

Cyber Landscapes

"What difference does that make, what channel you got?" complains Ed Lindsay while he flips the stations on a television in a boarding house common room. Lindsay, a character in a 1961 episode of *The Twilight Zone*, is frustrated with the rapt attention that his housemates pay to the television. Soon after this exchange, Lindsay retrieves his 1935 console radio from the basement, and he finds that it receives, literally, broadcasts from the past. The radio's mystical power eventually transports Lindsay into the past for which he longs.[1]

The episode, named "Static," avoids the usual, clichéd plot of fear of advancing technology coupled with eroding humanity, so often found in science fiction.[2]   Instead, it makes a more subtle point about technology that is implicit but often overlooked in these narratives, namely that technology shapes the social experience of time and space. Though a permutation of the same broadcast technology, the TV world has different spatial and temporal reference points than does the world of radio. This can be seen in Lindsay's characterization of a musical performance on TV as "ruining a perfectly good song." The values imposed by the TV (video) are different from the values imposed by radio (audio). This is more than just an issue of production quality; it changes the interactions of the individuals within those spaces. Television's visual values prompt Lindsay to refer to his housemates as "hypnotized" as they watch. This is different from the space of radio, which created an interactive social space around its speakers, so when Lindsay reconstructs his space to the 1940s, the radio is not the focal point in the room, instead the focal point is his love interest.

At the surface, this fictional tale is wrapped in a narrative of social fragmentation caused by mass media, but beneath this narrative lies a deeper

---

[1]   "Static," *The Twilight Zone*, season 2, episode 20 (1961).
[2]   *See, for example,* "A Thing About Machines," *The Twilight Zone*, season 1, episode 40 (1960).

theme that sits at the heart of inquiries into modernity: the effects of technology on the construction of social space. What Ed Lindsay observes is that, though analogous, these technologies each change how the world around him is ordered in unique ways. They literally shape the space of the boarding house.

Cyberspace, as a technology, is no different. It shapes space, and it does this because the technology creates unique spatial orientations. The goal of this chapter is to describe the spatial geography of Cyberspace in terms of its technical manifestations, and in terms of the dominant conceptual narrative through which Cyberspace is understood. This description will resist adopting a definition of "Cyberspace" in absolute terms. Part of this impetus comes from the diverse definitions that already exist in the literature describing Cyberspace, but never in complete terms.[3] As a result, the chapters in Part I will focus on describing Cyberspace to facilitate a richer understanding of its contours. This approach flows from a central hypothesis that Cyberspace is a geography in which social relations unfold. Description is thus prioritized over definition due to the difficulty in defining a dynamic space both accurately and coherently. Definition is a tool to simplify concepts. Description, on the other hand, reveals nuance and complexity critical to a rich understanding, as sought herein. This chapter will first use a layered model to describe the technical architecture of the Internet, which is distinct from Cyberspace. Once this technical space has been articulated, the spatial conceptualization of Cyberspace will be explored. Section II of this chapter argues that the dominant human understanding of Cyberspace is through a spatial narrative, and that this narrative has powerful implications for the social conceptualization of Cyberspace. Finally, the chapter will conclude by examining the inhabitants of Cyberspace and the implications of networked populations. The spatial geography of Cyberspace is critical to understanding the larger thesis that Cyberspace recodes borders and reprograms the world.

Networked Space

Ed Lindsay's question of "what does the channel matter" can be answered easily: a lot. The technology of TV is such that choosing a channel means

---

[3]   *For example*, Gompert & Saunders, *Paradox of Power* (2012) 115 ("Cyberspace [is] shorthand for the capabilities and content of computer networking."); Lessig, *Code 2.0* (2006) 9 ("But 'cyberspace' is something more. Though built on top of the Internet, cyberspace is a richer experience."); Toulouse, "Introduction" (1998) 5 (". . . a new transnational realm of civil society . . ."); Luke, "The Politics of Digital Inequality" (1998) 121 ("Cyberspace might best be understood as the latest manifestation of nature's pluralization."); and Betz & Stevens, *Cyberspace and the State* (2011) 13 ("Cyberspace is notoriously difficult to pin down.").

choosing a network – and choosing a network means accepting the content chosen by the network. Changing the channel changes everything, and it was the only way to change the output of the TV. The networks accessible on a given TV are limited by location since broadcast TV is a function of proximity to the transmitter. Furthermore, accessibility was limited to reception from the broadcaster, but not interaction with the broadcaster. The space that TV creates is one of viewers relegated to peering in.

If "Static" were updated for contemporary airing, one could imagine the boarding house crowd all gathered in the common room, but the focal point would be their own personal electronic devices. Ed Lindsay, instead, would yell because they were not taking part in the social act of watching the TV in the common area and building community through the shared experience of viewing. While Lindsay's technological skepticism would be built on substantially the same rhetorical claims, the space in which he would be making his claims would be very different. In this updated version, each individual would be focused on being in Cyberspace and, importantly, interacting with others in Cyberspace. Each individual will have chosen their own channel. Some of these channels, such as services like Pandora or Netflix, mimic previous information technologies. Other channels create vastly different opportunities for engagement and interaction. Indeed, many individuals in this alternate take would be interacting with more individuals as a result of this technology. This simple shift changes the constitution of the common room space, because "the Internet is not like TV – you use it, it doesn't use you."[4]

Technology, in particular information technology, changes human interactions.[5] This is because these technologies are capable of providing more and richer information, and information sits at the core of social interactions. Space is constructed by human technology, and humans experience spaces differently depending on how technology is deployed. Ed Lindsay experiences the common room of the boarding house differently when different technology is deployed. This is similar to trends noted by Cohen in which surveillance technologies alter public space. Surveillance technologies, beyond simple observation, achieve "the active production of categories, narratives, and norms."[6] Cohen argues that these technologies change space by "constrain[ing] the range of available behaviors and norms."[7] Surveillance technology is emblematic of how the "prolifera[tion]" of

---

4   Toulouse, "Introduction" (1998) 12.
5   *For historical examples see*, Burbank & Cooper, *Empires in World History* (2010) 109–110; Mattelart, *Networking the World* (2000) 1–13; and Kellner, "Intellectuals, the New Public Sphere, and Technopolitics" (1998) 175–79.
6   Cohen, "Privacy, Visibility, Transparency, and Exposure" (2008) 181.
7   *Id.* at 190.

"transaction points" changes the experience of physical geography.[8]

Before abandoning a happy Ed Lindsay in the 1940s, we should take a closer look at the nature of the technology that is defining the space in which he lives, or more precisely defining his transaction points. Mass communication in this world is the product of centralized, one-way communication. In this model, power is located at a central position, and is understood as the power to transmit. The entity that controls the transmitter also controls the content that the viewer or listener sees. The end device only receives; none of the knobs or buttons allow the user to send a message back to the transmitter. Mass media in this space is about transmission to the masses that receive it.[9] It is a one-way street, and the space at the receiving end of that street is shaped by this technology. The Internet dismantles this one-way paradigm and presents the user with an array of opportunities to engage in multi-way communication with other individuals, with the masses, and with nearly any other type of entity capable of communication. This fundamental difference creates dramatic changes for the nature of human interaction and social order, because transaction points become myriad and are distributed worldwide.

It is important to note that the Internet is distinct from Cyberspace. The Internet, for present purposes, can be understood as the technology that makes Cyberspace possible.[10] The technology of the Internet facilitates and is inseparably entangled with the phenomenon we know as Cyberspace, which inhabits broader social dimensions. This means that in order to describe Cyberspace, one must first describe the Internet.

A layered model is adopted herein to explain the technical architecture of the Internet. This model "was developed by computer scientists to explain the functional components of the Internet and how they work together to convey Internet traffic."[11] A number of legal scholars have adopted the layered approach to explain policy and regulation on the Internet.[12] While these regulatory aspects will be explored later, at present the layered model presents a useful model for breaking down the component systems that work in concert to make the Internet possible. The layered approach is a "conceptual tool" that "divides a networked information system into a

---

[8]   *Id.* at 200.

[9]   *See* Carey, "A Cultural Approach to Communication" (2002) 36–45.

[10]   Lessig, *Code 2.0* (2004) 9 and Kulesza, *International Internet Law* (2013) 31.

[11]   Goodman & Chen, "Modeling Policy for New Public Service Media Networks" (2010) 115.

[12]   *See* Goodman & Chen, "Modelling Policy" (2010) 116; Werbach, "Breaking the Ice" (2005) 78–80 and Solum & Chung, "The Layers Principle" (2003) 821.

hierarchical 'stack,'"[13] presenting the Internet as a combination of different technologies with different functions stacked together to form the whole. This approach is useful, because the "interconnectivity among networks" is "so complex that it is not easily understood."[14] Layering creates a model for categorizing diverse, yet interrelated, technologies by function and reveals how each "self-contained" category is linked to the layers above and below it.[15]

Different authors have used different stacks of layers. For instance, Post simplifies the Internet into two distinct layers, the network layer and the applications layer[16]; Kulesza uses three layers[17]; whereas Solum and Chung use a six-layer stack (See Fig. 1.1).[18] The differences in the models are not substantive in nature and are, instead, based on the resolution of the analysis of the "conceptual tool."[19] A medium grain four-layer stack will be used here to avoid both oversimplification and unneeded complexity. Werbach and others have identified a four layered stack, which contains a physical layer, a logical layer, an applications layer, and a content layer.[20] This four-layer stack will guide the analysis here.

	Physical Layer	Physical Layer	Physical Layer
Network Layer			Link Layer
	Logical Layer	Logical Layer	IP Layer
			Transport Layer
Applications Layer	Content Layer	Applications Layer	Applications Layer
		Content Layer	Content Layer
Post	**Kulesza**	**Werbach**	**Solum & Chung**

Fig. 1.1: Various Layered Models

---

[13] Werbach, "Breaking the Ice" (2005) 71, 66.

[14] Gompert & Saunders, *Paradox of Power* (2012) 116. *See also* Leiner *et al.*, "A Brief History of the Internet" (2012).

[15] Werbach, "Breaking the Ice" (2005) 66.

[16] Post, *Jefferson's Moose* (2012) 80–83.

[17] Kulesza, *International Internet Law* (2013) 125–126.

[18] Solum & Chung, "Layers Principle" (2003) 816.

[19] Werbach, "Breaking the Ice" (2005) 71.

[20] *Id.*; Werbach, "A Layered Model for Internet Policy" (2002) 37; Reed, "Critiquing the Layered Regulatory Model" (2005) 281; McTaggart, "A Layered Approach to Internet Legal Analysis" (2003) 573; and Lessig, *Code 2.0* (2004) 144–145.

The Physical Layer

At the bottom of the conceptual stack is the physical layer. The physical layer is made of the hardware on which the Internet runs. This hardware consists of routers, servers, cables (copper and fiber optic), cell towers, satellite links, and other telecommunications technologies.[21] This infrastructure is essentially the connective tissue of the Internet, providing the medium through which information is transmitted. The physical layer includes all the physical equipment associated with the Internet. This importantly includes the Internet backbones and telecommunications networks, which provide the physical means through which data flows.

Internet backbones are a group of services providers that connect to route information transfers between autonomous networks.[22] These providers sell internetwork connectivity access to other providers who provide services to third parties such as individual users or corporations.[23] This secondary set of providers are commonly known as Internet service providers (ISP). An Internet backbone

> essentially forms its own network that enables all connected end users and content providers to communicate with one another. End users, however, are generally not interested in communicating just with end users and content providers connected to the same backbone provider; rather, they want to be able to communicate with a wide variety of end users and content providers, regardless of backbone provider. In order to provide end users with such universal connectivity, backbones must interconnect with one another to exchange traffic destined for each other's end users.[24]

Backbones route the flow of information among networks. It is important to note that their function is only the transfer of data. Backbones do not store the information on the Internet; they transmit data among networks.

The backbone providers – and the providers to whom they sell – send data to users via telecommunications networks. For instance, most home users connect to the Internet via telephone wires or coaxial cable – both of which were installed to be used as a medium for different technologies. But users

---

[21]   Werbach, "A Layered Model for Internet Policy" (2002) 60.

[22]   Osgood, "Net Neutrality and the FCC Hack" (2004) 32.

[23]   *Id.*

[24]   Kende, "The Digital Handshake" (2000) 3.

can also connect to the Internet via cellular networks, radio frequency or Wi-Fi, or through dedicated lines. Two things should be noted at this point. First, the Internet is running on a diversity of networks that deploy different connective technologies. This means that it facilitates a high level of inter-operability among diverse technologies. Second, these networks are owned by a diverse group of actors, meaning there is a high level of interoperability among entities. The Internet's functionality is centered on this technological ambivalence towards the medium of transmission as well as the identity of the transmitter or recipient of the transmission. This is dramatically different from previous telecommunications technologies that were regulated according to the specific technological parameters that limited interactivity. For instance, broadcast was regulated according to principles that maximized the efficient use of the scarce electromagnetic spectrum, whereas telephone regulation was used to maximize public access.[25] Technological ambivalence is indicative of a trend that is visible at all layers of the conceptual stack: convergence. Convergence is a process through which the "historical distinctions between communications networks are melting away."[26] Convergence is a product of the logical layer, which is next in the conceptual stack of layers.

The Logical Layer

Convergence occurs at the physical layer because the logical layer re-configures how information is sent over the physical layer. The logical layer consists of the software protocols that define the data being transferred by the Internet. All telecommunications systems transfer data electronically, but traditionally this signal was analog and was limited by the strictures of the technologies that carried analog signals.[27] The advent of computers enabled digitization, which allowed for the same content to be encoded as standardized data or "fundamentally just a string of ones and zeros" that are "ultimately interchangeable, meaning any communications platform can in theory, offer any service."[28]

The heart of the Internet is the Transfer Control Protocol/Internet Protocol

---

[25] *See generally*, Krattenmaker, *Telecommunications Law and Policy* (1998) and Kennedy & Pastor, *An Introduction to International Telecommunications Law* (1996).
[26] Werbach, "Breaking the Ice" (2005) 61. *See also*, Kulesza, *International Internet Law* (2013) 53; McIntosh & Cates, "Hard Travelin'" (1998) 95, 102–03; Tambini, Leonardi, & Marsden, *Codifying Cyberspace* (2008) 3–4; Jayakar, "Globalization and the Legitimacy" (1998) 719.
[27] Leiner *et al.*, "A Brief History of the Internet" (2012).
[28] Werbach, "Breaking the Ice" (2005) 62; Post, "Against 'Against Cyberanarchy'" (2002) 1375–76.

(TCP/IP).[29] This protocol sets the standards for transmission of data on the Internet. It defines two distinct functions. First, it defines how the information being sent should be packaged. Digital information, unlike analog information, is easily severed and reassembled. When information is sent over the Internet, a computer program on the end user's device will slice it up into small packets of data. Each packet is labeled with the order in which it should be reassembled. The second function the TCP/IP describes is the Internet protocol, which places a distinct address on each packet that tells nodes on the network where it should be sent. This process is known as packet switching.[30]

Packet switching revolutionized telecommunications, which to that point transmitted analog signals and depended on circuit switching. Every device on the Internet has an IP address, a numeric identifier for all traffic to and from that device, which is similar to a phone number.[31] Historically when a call was made on a landline, an analog signal was sent that required constant connection to a circuit to the other end of the call.[32] That circuit is connected through a centralized operator, a process known as circuit switching.[33] A visual of this process was a common feature of early television programs, which would often use a split screen to show the operator physically connecting the continuous circuit on a switchboard with a patchcord. Packet switching on the other hand does not require a continuous connection because the information is broken into data packets instead of a continuous analog signal. This means that the packets can be routed via any combination of routes through the network in order to get them to the proper IP address. Instead of a centralized operator, there are decentralized routers and nodes through which a packet travels. This type of networking allows for more efficient transfer speeds by distributing loads across the network.[34] In other words, the packets do not need to travel along the same path or arrive in the same order, so packets are sent along the most efficient route possible. In practical terms this means that an email, for instance, once broken down into packets could travel through numerous different servers located in geographically disperse places. Packet switching avoids the strain on the central operator from which circuit switching suffers.[35]

A number of salient features of this system should be emphasized. First, the

---

[29]   *See* Post, *Jefferson's Moose* (2012) chapters 4–6; Lessig, *Code 2.0* (2006) 43–45, and Clark & Landau, "Untangling Attribution," (2010) 27.

[30]   Brate, *Technomanifestos* (2002) 104–05.

[31]   *See* DeNardis, *The Global War for Internet Governance* (2014) 37–41.

[32]   Leiner *et al.*, "A Brief History of the Internet" (2012).

[33]   *Id.*

[34]   *Id.*

[35]   *See* Post, *Jefferson's Moose* (2012) 47–59.

TCP/IP protocol is designed to transfer a packet regardless of the information it contains. Importantly, as currently configured, the routers on which the protocol runs do not register what is "in" the packet.[36] The router simply passes the packet along to the next waypoint on its journey. This is why the Internet is sometimes called "stupid."[37] The design of the Internet is simply to allow information to be freely transferred among the various nodes on the network meaning that the content of those packets is not stored in the logical layer.[38] Second, this means that the transmission of the data is neutral in regards to the technology on which it travels. The Internet can run over copper cable, fiber optics, electromagnetic frequency, or anything else that can carry electronic communications. TCP/IP provides a standardized manner for packaging and addressing data for transmission. Third, as a result of this technological ambivalence the Internet has the potential to be widely accessible. The Internet is not a single network, it is a network of networks facilitated through a standard protocol. The Internet, when viewed at the protocol layer facilitates the linking of dissimilar networks as data packets can ride on any telecommunication infrastructure.[39] Finally, since the standard protocol is meant to ensure interoperability, the network itself is rhizomatic in nature inasmuch as it is a non-hierarchical assemblage of networks.[40]

It was stated earlier that the logical layer functions as the heart of the Internet. This is because it serves as the vital link between the physical layer below it and the applications layer above it through an "open network architecture," which is the "key underlying technical idea" of the Internet.[41] Open network architecture provides a link among disparate physical layer technologies and disparate applications layer technologies by creating a common language of communication *among* them as opposed to *between* them.[42] The logical layer drives convergence at the physical layer because of these attributes, but this convergence is experienced at the applications layer.

The Applications Layers

The statement that the Internet is "stupid" is based on the logical layer's

---

[36]   This is how the Internet was designed to operate, but it should be noted that deep packet inspection technologies are used by some entities. *See* DeNardis, *Global War* (2014) 206–07.

[37]   Post, *Jefferson's Moose* (2012) 80.

[38]   Leiner *et al.*, "A Brief History of the Internet" (2012).

[39]   Mattelart, *Networking the World* (2000) 4.

[40]   *See* Betz & Stevens, *Cyberspace and the State* (2011) 38; Leiner *et al.*, "A Brief History of the Internet" (2012); and Fielder, "The Internet and Dissent in Authoritarian States" (2013) 168.

[41]   Leiner *et al.*, "A Brief History of the Internet" (2012).

[42]   *Id.*

functionality to be non-discriminatory in the transferring of data packets and is commentary on the popular conceptualization of the Internet as a vast archive of knowledge. The Internet is "stupid" because it is an end to end network, which means intelligence is "vested in the edge."[43] The devices and applications they run at the edges of the network are where the Internet "happens," so to speak. The data packets that the logical layer transmits are only intelligible at the ends of the network, because "the Internet ... was not designed for just one application, but as a general infrastructure on which new applications could be conceived."[44] Essentially, to use a buzz phrase ushered in by smartphones, "there's an app for that."

The World Wide Web (WWW) serves as an excellent example. If asked "what is the Internet?" many people would likely describe it as the WWW as this is still one of the most common ways that people experience the Internet.[45] The WWW is actually an application that runs on a device and functions at the applications layer.[46] A rudimentary explanation of how the WWW works will help to show how the applications layer functions as well as the end-to-end principle. If you want to view a web page you type a Uniform Resource Locator (URL), for instance – http://www.dudeism.com – into your web browser's address bar.[47] The first thing to be noted is that there are multiple web browsers made by a variety of entities including corporations, non-profits, and individual programmers. The web browser then sends a request via your Internet Service Provider (ISP) to a server that contains a file with a list of URL's associated with the .com root name.[48] It searches this list, called a root file, for dudeism.com, and finds the IP address of the device that is associated with dudeism.com through the Domain Name System (DNS). In simple terms, 'dudeism.com' is a text-based identifier for the IP address, which is 64.91.245.254 (as of this writing). The ISP, on your behalf, then contacts this device, which has been configured to act as a server,[49] and

---

43   Lessig, *Code 2.0* (2006) 111.

44   Leiner *et al.*, "A Brief History of the Internet" (2012).

45   *See* Toulouse, "Introduction" (1998) 2 and Betz & Stevens, *Cyberspace and the State* (2011) 13.

46   Leiner *et al.*, "A Brief History of the Internet" (2012) *See also,* Verizon v. FCC, No. 11–1355, 740 F. 3d 623 (Court of Appeals, Dist. of Columbia Circuit 2014) at 36.

47   The HTTP portion of the URL denotes the type of data being sought, in this case it stands for Hypertext Transfer Protocol. This portion of the address is a Uniform Resource Identifier (URI), and it identifies that a hypertext file is being sought. There are numerous URIs indicating the type of data a given application is seeking. These include the common File Transfer Protocol (FTP), Internet Chat Relay (IRC), and HTTP Secure (HTTPS).

48   Partridge & Lonardo, "ICANN Can or Can It?" (2009) 24–29 and DeNardis, *Global War* (2014) 41–44.

49   A server is an application on the applications layer. A server, though usually on specialized hardware, is simply a computer application that makes computer files

looks for a directory named "www." Once there, the browser will look for a default file, most commonly titled "index.html," and the ISP will transfer a copy of this file, which your computer downloads.[50] A copy of the file named index. html now exists on your computer, and your browser opens this file, which contains computer code that a web browser understands and executes. This code tells the browser what to display on your screen. This entire transaction is facilitated by the logical layer and is transferred as digital electromagnetic signals across the physical layer.

In this example, we can see very clearly that the information that we access while connected to the Internet is stored at the periphery. The web page is not "on" the Internet, rather it is accessible via the Internet, and it exists on a connected device. The file that you see is copied to your computer, meaning that information from afar becomes immediately localized, even if temporarily, in the memory of the user's device so that it can be manipulated by the software on that device.[51] This is the end-to-end principle in practice, which is "hard-wired into the Internet's architecture."[52] In technological terms, this is known as "peering."[53] Peering implies equality created between devices through the common protocol. Of course, this is equality in technological terms only and not to be confused with equality in a legal or political sense.

A practical effect of the end-to-end principle is that convergence is experienced by the user at the applications level. Indeed, the "there's an app for that" catchphrase captures this very idea. Convergence is experienced because information can be digitized, and technological ambivalence facilitates a diversity of applications with different outputs. This has resulted in a bloom of technological innovation as applications and networks have proliferated.[54] Possibly the best example is the Internet of Things (IoT)

---

available to other computers on a network. In this case the server has been configured to be open to requests from any network. Servers are essentially file systems configured in a hierarchical directory and can be understood to function in a substantially similar way to the file and folder system found in most desktop operating systems.

[50] Tambini *et al*, *Codifying Cyberspace* (2008)) 7. "index.html" is simply a filename and "index" is an arbitrary default filename for which browsers search as a result of their programming.

[51] Lessig, *Code 2.0* (2006) 268.

[52] Tambini *et al*, *Codifying Cyberspace* (2008) 2.

[53] Leiner *et al.*, "A Brief History of the Internet" (2012).

[54] *See* Tambini *et al*, *Codifying Cyberspace* (2008) 9; Leiner *et al.*, "A Brief History of the Internet" (2012); and Goodman & Chen, "Modeling Policy" (2007) 120. *Compare with* Jayakar, "Globalization and the Legitimacy" (1998) 722; Krattenmaker, *Telecommunications Law and Policy* (1998) 367–69; and American Broadcasting Company v. Aereo, 573 U.S. (2014).

concept in which devices other than traditional computers are being networked for applications such as home automation. IoT allows nearly any machine that can be manipulated by a circuit board to be networked into the spatial geography of Cyberspace. So, for example, there are now lightbulbs on the Internet.[55] Innovation at the applications layer is further driven by the decentralization of the logical layer, which gives more individuals access to information systems.[56]

Another reason that innovation happens at the applications layer is that in order to facilitate interoperability of networks, the protocols of the logical layer are open, allowing anyone with proficient skill in programming to be able to write an application that facilitates new types of information flows. This significantly lowers the cost of development of new products, but it also means that individual programmers can change how Internet communications work – or more precisely change the nature of communications through the applications layer. A good example is Phil Zimmermann, who wrote the Pretty Good Privacy (PGP) program. This public key encryption program was developed to allow users to send secure encrypted messages to other individuals via the Internet.[57] Interestingly, encryption programs like PGP are classified as weaponry under the US International Traffic in Arms Regulations (ITAR).[58] These regulations restricted the export of PGP as a defense article.[59]

The example of PGP illustrates three important things that will be seen in a variety of contexts within this research. First, a single coder changed the nature of Internet transactions. This means that a single individual, taking advantage of the innovation-friendly nature of the end-to-end network, was able to change the possibilities for human interactions on the Internet and in Cyberspace. Second, this technology was unable to be contained by the state. ITAR is specifically directed at the export of weapons technologies that appear on the United States Munitions List (USML). These regulations apply to technology crossing the border of the United States, yet PGP was freely available worldwide soon after its creation, indicating a breach of the space of the state. This availability is driven in part by the ephemeral nature of software, which is easily shared online. Finally, this application, for the purposes at hand, cannot be imbued with normative power. The descriptive bent of this chapter requires that PGP, like all programs at the applications layer, be recognized as a technology that can enable good interactions (e.g. giving voice to political dissidents in repressive regimes) as well as bad

---

[55] Wakefield, "Smart LED Light Bulbs Leak Wi-Fi Passwords" (2014).

[56] Verizon v. FCC (2014) at 36.

[57] Greenberg, *This Machine Kills Secrets* (2012) 70–76.

[58] *Id*. at 72–74.

[59] International Traffic in Arms Regulations, 22 C.F.R. 121.1 Category XII(b) (2018).

interactions (e.g. giving cyber criminals the ability to transmit illicit data free from scrutiny). The innovation facilitated by the applications layer is such that it creates openings for all entities – whether they be normatively good or bad; state or non-state; commercial or criminal; individual or collective – to engage in a variety of measures of control and liberation.

The Content Layer

Content is what concerns most people using the Internet. They neither care to know nor need to know the specifics of the code that is running beneath the content layer at either the application or logical layer. Nor do they likely understand the intricacies of the physical network past their connection to the ISP. They are concerned with content, and in a digital world, content can be just about anything. While sights, sounds, and words have been the traditional domain of the Internet, in no way is the Internet limited to transferring only these types of information.

The Thingiverse website is an online repository of 3D printable objects.[60] Or, more precisely, it is a repository for programs that will instruct a 3D printer to print a specific three-dimensional object. The object itself is not sent through the Internet, but the effect is the same since the object materializes at the user's device. Essentially, if hardware can be developed that can output a type of information digitally at the applications layer, then that data can be transferred across the Internet. The output of end devices is the content layer.

The content layer is, obviously, the layer where most of the public debate on Internet regulation occurs. This is because the interaction of the three layers below the content layer allow for large amounts of data to be transferred quickly to anyone no matter where they are so long as they have network access. The content layer of the Internet is dramatically different from the content layer of previous telecommunications sources, which disaggregated different functions. Broadcast is a one directional method that reaches mass numbers of people, whereas the telephone allowed for bidirectional interactions but not on a mass scale. The centralization of broadcast made it easily susceptible to societal controls over the content whether through regulations or norms. The telephone, on the other hand, offered little control over content, but architecturally minimized the possible reach of the communication.

Content on the Internet is both multidimensional and mass, meaning there is low control over the content and the reach of information. This can most

---

[60]   Thingiverse, https://www.thingiverse.com/ .

clearly be seen in the concerns that numerous states have about content coming in through their borders such as political propaganda or pornography.[61]

Much of the discussion around Internet governance focuses on issues of free speech and censorship centering debate on the content layer. This is because the three underlying layers in concert amplify traditional societal concerns with flows of information. Information now flows across networks that are distributed in nature, permeate borders, and maximize access by individuals. This is a paradigm shift in telecommunication technology, and its effects on society are broad. The content layer is the locus of these effects, as it is the content – whether the content is in the form of economic activity, religious ideology, political activism, or criminal conduct – transmitted via the Internet that creates societal issues.

Cyberspace

A genre of movies and songs from the late 70s and earlier 80s celebrate the culture of Citizen Band (CB) radio. In particular, the film catalog of Burt Reynolds is notable with *Smokey and the Bandit* (1977), *Smokey and the Bandit 2* (1980), *Cannonball Run* (1981), and *Cannonball Run II* (1984). Aficionados might also appreciate television series such as *The Dukes of Hazzard* (1979–1985), *B.J. and the Bear* (1979–1981), and *Movin' On* (1974–1976), and country music offered up a plethora of songs such as C.W. McCall's "Convoy" (1975), Red Sovine's "Teddy Bear" (1976), and Cledus Maggard's "CB Lingo" (1976). These cultural nuggets give a glimpse into a culture built around a network of people that interact on CB radio channels. In these narratives, news often spreads quickly across the network leading to collective group action, which usually finds expression in highway hijinks. The CB goes hand in hand with the automobile as both served as potent symbols of individual autonomy (and it is likely no coincidence that these narratives often glorify running from the law enforcement in high speed chases). One of the most notable things in this genre is that the CB has its own language that socializes the participants in the network. CB in these films is portrayed as more than just a communication technology. Instead, it is the glue that structures the social space of mobility-driven culture.

---

[61] *See generally* Eppenstein & Aisenberg, "Radio Propaganda in the Contexts of International Regulation and the Free Flow of Information as a Human Right" (1979) 54; Robertson, "The Suppression of Pirate Radio Broadcasting" (1982) 71–101; United Nations General Assembly, Res. 37/92: Principles Governing the Use by States of Artificial Earth Satellites for International Direct Television Broadcasting" (1982); and EUTELSAT, "Eutelsat condemns jamming of broadcasts from Iran and renews appeals for decisive action to international regulators" (2012).

If the Internet is a stack of functional layers, then Cyberspace is the Internet with the addition of a social layer.[62] This may seem a little obvious. After all, the Internet is not a natural phenomenon and is a human creation, meaning a social layer may be presupposed. While true, the point here is to highlight something more than just human usage of the technology. It is, instead, to highlight the scope and integration of the Internet into societies globally. The social layer creates a "structure of metaphors and visions" that conceptualize the space that the Internet creates.[63] The technology of CB radio still exists and is used, but when was the last time that a story about human activities on CB topped the news? The reason for the dearth of media coverage of the CB network is that much of the social layer has been removed as CB was supplanted by cellular phones, which better served most people's needs. The drop in scale of usage means that the network has less importance.[64] It is precisely the fact that 48% of the world's population is connected to the Internet and this number is rapidly growing that makes Cyberspace an important social phenomenon.[65] Social interactions of all sorts are taking place there, but where is there?

This section will first establish that a spatial narrative serves as the dominant conceptualization of Cyberspace. Then it will probe the attendant metaphors to this spatial narrative and attempt to identify Cyberspace in terms of location and place.

Cyberspace as Space

A great deal of the early literature on Cyberspace debated specifically whether it constituted a new space distinct from the space inhabited by states. The legal debate, focused on the multijurisdictional effects of Cyberspace, is best exhibited in the scholarly exchange between Jack Goldsmith and David Post. Goldsmith argues that Cyberspace presents no novel legal problems, and that "Cyberspace transactions do not inherently warrant any more deference by national regulators, and are not significantly less resistant to the tools of conflict of laws, than other transnational transactions."[66] Post on the other hand, a self-proclaimed "cyberexceptionalist," argues that Cyberspace should be approached as a new geography that humans inhabit. At the heart of this debate is one fundamental issue: is cyberspace a space?

---

[62] Lessig, *Code 2.0* (2006) 9 and Kulesza, *International Internet Law* (2013) x–xi.
[63] Streck, "Pulling the Plug on Electronic Town Meetings" (1998) 20.
[64] *See generally* Post, *Jefferson's Moose* (2012) 68–69.
[65] International Telecommunications Union, *ICT Facts and Figures 2017* (2017) at 2.
[66] Goldsmith, "Against Cyberanarchy" (1998) 1201.

Goldsmith's answer to this question is that since Cyberspace exists on the Internet, then Cyberspace exists where the physical links and users do. The physical layer and users exist within physical territory of the state. Through this lens Cyberspace only has a "space" to the extent that its physical components do. Post on the other hand would argue that something fundamentally different is happening, because Cyberspace mediates the vast number of human interactions without regard to the physical and political boundaries of the terrestrial sphere.[67] He argues that the difference between real space and Cyberspace is akin to the difference between "life on land" or "life in the sea."[68] In this model, Cyberspace's spatial dimension is defined by the entire layer stack, and not just the territorially grounded physical layer.

The problem is that, to some extent, both authors are correct. Most of Cyberspace's physical manifestations do exist within state borders. Thus, a regime such as that in North Korea can control the spread of Cyberspace by maintaining tight controls on the dispersion of physical technology at its borders – leading activists to attempt to send in technology using balloons.[69] Cyberspace, at the same time, defies containment by the state and seemingly exists everywhere. The Pirate Bay, a prominent torrent website carrying links to copyrighted material, has repeatedly evaded being shut down by state power structures through the use of mirror sites, which disperse the site across servers in various geographic regions.[70] The reality is that Goldsmith's argument while logically solid is often "more honoured in the breach than in the observance."

One of the problems with Goldsmith's view is that it ignores a simple fact: humans understand Cyberspace as a space. Cyberspace is conceptualized as space through a spatial narrative that serves as a dominant metaphor for human understanding of Cyberspace.[71] In other words, Goldsmith "presuppose[s] a hard division between a regulated physical layer and everything else."[72] Goldsmith's argument seems facile when applied to the Internet, but it becomes dissonant when applied to Cyberspace. This is because the spatial narrative makes technological reductionism impossible,

---

[67]   Post, "Against 'Against Cyberanarchy'" (2002) 1374.

[68]   *Id.*

[69]   Halvorssen & Lloyd, "We Hacked North Korea With Balloons and USB Drives" (2014).

[70]   Brown, "Pirate Bay Mirror Is Proxy-Friendly, Bypasses UK Ban" (2012); Mlot, "The Pirate Bay Is Back Online (Sort Of)" (2014); and Hamill, "Pirate Bay Is BACK" (2015). *See also* Domscheit-Berg, *Inside WikiLeaks* (2011) 21.

[71]   *But see* Gelernter, "The End of the Web Search and Computer as We Know it" (2013); Seife, *Decoding the Universe* (2007) and Lloyd, *Programming the Universe* (2006).

[72]   Werbach, "Breaking the Ice" (2005) 79.

as "the way we describe a thing can change the nature of that thing."[73] The spatial narrative that accompanies Cyberspace is very much a description of social experience in Cyberspace.[74] The spatial narrative "transform[s]" the "experience" of Cyberspace."[75]

The spatial narrative is found within the common vocabulary used to describe Cyberspace. Users go *online* and visit chat*rooms* or web*sites*. These can be found by typing in an IP *address* that is often denoted by a Uniform Resource *Locater* (URL) which includes a *domain* name. That name is understood to be *owned* by an entity, which will probably have a fire*wall* up to keep intruders out of its *local* server. Lessig notes that "cyberspace is something you get pulled 'into.'"[76] Ferguson and Mansbach note terminology such as "electronic highway, electronic mail, infobahn, infosphere, ... information superhighway ... online community, virtual community, and virtual reality."[77] Barlow's influential "Declaration of Independence for Cyberspace" declares that states have "no sovereignty" in the "new home of the mind."[78] Resnick refers to the "land of Cyberspace,"[79] and Post uses the metaphor of exploring a new territory to evaluate law in Cyberspace.[80] In short, Cyberspace has a "placeness."[81]

This metaphor is central to the social construction of Cyberspace, because "metaphors have a profound effect on computing."[82] As the Internet reached more users, these concepts could often be found in the iconography of Internet Service Providers (ISP). For instance, America Online (AOL) was one of the first mass market ISPs, and, as a result, AOL was the initial first online experience for a large portion of the Internet users that flooded the Internet when it was privatized in the mid-1990s.[83] AOL used skeuomorphs to orient these new users. For example, the sound of an opening and closing door was used to denote entrance and exit of users from chatrooms. Similarly, an icon of a traditional roadside mailbox denoted the email server thereby linking the email concept to its physical counterpart, which would have specific geographic location denoted by a physical address. AOL is not an isolated

---

[73] Streck, "Pulling the Plug on Electronic Town Meetings" (1998) 26.

[74] Fritsch, "Technology and Global Affairs" (2011) 31.

[75] Streck, "Pulling the Plug on Electronic Town Meetings" (1998) 26.

[76] Lawrence Lessig, *Code 2.0* (2006) 9.

[77] Ferguson & Mansbach, *Globalization* (2012) 10.

[78] Barlow, "The Declaration of Independence for Cyberspace" (1996).

[79] Resnick, "Politics on the Internet" (1998) 51.

[80] Post, *Jefferson's Moose* (2012).

[81] Johnson & Post, "Law and Borders" (1996) 1379; *see also* Betz & Stevens, *Cyberspace and the State* (2011) 13.

[82] Gelernter, "The End" (2013) and Streck, "Pulling the Plug on Electronic Town Meetings" (1998) 26.

[83] *See* Lessig, *Code 2.0* (2006) 88–94.

example; skeuomorphs have been used extensively in digital design to help orient users.[84] The desired effect is the creation of a visual, spatial geography that new users can easily orient themselves using concepts associated with physical geography.

The pervasiveness of the spatial metaphor illustrates something very important that is often overlooked in Goldsmithian type arguments. No matter whether Cyberspace exists in a physical place, it is conceptualized and understood as a space by its users. Cyberspace is experienced as space, and it is "different from real space."[85]

Cyberspace as a Place

If Cyberspace is a space then where is it? Space is intrinsically linked to the idea of location. Locating Cyberspace is a difficult task, and the spatial narrative can only be pushed so far.[86] Part of the problem is that an individual can never be wholly in Cyberspace, yet this has not kept Cyberspace from being understood in terms of spatial concepts. The Internet's layers, discussed above, construct the spatial geography of Cyberspace by setting the metes and bounds of human interaction online. In the same way that rivers and mountains create natural boundaries, Internet technology creates boundaries for human interactions. The spatial metaphor invokes a number of important concepts that shape social understanding of Cyberspace.

Cyber-realists will claim that Cyberspace is located within the physical bounds of the state. For instance, in terms of the WWW, URLs denote a specific server on the Internet, which does exist in a physical location and is owned by an entity. The URL is conceptually very similar to the idea of an address, which denotes a specific geographic location, so the URL points to a place with a location that is within the borders of a state, and to a specific *res* within that state. This answer to the location problem is not without issues, though. URLs are freely associable to other servers that can contain either the same information or different information. The server itself may be static, but the website that is visited in Cyberspace is not. It can move with a simple change to the DNS root file, which will resolve the URL to a different IP address, and to a different *res*. The distinct *site* that the user *visits* is indeed fluid in a spatial sense. Cyberspace exists in a geographic duality. Like Papa Legba with one foot in the grave, Cyberspace has one foot firmly planted inside state borders, but the other foot is planted somewhere outside those borders.

---

[84]   Heddaya, "See a Map, Not a Territory" (2013).
[85]   Kulesza, *International Internet Law* (2013) xii.
[86]   *For instance*, Johnson & Post, "Law and Borders" (1996) 1378.

The spatial narrative is a social conceptualization that renders Cyberspace as a "distinct 'place.'"[87] As a place, it exists concurrently yet separately from the state, meaning it both borders and intersects the state. Because Cyberspace has transnational effects that are unbounded by physical geography, it is submitted here that Cyberspace constructs and is located in a global space.[88] A global location implies two things. First, Cyberspace is a space with world scale, and its growing level of integration into societies worldwide is hardly deniable. Second, Cyberspace is a geography that is exterior to international space. The network architecture that underlies Cyberspace allows it to evade the strictures of national borders. Global space is located where internationally defined territory thins and runs out.

To understand this, one must first recognize that the concepts of space and location also implicate further notions such as borders and property. The often-quoted trope from the early days of the Internet that "borders are just speed bumps on the information superhighway" points directly to Cyberspace's spatial character and global location. Indeed, the spatial metaphor of a highway is a reminder that all the locales in Cyberspace exist in the same place, or maybe better stated, they all have addresses on the same street. All IPs on the Internet are equally close to the user. While the ability of states to raise borders in Cyberspace is not completely absent, the user's ability to thwart those mechanisms allows for penetration of those borders at will, showing that software borders are indeed soft. The rhetoric of the spatial narrative supports this. For instance, John Perry Barlow's "Declaration of Independence for Cyberspace" declares explicitly that "Cyberspace does not lie within [a state's] borders."[89] Barlow is linking the independence of Cyberspace to its own territorial sovereignty, stating later that he "felt like the answer to sovereignty was sovereignty. To fight them on their own terms."[90] The spatial narrative gives conceptual credence to extraterritoriality of Cyberspace.

The concept of property is also implicated. The Western norms of ownership and exclusion are set on end in Cyberspace, which "makes a hall of mirrors out of conventional understandings of what constitutes private and public property."[91] Take the website example used above. Users often reference ownership of a website, but this is inexact at best. What these users are describing is two different phenomena of "ownership." First, they are describing the URL which indicates location of the website, but this domain

---

[87]   *Id.*
[88]   *See* Kulesza, *International Internet Law* (2013) 29.
[89]   Barlow, "A Declaration" (1996).
[90]   Greenberg, *This Machine Kills Secrets* (2012) 256.
[91]   Toulouse, "Introduction" (1998) 13.

name is only registerable and not owned so an individual's rights in it do not represent traditional property rights. While entities may own intellectual property rights to attributes of the URL,[92] they must maintain their registration in order to keep the URL, whether they use the URL or not. Interestingly, this means that it is possible to register a URL to keep it from becoming a place in Cyberspace. Furthermore, the URL can easily be pointed to another server by associating it to a new IP address, meaning that the URL as an owned space is to some extent ephemeral. This points to the second phenomenon of ownership that users are describing when they discuss ownership of a website, which is ownership of the content that is displayed in the browser window, which can be thought of in terms of intellectual property.[93] Since the webpage is available worldwide, questions about the territory that protects those intellectual property rights arise. This becomes messier when one takes into account that a great deal of web content is copied and stored on the local machine, and when one contemplates that the success of social networking websites is often predicated on serving content that is sourced from somewhere other than the website's "owner." Interestingly, a third concept of ownership is not usually invoked when referencing website ownership, which is ownership of the server in the physical layer, where the cyber-realist focuses their analysis. This type of ownership is diminished in importance since a URL and data can be moved to new servers at will, meaning that the physical location changes fluidly.[94] Additionally, the entity that places the content on the server often rents that server space from a third party and has no physical control over it further muddying the ownership waters.[95]

The website example hints at the underlying issue for property narratives in Cyberspace: hard physical location is ephemeral because property in Cyberspace is practically infinite. Western understanding of property is predicated on scarcity, which rests on the idea that "they aren't making anymore of it." In Cyberspace, property is fragmented across physical space and metaphysical space resulting from the effects of the logical layer which makes data fungible such that it can move freely from place to place and exist simultaneously in all those places. Property in Cyberspace expands simply by adding devices with computer memory to the network, or by adding new files to established servers (e.g. adding a new post to a blog).[96] Notions of

---

[92]   See generally, Merges, Menell, & Lemley, *Intellectual Property in the New Technological Age* (2012) 911–930.

[93]   See Lessig, *Free Culture* (2004); Partridge & Lonardo, "ICANN Can or Can It?" (2009); and Ranieri, "EFFecting Digital Freedom" (2014) 52–53.

[94]   Domscheit-Berg, *Inside WikiLeaks* (2011) 21.

[95]   See Bearman, "The Untold Story" (2015).

[96]   Spar, "The Public Face of Cyberspace" (1999) 348 and McIntosh & Cates, "Hard Travelin'" (1998) 95.

property based on scarcity and ownership become tenuous as scarcity decreases and ownership fragments.[97] So, for instance, scarcity of land is central to Schmitt's conception of the land generating the law – as it is the scarcity of land that drives its division. However, when territory is infinite the need for division is functional as opposed to economic. This is not to argue that there is no economic value in domain names, but that value is derived not necessarily from scarcity, but from the idea contained in the domain name, which is most often linked to the name recognition associated with a company or brand. Thus any URL, in theory, has the potential to be of high value if it achieves high recognition, whereas real properties value is linked to physical attributes.

None of this is to say that traditional notions of borders and property do not still have sway. As noted earlier, Goldsmith's observation of physical location granting state's territorial control over Cyberspace technologies is relevant, because users are "always in both places."[98] This, however, is only part of the story. States can only control the parts of the Internet they can literally touch, but not necessarily all the parts of the Internet that can touch them. The technological landscape that intersects state territory is architected in such a way that much of Cyberspace is located outside the state.

Metaphysical Geographies

The critical notion in this chapter is that Cyberspace is understood by humans as a space and as such it also has location and place. Despite its metaphysical nature, individuals cannot help but envision Cyberspace in terms of its spatial characteristics. This is no surprise to anyone familiar with the literature on Cyberspace, which struggles with the ethereal nature of a place that is both there and not there in the sense of "traditional dimensionality."[99] Indeed, the concept of virtual reality embeds the spatial narrative quite deeply into understandings of Cyberspace. At its inception, virtual reality was portrayed as the ability to go into a new space and to experience it as real.[100] This concept materialized in applications such as Second Life, which allowed a user to explore and interact in a virtual world that was created by the individuals that inhabited it.[101] Virtual reality's current inception through devices such as Microsoft's Hololens allows the users to

---

[97] *See* Tambini *et al.*, *Codifying Cyberspace* (2008) 68 and Goodman, "Media Policy and Free Speech" (2007) 1221.

[98] Lessig, *Code 2.0* (2006) 298.

[99] Betz & Stevens, *Cyberspace and the State* (2011) 35.

[100] *For example compare*, The Lawnmower Man (New Line Cinema 1992) and *The Matrix* (Warner Brothers 1999).

[101] *See* Lessig, *Code 2.0* (2006) 108–111.

visit virtual spaces as well as real spaces.[102] Additionally, led by the pornography industry, devices are being created that allow for richer interactions of individuals in Cyberspace.[103] These technologies move beyond an audio/visual experience in Cyberspace and allow users to take part in the experience portended by AT&T's 1980s ad slogan "Reach Out and Touch Someone."[104] The ability to physically "touch," even through an Internet connected device means that the metaphorical has become the experiential. Physicality is now freely transportable beyond borders, which become much less benign in an example like Stuxnet where code was used to physically and surreptitiously manipulate centrifuges in an Iranian nuclear facility.[105] Cyberspace cannot remove a mountain in between two places, but it can render many of the mountain's effects irrelevant.

The idea of touch leads to a final observation that must be made about Cyberspace: as a space it has inhabitants.[106] Granted these individuals live both in Cyberspace and out. There is developed rhetoric that refers to netizens and cybercitizens, both of which implicate a core concept of citizenship that is traditionally linked directly to territorial authority.[107] Arguably the term "global citizen" found in the literature on global governance can only be conceptualized with a technology that can free the individual from the strictures of their national citizenship. While such ideas might be dismissed as purely rhetorical, we can see that they indeed do have manifestations such as Estonia's e-Residency campaign, which extends digital rights to registered entities.[108]

Digital natives may be the most potent of these metaphors for inhabitation, as society has not yet entered a time in which individuals have no concept of what it is like to not be contained within networked space. Digital natives, a naturally rising part of the population, will not conceptualize spatial organization without the inclusion of Cyberspace. Rhetorically, the term 'digital natives' indicates that these individuals are more than just transitory surfers. Their geographic experience will always be networked and machine mediated. In such a world, a digital-self existing on the network becomes a normalized human attribute, and the population as a whole becomes respatialized as social constructions of space become morphed by networks.

---

[102] Microsoft, "HoloLens" (2015).

[103] Stadtmiller, "Virtual Reality Sex Is Coming" (2015).

[104] Ramey, "When AT&T Asked Us to 'Reach out and Touch Someone', Did They Mean That Literally?" (2008).

[105] Oliver, "Stuxnet" (2013) 127–59.

[106] Post, *Jefferson's Moose* (2012) 31–36 and Lessig, *Code 2.0* (2006) 298.

[107] Luke, "The Politics of Digital Inequality" (1998) 123.

[108] e-Estonia, "What is e-Residency?" (2015).

Machine mediated space means that new and different boundaries are experienced based on the architecture of those machines. This is not to imply a dystopian science fiction plot, such as that of *The Matrix*, in which the human conscience only exists within digital bounds. The individual will certainly still exist and move through physical space, but there will be new understanding of the nature of boundaries and borders as individuals recognize an "extraordinary possibility for many to participate in the process of building and cultivating a culture that reaches far beyond local boundaries."[109]

As already noted, IoT is indicative of such networked space. IoT allows the networking of devices that can be controlled by electrical current, thus a small computer known as a microcontroller can be used to spin motors, adjust electrical current levels, flip switches, and accomplish a variety of other tasks. Microcontrollers with a network connection allow a user to exert control over physical space through a network connection.

One of the most popular applications of IoT is enabling home automation via the Internet, effectively networking an individual's physical personal space. Transaction points literally proliferate through the space of the home. For instance, lights have traditionally been controlled with a physical switch implicitly requiring a person to move through the physical in order to operate it. IoT, though, ends the "who is turning off the lights" debate that so many couples have by removing the distance to the switch. More striking, it allows the user to turn the lights on or off from a foreign country and even allows an outside party to control the lights. The interior space once defined exclusively by the walls of a room is now open to new forms of control as those walls are breached. The borders physically defined by walls are no longer boundaries to certain types of computer mediated changes in that space. Needless to say this changes the experience and perception of the space of "home" for that user.

This chapter has described the spatial geography of Cyberspace, focusing on both its technical and conceptual landscapes. The spatial orientations that are employed in Cyberspace create strong metaphors that steer social understanding. One of the attributes discussed in this chapter was the dynamism of Cyberspace, and its ability to expand nearly infinitely, making the contemplation of its borders difficult.

---

[109] Lessig, *Free Culture* (2004) 9.

The next two chapters in Part I will use the concepts of legal geography and political geography to better understand the true limits of Cyberspace and define its borders.

3

Legal Terrains

One of the most striking things about air travel is the labyrinthine airport layouts that create and demarcate a variety of distinct spaces for the traveler. Passengers move through underground passageways and shopping mall-esque avenues en route to boarding their airplane. They move from a non-sterile zone to a sterile zone after crossing security borders that demarcate changes in rules. While travelers experience these layouts as minor annoyances, they often fail to recognize how airports are architected to control the travelers within them. Airports by design demarcate and produce the rules of behavior within different zones of space. This is not a characteristic unique to airports, as nearly all architecture deploys some sort of control.[1]   For instance, architected control is the underlying premise of Jeremy Bentham's Panopticon, but it can be also seen deployed in the layouts of public spaces such as Walmart stores and museums.[2] Architected control is visible in private spaces as well, as doors and walls are architectural mechanisms that help to maintain privacy. Architecture controls how individuals experience space by enabling and disabling them in a variety of ways, and Cyberspace's open network architecture is no different.

Along these same lines, airports use architecture to segregate international passengers, particularly international arrivals, from the rest of the airport population. International passengers are ushered into arrivals halls that are designed with a series of counters at which sits an authority of the state that checks the passport and documentation of each traveler. There are signs that indicate that this line of counters is the border of the country at which the plane has landed. Despite the fact that these travelers are usually deep within the interior of the territory of that state, they have not yet entered the state. In this case, the geography of the border is warped to match the legal geography of jurisdiction, creating nearly unmappable zones of exclusion on a map of national borders.

---

[1]   Lessig, *Code 2.0* (2006) 38–60.
[2]   Cohen, "Privacy, Visibility, Transparency, and Exposure" (2008) 184.

These examples illustrate different sides of the same coin. Legal geographies can be deployed by technologies of enforcement to limit individual ability to transgress the norm being enforced. Additionally, these geographies can also be reimagined to include or exclude space despite the physical location of that territory. The state's ability to dynamically conceptualize its borders in such a way as to create legal fictions within territory renders borders into markers of a legal geography based on jurisdiction.[3] This is why architectures of control are used at borders: they give materiality to imaginary lines, because state's borders are only as solid as the state itself can make them.

The legal geography of Cyberspace is a question of how architectures of control are deployed within it. The analysis here applies across the layered model established in Chapter 2. First, it will probe the idea of jurisdiction as a type of geography. To do this it will examine the traditional link between territory and jurisdiction. The second section will use the link between architecture and control to examine a fundamental principle of how regulatory power is distributed in Cyberspace through examination of Lessig's principle that "code is law." Finally, this chapter will turn to the idea of code as a constitution of Cyberspace and explore the governance implications that flow from such an idea. This final section will then draw conclusions on the dispersion of jurisdiction in Cyberspace.

The Space of Law

Jurisdiction is the space of law. It can be understood, in at least one sense, as the literal geographic limitations of the law.[4] As a legal concept, jurisdiction can seem ephemeral, but it is literally part of the language that we use to locate ourselves within the world. "I'm from ..." is a phrase that is likely to end with a designation of a legal jurisdiction such as a state or its political subdivisions such as provinces, counties, or municipalities. These subdivisions, which are often nested like matryoshka dolls, each denote space with a particular set of legal characteristics. This is what is meant by legal geography. Importantly, these nested jurisdictions overlap in such a way that an individual is often standing in a hierarchical stack of overlapping jurisdictions. It is argued herein that Cyberspace also deploys a legal geography of jurisdiction over the individual, but this geography resists containment within jurisdictions as conceptualized in the international governance regime.

As noted in Chapter 2, Cyberspace alters our spatial experience. Jurisdiction,

---

3   *See* Bowman, "Thinking Outside the Border" (2007) 1192–95.
4   Kulesza, *International Internet Law* (2013) 2–3.

in the modern state system, is linked directly to territory. Territory serves as the critical link between jurisdiction and power in a state's deployment of governance, because historically there has been "a general correspondence between borders drawn in physical space ... and borders drawn in 'law space.'"[5] This is by no means a 'natural' connection, but it has been a de facto connection based on technologies through which power is exerted and through which global order unfolds.

To this end, international law has recognized five bases from which a state may extend its jurisdiction and thereby exert its power: territorial, personal, protective, passive personality, and universal.[6] Each of these principles for extending jurisdiction has their own internal logic, but all – save one – are tied back to physical territory. This embeds territorial understandings into the concept of   jurisdiction within international space.[7] Personal jurisdiction is linked back to a territory via auspices of nationality; protective jurisdiction is linked to protecting the territory of the state from harm; and passive personality links to the concept of nationality, which in turn links to territory. Only universal jurisdiction seems to evade the territorial link, because its original incarnation was as a mechanism to address actors external to the territorial borders of any state, such as pirates.[8] Universal jurisdiction, though, does require that malefactors be brought into the territorial jurisdiction of the state in order for it to exert legal power.[9]

What these accepted principles of jurisdiction exhibit is that territory is foundational to jurisdiction in the international system, and that jurisdiction can be understood as the space in which the state can exert its power, both juridical power and through its monopoly on violence.[10] It is important to understand the territorial limitation of state power, because territory sits at the heart of the international legal system. The borders drawn by that system show a particular configuration of jurisdiction superimposed on the space of the world. While "[w]e take for granted a world in which geographical borders ... are of primary importance in determining legal rights and responsibilities," this configuration is only a static rendering of a dynamic set of lines that

---

[5]   Johnson & Post, "Law and Borders" (1996) 1368.

[6]   Akehurst, "Jurisdiction in International Law" (1972) 145; Schabas, *Genocide in International Law* (2009) 409; and Blount, "Jurisdiction in Outer Space" (2007) 299.

[7]   Kulesza, *International Internet Law* (2013) 4.

[8]   *See* Schmitt, *Nomos of the Earth* (2003) 42–44.

[9]   *See for example* the cases of Adolf Eichmann: Arendt, *Eichmann in Jerusalem* (1963) 262–263; Augustus Pinochet, Roht-Arriaza, "The Pinochet Precedent and Universal Jurisdiction" (2001) 311–19; and Humberto Álvarez Macháín, Zaid, "Military Might versus Sovereign Right" (1996) 829.

[10]   Kulesza, *International Internet Law* (2013) 6.

indicate a variety of fluid spaces.[11]

The argument advanced by this section is that jurisdiction, understood as a legal geography, is neither a continuous nor a static space, and that it is reconfigurable not only through a state's own conceptualization of its borders, but also through external processes that reshape the nature of legal space. This section will proceed in two parts, both of which are designed to show the gaps in the link between territorial space and regulatory space. First, this section will show how Cyberspace fractures national jurisdiction, and then, it will pursue the same goal in terms of international space. It should be noted that the claim made in this section is not that state jurisdictions have wilted away, but that jurisdiction is not "already, and forever, 'settled.'"[12] The state retains a great deal of power in relation to objects and individuals within its territory. However, Cyberspace creates a spatial situation in which regulatory power associated with territory runs out, and at this point we can see where Cyberspace's legal geography begins.

National Space

The debate on the nature of Cyberspace, typified by the exchange between Post and Goldsmith discussed in Chapter 2, is important in the discussion of legal geography. The debate was centered on whether or not Cyberspace was a new space, but specifically as legal scholars, the dispute centered on whether Cyberspace created new alternative legal geographies of jurisdiction. Such claims had been advanced in Barlow's "Declaration of Independence for Cyberspace." Barlow's claim that states "were not welcome" in Cyberspace, is rooted in the notion of an independent territorial sovereignty as the source of legitimate governance in Cyberspace.[13]

While Goldsmith rejects such rhetoric outright, Post takes a more nuanced position. He claims that "cyberspace is somehow different" and that this difference "matters for the purposes of understanding these jurisdictional questions."[14] Post's argument is rooted in the idea that Cyberspace creates a world "of inter-connected and geographically complex cause and effects."[15] He notes that

> transactions in cyberspace can take place at much greater physical remove; they are consummated by means of the

---

[11]   Johnson & Post, "Law and Borders" (1996) 1368.

[12]   Post, "Against 'Against Cyberanarchy'" (2002) 1373.

[13]   Barlow, "Declaration" (1996).

[14]   Post, "Against 'Against Cyberanarchy,'" (2002) 1368.

[15]   *Id.* at 1381.

movement of bits rather than atoms; they are digitally encoded; they are unaffected by the participants' sense of smell; they are embedded in and mediated by computer software; they travel at the speed of light, etc.[16]

Massively distributed computer mediation of transactions, in Post's view, requires reevaluation of "settled understandings" of concepts such as jurisdiction.[17]

To understand Post's arguments, the critical gaze must again turn to the borders that define the state. Older transborder technology was often controlled by technological standards that were adopted by a given state. This was a unique function of legal jurisdiction that could create architectural controls at the border of a state. For example, by adopting a different standard railroad gauge a state could ensure that all train shipments were disembarked and reloaded under the state's watchful eye.[18] Standard setting is a tool by which technology is directly regulated. The logical layer of the Internet adopts standards that enforce universal interoperability, meaning that the logical layer bypasses borders by rendering a state's physical telecommunications standards irrelevant. The physical technology of the border is undermined as Cyberspace reroutes border crossings to the applications layers running of the Internet. The proliferation of transaction points also drives the proliferation of border intersections. For the territorial border, "[d]igitization means dematerialization."[19]

This is not to say that border crossing technologies have not been issues for the international community before. Indeed, radio transmissions[20] and satellite broadcasting[21] both caused debate in the international arena. As Post notes though, the scale of Cyberspace is dramatically different from previous technologies.[22] The ability to instantaneously communicate with the entire online population forces new understandings of jurisdiction, since this means that data transmissions cross all borders at once.

The architecture of Cyberspace is such that it forces geographically remote

---

[16] *Id.* at 1375–76.

[17] *Id.* at 1373.

[18] Mattelart, *Networking the World* (2000) 1–13 and Werbach, "Breaking the Ice" (2005) 60.

[19] Luke, "The Politics of Digital Inequality" (1998) 125.

[20] Robertson, "The Suppression of Pirate Radio Broadcasting" (1982) 71–101 and Eppenstein & Aisenberg, "Radio Propaganda" (1979).

[21] *See* Lyall & Larsen, *Space Law* (2009) 256–269 and UNGA, Res.3 7/92 (1982).

[22] Post, *Jefferson's Moose* (2012) 60–89.

states into direct contact with each other by bringing their borders together. This often means that "multiple noncoordinating jurisdictions" are brought into proximity as the Internet networks those jurisdictions into contact.[23] Cyberspace creates contact points between and among all networked physical space. This is problematic because laws "mostly concern national spaces."[24] This can be seen in the quintessential France v. Yahoo! case.[25] Suit was brought against Yahoo! in France because Yahoo! maintained an auction website that facilitated the sale of Nazi paraphernalia, which is illegal in France.[26] Yahoo!, an American company, was held culpable in France for the availability of this website within France's territory.[27] Two things should be made clear. First, this website was available to anyone with an Internet connection and a web browser regardless of location. Second, France's legal claim was only that the availability within the territory of France was illegal. If Yahoo! capitulated to the French demand for removal, the website would not be available anywhere in the world, including places where sale of such memorabilia is legal, leading to French law and values being enforced globally. Yahoo! sought a declaratory judgement in a United States federal court to render the decision unenforceable, but the 9th Circuit declined to grant the declaratory judgement on the grounds that it did not have jurisdiction over the French entity LICRA, which brought the original suit.[28]

While the cyber-unexceptionalist might argue that this is indicative of courts being perfectly capable of applying law to cases involving Cyberspace, the Yahoo! case has deeper implications that make such a stance tenuous. If this transaction were to occur in a pre-Internet environment there are a number of factors that would have made it different. First, a French citizen would need to leave France in order to take part in the auction making it a costly

---

23   Lessig, *Code 2.0* (2006) 300.

24   Kulesza, *International Internet Law* (2013) 86.

25   Post, *Jefferson's Moose* (2012) 164–71; Lessig, *Code 2.0* (2006) 294–97; and Kulesza, *International Internet Law* (2013) 107–08. A similar case is the German *CompuServ* case which addressed the availability of pornography via CompuServ services. *See* Kulesza, *International Internet Law* (2013) 106–107 and Lessig, *Code 2.0* (2006) 39.

26   Kulesza, *International Internet Law* (2013) 107.

27   The technology that led to the *Yahoo!* case predated technology that allowed for geolocation of users through their IP addresses. Kulesza, *International Internet Law* (2013) xiii. Debates on the geographic control of IP addresses persist Leiner *et al.*, "A Brief History of the Internet" (2012); ITU, "Resolution 102 (Rev. Busan, 2014) ITU's Role with Regard to International Public Policy Issues Pertaining to the Internet and the Management of Internet Resources, Including Domain Names and Addresses" (2014) 148; and ITU, "Resolution 133 (Rev. Busan, 2014) Role of Administrations of Member States in the Management of Internationalized (Multilingual Domain Names)" (2014) 183.

28   Yahoo! Inc. v. La Ligue Contre Le Racisme, 433 F. 3d 1199 (9th Cir. 2006).

endeavor. That citizen would then need to physically transport the item over the French border and negotiate regulatory pressure points applied at border crossings. The Internet on the other hand allows all French citizens to take part in auctions that are "in" the United States in terms of server location. Three things are important here. First, the border crossing is not physical. This means that the state has lost some control over where its border is drawn. Second, the border crossing occurs on a private network. The state's apparatus for controlling borders is located physically at the borders in the form of checkpoints, which are places of inclusion and exclusion. In this case, the "checkpoint" has been routed around and the state has been excluded from its usual control function. Finally, the scale of Yahoo!'s actions are at a much different level of magnitude, as actions in Cyberspace have a "multi-site effect" fragmenting the idea of the *lex loci*.[29]

Yahoo!'s auction site allowed everyone in France with Internet access to take part in these auctions by minimizing the transaction costs associated with borders. The physical geography pre-Internet stood as a barrier to all but the wealthiest and most dedicated of collectors. Now technology facilitates easy access by all to these auctions. Yahoo! was acting within the jurisdiction of France, yet France lacked the jurisdictional capacity to reach out and physically touch Yahoo! meaning that jurisdiction tapers as France's territory runs out. Before the Internet such interactions were marginal, but post-Internet they are facilitated.[30]

Jurisdiction as a function of territory requires that transactions be located "geographically somewhere in particular," which is "most unsatisfying."[31] The enduring lesson from Yahoo! is that state control over persons and property is being diminished as the borders that define that jurisdiction no longer represent a barrier to social transactions.[32] The space of the state runs out as a social space beyond its control opens.

International Space

Since the scale of transactions on the Internet is global in scope, many scholars have turned to international law as the way in which Cyberspace can be appropriately regulated. This approach is seemingly a natural one, since flows of information in Cyberspace are often transnational in nature, but this

---

[29] Kulesza, *International Internet Law* (2013) 103. *See also* Spar, "The Public Face of Cyberspace" (1999) 345.

[30] Post, "Against 'Against Cyberanarchy'" (2002) 1383.

[31] Johnson & Post, "Law and Borders" (1996) 1378.

[32] *See* Kulesza, *International Internet Law* (2013) 14 and McIntosh & Cates, "Hard Travelin'" (1998) 85.

too presents several issues, and the dearth of international law addressing Cyberspace is telling.

First, it should be noted that the national is embedded in the international and vice versa. International space is a conceptual extension of national space.[33] The international system itself is made up of states that participate based on principles of nonintervention and sovereign equality.[34] As a result, modern international law is oriented toward the "territorial integrity" of the state itself.[35] International law reifies the geography of the state by rendering jurisdictional edges as borders of exclusion through the principle of nonintervention.[36] Indeed, until very recently, international law's regulatory focus was the border of the nation state, and only the most marginalized of territories are without legal standing in international law.[37]

States have long debated the control of transborder information flows as a matter of international law. Radio Free Europe and Voice of America are excellent examples of state attempts to penetrate the borders of other states with telecommunications technology.[38] But these interventions were limited in scope as both technology and geography ran out. Radio technology is limited by the ease of jamming as well as geographic constraints on the transmission power of the station.[39] Similarly, satellite technology raised issues resulting in a controversial set of principles adopted by the UN General Assembly.[40] Cyberspace is a new context for these same issues as it gives users "new opportunities for exchanging information and opinions."[41]

Concern with international communications is reflected in the international forum for addressing such issues – the International Telecommunication Union (ITU) – which is the "oldest international organization in the world."[42] The ITU is the international organization (IO) tasked with coordinating international telecommunications with the "object of facilitating peaceful relations, international cooperation among peoples and economic and social

---

[33] Habermas, *The Postnational Constellation* (2001) 63.
[34] Clapham, "Degrees of Statehood" (1998) 145 and Walzer, "The Moral Standing of States" (1980) 212.
[35] UN Charter (1945) Art. 2(4).
[36]   Habermas, *The Postnational Constellation* (2001) 64.
[37] Sassen, *Territory, Authority, Rights* (2006) 54.
[38] Eppenstein & Aisenberg, "Radio Propaganda" (1979).
[39] *Id.* at 154–156.
[40] UNGA, Res. 37/92 (1982).
[41] Council of the European Union, "EU Human Rights Guidelines on Freedom of Expression Online and Offline" (2014) I.D.35.
[42] *See* Codding, "International Telecommunications Union" (1994) 501. For other historical IOs *see* Mattelart, *Networking the World* (2000) 6–8.

development by means of efficient telecommunications services.[43] The ITU has three sectors,[44] each with its own mandate: the Radiocommunication Sector "ensur[es] the rational, equitable, efficient, and economical use of the radio-frequency spectrum"[45]; the Telecommunications Standardization Sector which promotes standards that work across national borders[46]; and the Telecommunication Development Sector which promotes the development of telecommunications systems in developing countries.[47] Cyberspace, while clearly a form of international telecommunication, does not fit distinctly within these well-defined silos of the ITU. As a result, the ITU has had little power to assert any sort of direct governance over Cyberspace.[48]

The gap that the ITU cannot fill has also been left empty by other international law-making processes. There is a notable dearth of treaty law. The only cyber-oriented, multilateral treaty is the Budapest Convention on Cybercrime, and it is weak at best.[49] The Budapest Convention attempts to set standards on the prevention and prosecution of cybercrime, but it falls short of being a document with any teeth to compel state action. Instead of strong international obligations, the treaty shifts implementation and enforcement burdens to states and extends no jurisdiction by any international entity. By vesting right and obligation in the domestic system of the states, the Convention on Cybercrime reifies the central position of the state and ignores the vastly different governance dimension that Cyberspace presents. In fact, much of the scholarship on international law and Cyberspace seems to imply that it is an ineffective mechanism.[50] Sofaer *et al.* suggest that cyber war, cyber intelligence, content restrictions, human rights, and national security will all remain outside the scope of international agreements.[51] Notably, conflict and human rights are specifically within the scope of extant international agreements, indicating a significant shift in power.

It is precisely the orientation to the national that has rendered international law ill-equipped to deal with the global nature of Cyberspace as it uses a siloed regulatory paradigm based on physical territory. While scholars have looked to both customary international law[52] and soft law principles,[53] there is

---

[43] Constitution of the International Telecommunication Union (2010), preamble.

[44] *See* Codding, "International Telecommunications Union" (1994) 508.

[45] ITU Constitution (2010) Art. 12.

[46] *Id.* at Art 17.

[47] *Id.* at Art 21.

[48] Kulesza, *International Internet Law* (2013) xiii–xiv.

[49] *Convention on Cybercrime* (2004).

[50] Kulesza, *International Internet Law* (2013) 29, 60.

[51] Sofaer, Clark, & Diffie, "Cyber Security and International Agreements" (2010).

[52] Zalnieriute, "An International Constitutional Moment" (2015) 99–133.

[53] *See generally,* Power & Tobin, "Soft Law for the Internet" (2011) 31–45;

little consensus on how cyber should be treated by nation states. The terrain seems to be frozen in terms of international law making.[54] This is not to say that states are unable to negotiate a treaty aimed at governing Cyberspace. They could do just that. The claim, instead, is that states are unable to deliver such a treaty, because they understand their own limitations in effectuating control in a sphere marked by severe jurisdictional uncertainty.[55] The non-territoriality of Cyberspace disembowels the notion of jurisdiction as contained in international law.[56]

A final distinction must be made. Chapter 2 posits a global location for Cyberspace, and it must be acknowledged that there are areas external to the state that exist within international space and are fully contemplated by international law. A group of areas known as global commons are defined within the bounds of international law, but outside the bounds of the national. The high seas, Antarctica, and outer space are all territories delineated by international law as global in nature.[57] Cyberspace does not fit within this category because it lacks a key common element with the global commons: Cyberspace is not a *res communis* in the sense contemplated by international law.[58] Global commons share a core legal prohibition against appropriation by a state. Cyberspace though, throughout the layered model, is marked by a dispersion of ownership with some components being owned by states themselves.

Cyberspace emerged appropriated and is therefore not a global commons within the legal sense of the word, making it difficult to classify within the international system.[59]

Yannakogeorgos & Lowther, "The Prospects for Cyber Deterrence" (2013) 49–77; and Hurwitz, "A New Normal?" (2013) 233–64. *See generally* Finnemore & Sikkink, "International Norm Dynamics and Political Change" (1998) 887–917.

[54]   *See* Kulesza, *International Internet Law* (2013) xiii–xiv and Hurwitz, "A New Normal?" (2013) 243.

[55]   *See* Power & Oisín Tobin, "Soft Law for the Internet" (2011) 35. On uncertainty, *see generally*, Clark & Landau, "Untangling Attribution" (2010) 25; Libicki, "Two Maybe Three Cheers for Ambiguity" (2013) 27–34; Lessig, *Code 2.0* (2006) 25; McDermott, "Decision Making Under Uncertainty" (2010) 227–41

[56]   Kulesza, *International Internet Law* (2013) 15 .

[57]   *Id.* at 20.

[58]   *But see* Betz & Stevens, *Cyberspace and the State* (2011) 107.

[59]   *But see,* Kulesza, *International Internet Law* (2013) 69. *See also* the related concept of global public goods Stiglitz, "Knowledge as a Global Public Good" (1999) 308–25; Sy, "Global Communications for a More Equitable World" (1999) 326–43; Spar, "The Public Face of Cyberspace" (1999) 344–62; and Tambini *et al*, *Codifying Cyberspace* (2008) 10.

Codes

The inability of national and international legal space to contain Cyberspace is rooted in the fact that users are "[s]eparated from doctrine tied to territorial borders."[60] In order to articulate a legal geography of Cyberspace, an inquiry into what regulatory mechanisms pick up when the territory of the state runs out must be made. Despite the fact that Cyberspace is sometimes compared to the Wild West[61] implying a degree of lawlessness, there are a number of sources of regulation in Cyberspace that exert control when and where the state cannot.[62]

As discussed in Chapter 2, Cyberspace has a technical architecture that sets its spatial boundaries and borders and serves to constrain inhabitants of that space. In the same way that a mountain range can prevent migration, the geography of Cyberspace is such that individuals can be stopped from migrating to certain networks as the result of virtual walls. The major difference, aside from one being virtual and the other existing in "meatspace", is that Cyberspace is an architected geography.[63]

Cybergeography – i.e. its mountains and valleys and other "natural" attributes – is a manifestation of the code and hardware deployed across the layered conceptual model.[64] To conceptualize how code restricts, consider a simple example of the early arcade game *Pong*, which was a simple game that was released for the Atari game system in 1972.[65] In *Pong*, two players control blocks on the screen that function as paddles. These paddles are used to hit a dot on the screen, which represents a ball. The paddles that the players use move across a single axis, up and down, on the lateral ends of the screen, and the ball bounces off the top and bottom of the screen. Game play continues until one player misses the dot allowing it to pass the paddle and touch the left or right edge of the screen.

In other, less convoluted terms, *Pong* is an electronic version of ping-pong or table tennis. There is a critical difference, for the purposes at hand, beyond just the equipment needed for each version: in ping-pong a player can break

---

[60]   Johnson & Post, "Law and Borders" (199) 1367; Kulesza, *International Internet Law* (2013) 124; and McIntosh & Cates, "Hard Travelin'" (1998) 114.

[61]   *See, for instance*, Mattice, "Taming the '21st Century's Wild West' of Cyberspace?" (2013) 9–12.

[62]   Tambini *et al*, *Codifying Cyberspace* (2008) 5.

[63]   Lessig, *Code 2.0* (2006) 6.

[64]   Tambini *et al*, *Codifying Cyberspace* (2008) 5 and Hayden, "The Future of Things Cyber" (2013) 4.

[65]   "About Pong," www.ponggame.org (2016).

the rules. It is a game with a set of rules. Those rules constrain the players through threat of penalty, but there is possibility that the players can subvert and violate those rules.[66] In *Pong*, on the other hand, players are incapable of cheating. *Pong's* rules are enforced perfectly in the sense that players are compelled to obey them, not through threat of consequences for violation, but through compulsion of the game's architecture implemented through the computer code that sets constraints on the player within the game space. The rules are enforced perfectly, so players need not be given a rulebook or even notice of the rules to avoid violating them.

This example is used to illustrate Lessig's "code is law" principle.[67] Lessig's principle states that when technology of any sort mediates transactions, the code, or architecture, of that technology also regulates the possibilities for those transactions.[68] Regulation embedded into architecture can achieve near perfect enforcement because rules are compressed into the structure.[69] At the heart of Lessig's theory is the concept of regulability. He argues that individuals are "regulated" by a variety of forces including markets, law (in the formal sense), norms, and architecture or code.[70] Each of these forces exerts limitations on an individual's actions. Lessig posits that in Cyberspace "regulation is imposed primarily by code"[71]

Code regulates Cyberspace because it "defines the terms upon which cyberspace is offered."[72] The code is law principle requires analytic focus to be returned to the layered model wherein we can see the variety of architectures through which code is deployed. The layered model reveals specifically that there is code running across the bottom three layers that, combined, influence the user experience at the content level. These layers "are the unacknowledged legislators of cyberspace."[73] A benign example is Netflix, a website that streams movies to subscribing customers.[74] Netflix licenses distribution rights for intellectual property and makes that intellectual property available to view by its customers. Netflix has several core concerns

---

[66] International Table Tennis Federation, "The Laws of Table Tennis" (2016).

[67] Lessig, *Code 2.0* (2006) 5.

[68] *Id.* at 77–78, 124; Tambini *et al*, *Codifying Cyberspace* (2008) 11; Cass R. Sunstein, *Republic.com 2.0* (2007) 95. *See also* Eppenstein & Aisenberg, "Radio Propaganda" (1979) 155–56.

[69] Lessig, *Code 2.0* (2006) 110; Noveck, "Designing Deliberative Democracy in Cyberspace" (2003) 7.

[70] Lessig, *Free Culture* (2004) 123 and Lessig, *Code 2.0* (2006) 16. *See also*, Tambini *et al*, *Codifying Cyberspace* (2008) 11–12.

[71] Lessig, *Code 2.0* (2006) 24.

[72] *Id.* 84.

[73] Greenberg, *This Machine Kills Secrets* (2012) 148 (quoting Nick Mathewson).

[74] http://www.netflix.com.

in making its business model operate effectively and profitably. The first is avoiding theft in the sense of nonsubscribers gaining access to the Netflix collection. Netflix does not rely on a notice forbidding non-subscribers from entering the website under force of prosecution. This would plainly be futile. Instead, Netflix uses code at the applications layer that requires a subscriber to verify their identity in the form of a login using a username and password. Netflix discourages widespread sharing of these credentials by deploying code that limits the number of IP addresses (and therefore devices) that can access the collection from a single account at a given time. Second, Netflix is concerned with abiding by the terms of the distribution license it has with the owners of the intellectual property it streams. Netflix uses code at the applications layer to make movie files stream to user devices instead of fully downloading, which keeps Netflix from distributing unauthorized copies of the files.[75] License agreements are also likely to contain geographic restrictions on distribution. Netflix uses the user's IP address, which is part of the code of the logical layer, to filter out devices logging in from outside the territory in which the distribution license applies. Finally, Netflix wants its service to work for its subscribers. To do this it analyzes the bandwidth of the subscriber's connection and adjusts the resolution of the display accordingly to ensure smooth streaming. Bandwidth is highly dependent on the architecture of the physical layer through which the subscriber connects to Netflix. Netflix's user experience is shaped by the layered architecture. The user likely does not experience the code as regulations or rules that command compliance. Instead, all of the regulatory mechanisms – save IP filtering, which maps to territorial concerns – are likely experienced as functionality of the service.

Netflix is a benign example, but it highlights one of Lessig's key insights. Coded regulations are hidden in the architecture of the space. This means that regulatory effects are often experienced as functionality rather than limitation, meaning that hidden regulations can be developed and imposed outside of public scrutiny. Code hides from the user, and there is rarely conversation between the user and the developer as to how code is to function. Indeed, users may not have any notice at all of the rules or how they are being applied. In applications such as *Pong* and Netflix this can be of little importance to the user, but when considered in terms of a global network that interconnects individuals such hidden rules become problematic as machine mediated interactions proliferate. The "code is law" principle explains how the regulatory space is shaped, but opens the questions of the sources of code and how code is implemented.

---

[75]   Streaming technology allows services to send only parts of a media file being actively watched to a user's devices, and it avoids local caching, so that the user's device does not retain the data that is sent.

Source Code: Software and Softlaw

Law comes from lawmakers. In a liberal democracy, it is, in theory, meant to be very easy to see from whence law comes.[76] Transparency in law and regulation is a function of the liberal democratic system of governance. This system implements a standardized process for lawmaking, which creates openness in the public forums in which law is made and adjudicated. The standardized procedure allows for individuals to access the law. The coupling of transparency and procedure allows citizens to peer in and see how the laws that govern them are constructed and applied. This process hinges on legitimacy in the substance of the law being confirmed through the legitimating act of proper procedure. It also opens political space by setting a framework for government action.

Code comes from coders; that is, people who write code. Coders are everywhere. They can be employed by a government, contracted by a private entity, working as a collective for the public good, part of a criminal cartel, or working on their own for simple personal satisfaction. The motivations and goals of coders are non-uniform. They can be writing code for economic gain or public benefit. The code they release can be proprietary and secret, or it can be open and transparent. Code can be deployed at any of the layers of the layered model. The implication being that there is no standardized procedure for developing code and there is no open and transparent forum in which code as a category of regulation is debated. This is because in Cyberspace code is ubiquitous and non-monolithic.

Code, like the Internet itself, is rhizomatic in nature. It develops irregularly across space and time from multivariate, unpredictable sources, and it is deployed dynamically across networks that mediate interactions. This is a function of the end-to-end network, which has already been demonstrated to facilitate innovation at the edges of the network. Coders working at the applications layer to proliferate transaction points through the development of innovative applications. The open architecture literally allows an individual to change the legal geography of Cyberspace by writing code. For example, the Silk Road, an online marketplace for black market goods was programmed and operated primarily by a single individual.[77] The Silk Road changed the space of the online marketplace by facilitating anonymous transactions to remove the burden of state regulation.

Code must be understood as dispersed: across layers, across actors, across motivations. At any given time, a user in Cyberspace is being regulated by

---

76   Rawls, *A Theory of Justice* (1971) 56.

77   Bearman, "The Untold Story of Silk Road" (2015).

multiple layers of code. Operationalized, the 'code' is law principle means that it is difficult to discern applicable regulations when analyzing user level interactions. There is literally too much code for the user to evaluate, and the user must find ways to extend trust in code without needing to understand all code structuring interactions. Users can do this by using a variety of mechanisms such as user agreements, security certificates, trusted sources, etc. The practical result of this dispersion of code is that Cyberspace is embedded with a preference for self-regulation.[78] This result flows from the non-hierarchical architecture implemented in the logical layer.

States have significant power to oversee parts of this architecture, but not enough to regulate Cyberspace as a whole, because the decentralized nature of the network gives "all actors ... an equally strong position in defining its nature."[79] It facilitates multiple entry points for co-regulators to deploy code. While states might use a device's IP address to reveal the identity of the individual using that device, Tor browser technology can be deployed at the applications level to encrypt and obscure a device's IP address thereby diminishing the reach of the state's regulatory power and giving the individual the ability to choose rights inconsistent with those defined in the legal geography of the state.[80] Self-regulation allows for the dispersion of governance over a complex system, and it "is the laboratory of law and regulation for the Internet."[81]

The self-regulatory preference is salient because law has traditionally been an inefficient means of governing rapidly developing technology. Law moves slowly compared to technology, thus law can be slow to react to technological developments, and changes in technology can warp legal terms and entrench outmoded legal provisions.[82] This is one of the reasons that, in the modern bureaucratic state, lawmakers pass specificity down hierarchically to regulators, whose procedural rules make them more dexterous in rulemaking. These more dexterous means though are still burdened by formal procedure. Self-regulatory mechanisms perform a similar function, but are able to implement standards (i.e. regulatory mechanisms) by stripping process to a minimum and focusing on narrowly defined problems.

Cyberspace is big, and its architecture is designed to handle its massive

---

[78]   Johnson & Post, "Law and Borders" (1996) 1388 and Kulesza, *International Internet Law* (2013) 60.

[79]   Kulesza, *International Internet Law* (2013) 125.

[80]   Greenberg, *This Machine Kills Secrets* (2012) 139–143.

[81]   Tambini *et al*, *Codifying Cyberspace* (2008) 4.

[82]   *For example, see* Gellman, "Civil Liberties and Privacy Implications of Policies to Prevent Cyberattacks" (2010) 273–309.

scale.[83] One of the ways that it does this is by dispersing governance across public, private, and civil society networks and devices. As noted, the state holds significant regulatory power over individuals and physical property, but Cyberspace governance is an assemblage, and the state is only one component of that assemblage. Similarly, international institutions such as the ITU and UN, despite their limitations, constitute another component of the assemblage as an expression of consensus, or lack thereof, of member states. The rest of the assemblage is composed of a variety of actors that work across the Internet's layers and exert different degrees of self-regulatory powers. For the purposes at hand, these non-state actors will be divided into three groups: commercial actors, civil society, and the individual. These groups are not discrete, and are chosen as representative points on a spectrum of actors.

Commercial Code

Commercial actors have long been considered to wield regulatory power, primarily through market forces. Indeed, Western European empires were built around private companies with the ability to extend regulatory authority through a lex mercatoria.[84] Commercial power is central to critiques of neoliberalism and the rise of the multinational corporation (MNC). One of the key lessons from globalization literature is the embeddedness of the MNC throughout the world, and its ability to skew law and policy through the extension of economic power has been confirmed.[85]

Cyberspace is, of course, no different. Commercial interests pervade three layers of the Internet. Corporations own physical infrastructure; corporations develop software at the applications layer; and corporations own content at the content layer. Only the logical layer is relatively free of direct corporate ownership and that is because the principle of interoperability requires the logical layer to be open, transparent, and the code free of proprietary claims. Corporations though are invested in the logical layer and are active in Internet Governance Communities (IGCs).

Tambini *et al.* show that corporate self-regulation happens along industry divisions and is rooted in the notion "that conventional regulation involving legislative lag and inexpert courts, would be inappropriate and would risk breaking the architectural principles of this new technology."[86] Different

---

[83]   Post, *Jefferson's Moose* (2012) 60–79.

[84]   Burbank & Cooper, *Empires in World History* (2010) 153–162.

[85]   For a salient example, *see* Saro-Wiwa, "On Environmental Rights of the Ogoni People in Nigeria (1995)" (2007) 360–363.

[86]   Tambini *et al.*, *Codifying Cyberspace* (2008) 30 and Jayakar, "Globalization and the

industry divisions deploy self-regulatory mechanisms to ensure compatibility, user trust, and accountability. These groups use mechanisms such as codes of conduct, industry standards bodies, and interfaces that allow users to report norms violations in order to ensure compliance with the law as well as user satisfaction.[87] Self-regulatory activities by corporations are subject to the same critiques as self-regulatory bodies in other commercial areas. Questions of democratic deficits, the reification of power structures based on concentration of capital, and legitimacy are all raised for obvious reasons.[88] In Cyberspace, as Tambini *et al.* observe, one of the central problems is that commercial bodies maintain control over information and how it flows, meaning that private interests become the arbiters of the "freedom of expression."[89] Importantly, corporations that exist in the global space of Cyberspace at a sufficient scale become the arbiter of this right across global spaces not linked to territorial jurisdictional limitations.

A second analytical problem caused by corporate self-regulation is that there are numerous different types of corporate actors. Phrases like "corporate interests" and "commercial interests" often indicate a unitary set of interests, but no such unitary interests can be identified for the 'Internet industry.' Self-regulation by commercial actors is architecturally dispersed and dependent on where a corporation functions within the layered model. Commercial actors innovating at the applications layer have an interest in maintaining open, end-to-end data transfers in the logical layer. This means that commercial interests owning physical infrastructure, like backbones and ICT networks are, due to market forces, required to maintain bandwidth sufficient to pass along the data required by the applications layer. The mismatch of interests, between content and bandwidth, can be seen in the net neutrality debate taking place in the US and Europe. The rise of streaming applications, such as Netflix, led to a steep rise in bandwidth requirements at the backbone level.[90] Due to the nature of agreements that arrange peering between backbones, the commercial owners were experiencing costs associated with increased bandwidth. The natural commercial solution to this problem is to pass those costs along to the entities using the bandwidth, and ISPs in turn want to pass those costs on to users. From a commercial perspective this is exactly how a market economy works, but this means that the ISP is also

---

Legitimacy" (1998) 726–29.

[87] *See generally*, Tambini *et al*, *Codifying Cyberspace* (2008).

[88] *Id.* at 112.

[89] *See*, UN General Assembly, Res. 217 A(III). Universal Declaration of Human Rights (1948) Arts. 18 & 19; International Covenant on Civil and Political Rights (1976) Art. 19; European Convention on Human Rights (2010) Art. 10; and American Convention on Human Rights (1978) Art. 13.

[90] Osgood, "Net Neutrality and the FCC Hack" (2014) 33–34 and Verizon v. FCC (2014) 5–6.

incentivized to give preference to some types of bandwidth usage.[91] As a result, an ISP and an Internet Content Provider (ICP) might enter into a contract that gives that ICP's content a priority to bandwidth or even excludes bandwidth traffic from a competitor. This could prove to be a viable profit stream to an ISP as well as potentially fatal to an ICP that lacks sufficient market power. ICP interest in providing content implicates free expression issues as well as the innovative architecture of the Internet itself. If the end-to-end architecture fails to connect ends, then the space created by the technological landscape is dramatically changed. The point here is not necessarily to discuss the merits of net neutrality, but to show how corporate interests at different points in the stack of layers diverge. Net neutrality shows how a simple supply and demand issue at the physical layer permutates across the other Internet layers and reveals deep governance issues concerning the nature of the network and core human rights.

The net neutrality example reveals divergence of corporate interests, but it also reveals a convergence as well, namely that as technologies converge, corporations often merge. Many ICPs are not owners of the intellectual property rights in the content that they provide.[92] The control of intellectual property has been key contestation in Cyberspace and has a pedigree that includes ICPs such as Napster and Pirate Bay. Successful ICPs such as YouTube, push content controls to users, which has been a thorn in the side of content owners who want to be the sole arbiters of that property. Net neutrality serves as a reminder that companies, such as Time Warner, are both content owners and ISPs.[93] Such corporate convergence without net neutrality would allow these companies to constrain ICPs from both directions in the layer stack. Such corporate convergence can create new sources of regulatory power as diversified companies seek to leverage different mechanisms to maximize profitability and filter out the competition.

Public Code

Public spaces are coded. As an example, Lessig cites the Americans with Disabilities Act, a law that recoded public space in order to increase access.[94] Similarly, newly constructed public and private places must be built "to code."

---

[91]   Rick Osgood, "Net Neutrality and the FCC Hack" (2014) 34; Verizon v. FCC (2014) 740 F. 3d 623 SLIP (Court of Appeals, Dist. of Columbia Circuit 2014) 6. *See also* Spar, "The Public Face of Cyberspace" (1999) 352; and Tambini *et al*, *Codifying Cyberspace* (2008) 8–9; Werbach, "Breaking the Ice" (2005) 78–9; Ranieri, "EFFecting Digital Freedom," (2014–2015) 52–53.
[92]   Osgood, "Net Neutrality and the FCC Hack" (2014) 35.
[93]   *See* Stout, "Comcast-Time Warner Cable Deal's Collapse Leaves Frustrated Customers Out in the Cold" (2015). *See also*, kliq, "Xfinite Absurdity" (2014) 51.
[94]   Lessig, *Code 2.0* (2016) 127.

Building codes ensure a number of different things: they ensure compatibility between structures and public utilities such as the electrical grid; they ensure safety by describing construction techniques that will give the building the required structural integrity, and these codes also enforce certain types of spaces. Helen, GA is an example. Helen, GA is a small tourist town in the Appalachian Mountains of Northeast Georgia. It has all the amenities of a vintage tourist town from an age when road trips were forced down winding highways: restaurants, including fast food chains, mini-golf, wine shops serving local rotgut, and motels for weary travelers. Popular with bikers on long mountain drives and summer camp field trips to "tube the Hooch," Helen sounds like numerous other outposts across Appalachia, but Helen looks different. Specifically, Helen looks like a Bavarian village lifted out of Germany – even the McDonald's conforms to the aesthetic. Helen uses its building code to transform itself into a particular type of public space, which is designed to structure an economic space built around tourism. The building code enforces architectural predictability in both the public space and the private commercial space.

ISPs and ICPs own and operate networks on the network of networks. To extend the 'information superhighway' metaphor, these are the private spaces that you see as you drive along the highway. They consist of businesses with their doors open to the public, and businesses that are closed to all but those authorized to enter. Additionally, there are mom and pop stands, yard sales, and other roadside attractions. There are also private residences that remain closed to the public, and churches that are open to all. As you drive, though, you are in public space. You are on a road, that is maintained by a public authority for the public good, but this authority is not a government authority enforcing local zoning standards.

Public space on the Internet is most visible at both the logical layer and the applications layer. These layers are where interaction points proliferate, but those interaction points must be architected. This has led to an interesting assortment of entities that maintain this public space through standardization procedures that are meant to ensure many of the same things building codes accomplish, namely interoperability, stability, and maintenance of the public space. Standardization is the means through which these entities work to structure the parameters of online interactions, because standardization makes architecture predictable.

Standard setting bodies are by no means an innovation. Government and commercial standards settings bodies have always been a feature of market economies. Government interest in setting such standards is in the maintenance of public space. While commercial interests are often vocal in the standards adoption process, they can be met with skepticism when they become the arbiters of rights within the public space. As already established, states only have partial control of the public space of the Internet, so as the state's territory runs out, a different type of self-regulatory body has stepped in: Internet Governance Communities (IGCs).[95] These governance bodies are self-regulatory in nature, and are marked by various levels of open membership that allows anyone with an interest and sufficient technical skill to take part in their deliberations. IGCs have grown organically with the development of Internet technology, and they constitute a community in which standard technical structures are negotiated.[96]   Unlike the ITU, which has been unable to extend its regulatory power over Internet protocols, IGCs routinely adopt standards that affect functionality across all layers of the Internet. IGCs will be central to the analysis found in Chapter 7, but two brief examples are offered here as illustrations.

The heart of the protocol stack, the logical layer creates a public space through its open code. It facilitates the digital handshake between devices on the Internet, and the open standards that create the logical layer allow entities to set up shop on the information superhighway. The standards that facilitate such interoperability need to be open, nonproprietary, and accessible, and they must work well enough to ensure wide adoption, which facilitates architectural predictability. These standards are developed by the Internet Engineering Task Force (IETF). The IETF was established by the researchers initially developing the Internet, and "probably has the largest influence on the technologies used to build the Internet" despite its lack of "formal authority."[97] Originally a group of computer scientists hailing from universities and making contributions to the early network architecture, the IETF now allows anyone to join and take part in deliberations on its non-binding standards.[98] Though non-binding, these standards are adopted under a decision procedure that emphasizes "rough consensus and running code," a deliberative stance that values agreement and functionality equally.[99] The IETF places great emphasis on transparency in decision making, and it's essential "read me" document states explicitly a rejection of "kings and tyrants."[100]

A second example is the World Wide Web Consortium (W3C). The innovation enabled at the logical layer means that other public spaces can be opened in Cyberspace through the use of the applications layer. As examined before,

---

[95]   IGCs is used to delineate these from IOs and to denote them as a distinct type of NGO (to the degree that they fit the definition of NGO).

[96]   *See* Leiner *et al.*, "A Brief History of the Internet" (2012).

[97]   Alvestrand & Lie, "Development of Core Internet Standards" (2009) 126.

[98]   *Id.* at 129.

[99]   Internet Engineering Task Force, "The Tao of IETF" (2012).

[100]   *Id.*

WWW is an applications layer code, and its basic language is HTML. Specifically, HTML enables the concept of hypertext, which allows connections to be made among digital documents, a function commonly called linking.[101] In order to facilitate such hypertext linking, HTML needs to be standardized and open. The W3C is the standards setting body that ensures the publicness of the WWW.[102] W3C describes itself not as an organization but as an "international community that develops open standards to ensure the long-term growth of the Web."[103] It too has open membership allowing both organizations and individuals to join, and its decisions are taken by "community consensus."[104]

Both of these examples exhibit key characteristics that make IGCs difficult to characterize in organizational terms, making their evolution as a governance mechanism significant to understanding the legal geography of Cyberspace. First, IGCs are a reflection of the distributed, open nature of Internet architecture. Their open membership schemes potentially distribute decision making globally, and their process is open in order to ensure goals of interoperability.[105] Second, as communities – rather than organizations – their decisions impose community values into architectural design. In IGCs, the public, as a collective, creates and maintains the code of public space.

Personal Code

The end-to-end network reduces barriers to innovation as does open code at the logical level. These innovative edges open up spaces in which individuals can act at a global level and change the nature of interactions in Cyberspace at the applications level. Both PGP and the Silk Road, discussed above, are examples of coders rewriting state regulatory power. These application layer codes inscribe new rules on the state's ability to control information using cryptographic technologies, or as one commentator claims, the user is empowered to "[c]reate the digital world, and with it, [one's] own rules."[106] The individual is given direct access to implementing innovations that can reconstruct the legal geography the user inhabits. The implication that the individual can directly regulate in Cyberspace is controversial at best, and many would outright reject such a notion. Alternate readings would likely suggest that the code deployed by these individuals will be the subject of criminal or commercial law. Such readings inscribe national jurisdiction

---

[101] On hypertext see Brate, *Technomanifestos* (2002) 33–52, 220–225.

[102] Alvestrand & Lie, "Development of Core Internet Standards" (2009) 138–139.

[103] World Wide Web Consortium, "About W3C" (2016).

[104] *Id.*

[105] *See* Lessig, *Code 2.0* (2006) 148.

[106] Greenberg, *This Machine Kills Secrets* (2012) 148.

around the individual as the subject of the law.

These readings are rooted in territory and overlook ways in which these technologies re-architect legal geography. Applications extend to individuals the ability to be the arbiter of their own rights in terms of informational freedoms. They are an "arbiter" in the sense that they can effectively hide personal interactions and remove them from the legal geography of territory. The logical layer allows applications layer code to bypass the state jurisdiction. The user respatializes to a legal geography that exists outside of the state's territorial gaze. The user as coder chooses the values contained in the code that he or she writes. This means that some may use these technologies to assert a freedom of political expression, but others can imbue the right with more nefarious content such as child pornography or terrorism. Such uses will be the subject of Chapter 8.

WikiLeaks serves as a good example. WikiLeaks is more than just a webpage. It is applications level code that allows individuals to send information to WikiLeaks while preserving anonymity.[107] Developed and deployed by Julian Assange with the help of a handful of other programmers, WikiLeaks became a global actor after it published a number of prominent leaks. This media attention peaked with the publication of thousands of State Department cables leaked by Chelsea (formerly Bradley) Manning.[108] Two things are important here, first Julian Assange's purposes for developing WikiLeaks specifically to invoke changes in world order and, second, the re-empowerment of the individual.[109] WikiLeaks is "a platform, a tool, an instance of technology," but it has an explicit legal purpose of diminishing the state's enforcement jurisdiction by reducing "incalculable legal costs" by transporting leakers to a new legal geography.[110]

The second thing to note is the power of the code. Cablegate leaker, Manning, was not caught as a result of the state following her digital trail. Instead, Manning revealed herself to a fellow coder, Adrian Lamo, who turned him in. Until that point, the United States had no evidence against Manning. Manning's own revelations returned her act to the interior of the legal geography of the state. Only when Manning spoke the crime did it materialize in a territorial sense.

---

[107] *See generally*, Domscheit-Berg, *Inside WikiLeaks* (2011).
[108] *Id.*
[109] *Id.* at 160 (quoting Julian Assange as stating "I'm off to end a war" in relation to the Collateral Murder leak from the U.S. occupation of Iraq.)
[110] *Id.* at 174–75, 137.

The legal landscape of Cyberspace, as described above, is a multi-dimensional geography that can rewrite the jurisdictional patterns established as accepted in international governance. Multidimensionality is the result of the dual geography implicit in the layered architecture of the Internet. This reveals why the layered model carries force as an explanatory tool: through dissection of the network architecture, interconnected points of control can be identified and observed. The layered model facilitates "layered thinking," which can reveal how the spatial characteristics of Cyberspace can ripple across the conceptual stack and change other geographies, as has been shown in relation to the legal geography addressed above.[111]

The airport analogy that opened this chapter took us to an international frontier found in an airport's international arrivals hall. There is another aspect of this room that should be noted before moving to the final chapter in Part I. If you listen while in the arrivals hall, you can hear the muffled, a-rhythmic beat of stamps hitting passports. As observed above, jurisdiction, or legal geography, is usually mapped across space using a state's territorial borders as indicators of its limits. These borders represent another notion as well. In the airport arrivals hall, the border is as much about territory and law as it is about individual identity. The border is an expression of political identity, and passports are opened in order to check political identity. The next chapter will take up this notion through examination of political geography.

---

[111] Werbach, "Breaking the Ice" (2005) 69.

4

Political Places

In the novel *Midnight's Children*, Salman Rushdie interweaves his signature magical realism into the political geography of India surrounding the specific time, 12:00am 15 August 1947, that India came into existence as a nation state.[1] Rushdie identifies this moment of national political identity as inseparably linked to individual identity. In one of the many turns of the novel, the reader is presented with the sale of Methwold's Estate. In the story, William Methwold sells his estate to an Indian family with the contractual stipulation that the family must continue to live exactly as the English inhabitants before them had until the moment of Indian independence, at which point the family could again live as Indians. The fictional contract imposes an English (read colonial/imperial/Western) geography over the estate being sold. The contract extends a political identity as well by defining the identity of the inhabitants concurrently with the state's political borders. The family lacked the possibility to live as and be Indian until the stroke of midnight, because until that point there was no such place to bound such an identity. Borders are what Kamal Sadiq, borrowing Rushdie's phrase, calls "midnight's children." Decolonization led to "[n]ew borders," and "paths that were legal and customary became illegal overnight" forcing, through both inclusion and exclusion, new identities on the local inhabitants as the result of international geopolitical shifts.[2] In Rushdie's tale law enforces political identity congruent with state geography. At midnight, though, everything changes.

In this example, we can see that the law (i.e. the contract) is the expression of political identity across a territory, rendering a condition in which "[l]ocation equals identity."[3] Rushdie illustrates that an individual's location is a construct that can change without physical movement. In other words, "space changes

---

[1]   Rushdie, *Midnight's Children* (2006).

[2]   Sadiq, *Paper Citizens* (2010) 39. *See also*, Cooper, "What Is the Concept of Globalization Good For?" (2001) 206.

[3]   Greenberg, *This Machine Kills Secrets* (2012) 141. *See also*, Clark & Landau, "Untangling Attribution" (2010) 25.

... meaning."[4] Political space is the space in which negotiations about how social rights and obligations will be allocated among the governed and the government. This negotiation itself gives identity to the participants in terms of membership, which legitimates their role in such negotiations. International borders, therefore, are expressions of legal geography mapped onto spatial geography through an expression of a political geography bounded by common community.[5] As a result, legal arguments "presuppose spatial knowledge," and human rights actions are "struggles for spatial normativity."[6] These values structure public space in which discourse and deliberation take place. Of course, such uniform identification of individuals with political values compartmentalized by borders is a mythical construction, but it is the construction that underlies international space.[7]

Thus far in this research, Cyberspace has been described in terms of its spatial and legal geography. Legal space is not sui generis; it has origin and history. Specifically, law is the product of negotiations that occur within the constructed public space of the state. Law is a mechanism used to articulate the parameters of public space as a reflection of the values negotiated by the political membership of the space.[8] At the heart of the concept of legal jurisdiction are "fundamental questions of order and legitimacy," which describe the political geography.[9]

This chapter turns its attention to the project of identifying how values shape the political geography of Cyberspace through its code and architecture. If code is law, then the coder makes political "[c]hoices among values, choices about regulation, about control, choices about the definition of spaces of freedom."[10] This section argues that there are underlying values that organize Cyberspace as well as guide and legitimate power distribution in the governance of Cyberspace. First, this chapter will build a framework for understanding how constitutional values structure political space and legitimate action therein. Then, it will analyze how constitutional values were implemented into the open network architecture through a historical analysis of its design across the technical layers. The final section reflects on the

---

4   Lessig, *Code 2.0* (2006) 87.
5   Coicaud, *Legitimacy and Politics* (2002) 12. *See also* Streck, "Pulling the Plug on Electronic Town Meetings" (1998) 39.
6   Liste, "Transnational Human Rights Litigation and Territorialised Knowledge" (2014) 1–19.
7   *For instance, see* Ferguson, *Global Shadows* (2006) 113–154. *See also,* Clapham, "Degrees of Statehood" (1998) 154; Walzer, "The Moral Standing of States" (1980) 214; and Mattelart, *Networking the World* (2000) 1.
8   Coicaud, *Legitimacy and Politics* (2002) 83.
9   Post, "Against 'Against Cyberanarchy'" (2002) 1387.
10   Lessig, *Code 2.0* (2006) 78.

value of interoperability, arguing that it is the core organizing logic for the political geography of Cyberspace.

Code and Constitution

At the heart of modern governance is the idea of the constitution. Constitutions are legal documents that are foundational in scope. They serve as the blueprints for the construction of public space, and are distinct from the legal geography they deploy.[11] Effective constitutions organize and distribute power among the actors within a governance space in such a way that a tenable imbalance of power is created between the citizen and the state.[12] So for instance, Sajo argues that constitutions embody shared emotions and values of the political community that it organizes,[13] and as such, constitutions can be seen to organize the "communicative conditions for a reasonable political will formation."[14] These value-laden "communicative conditions" are a political geography that structures public discourse and deliberation. The flow of information and boundaries to its flow are connected to build the "public sphere" within which political identity is formed.[15] Constitutions set the limits of jurisdiction, meaning that they extend communicative conditions across space, and demarcate the limits of community as defined by values embedded through founding political practices.[16] The constitution shapes the political geography in which "the process by which we reason about how things ought to be" takes place.[17]

Political geography can be observed in the communicative conditions deployed by code. Code when observed in the layered model constitutes both the spatial geography of Cyberspace (i.e. its architecture) and the legal geography of Cyberspace (i.e. its architecture). This compression is important. In physical space law and politics are extended over and, thus, contiguous with territory. In Cyberspace, space is extended by code, and

---

[11]   Rawls, *A Theory of Justice* (1971) 7. *See also*, Habermas, *The Postnational Constellation* (2001) 116 and Noveck, "Designing Deliberative Democracy in Cyberspace" (2003) 11.

[12]   Rawls, *A Theory of Justice* (1971) 28 and Clark, *Legitimacy in International Society* (2005) 19.

[13]   *See generally*, Sajo□, *Constitutional Sentiments* (2011).

[14]   Habermas, *The Postnational Constellation* (2001) 117.

[15]   *See generally*, Kellner, "Intellectuals, the New Public Sphere, and Technopolitics" (1998) 147–86; Noveck, "Designing Deliberative Democracy in Cyberspace" (2003) 11; Clinton, "Internet Rights and Wrongs" (2011); and Jayakar, "Globalization and the Legitimacy" (1998) 713.

[16]   *See, for example*, Whitehead, *Science and the Modern World* (1967), 13 ("Law is both the engine for government, and a condition restraining government").

[17]   Lessig, *Code 2.0* (2006) 78.

code is law. It should be no surprise then that code imposes communicative conditions as well, which requires probing the extent to which code functions as a constitutional force. This will reveal how values are architected directly into Cyberspace. Code is of course not the same as a formal constitution, but code does perform many of the same functions as a constitution, which makes the analogy tenable.[18]

The concept of legitimacy will be helpful in articulating the constitutional values that define a political geography. Legitimacy addresses the "justification of power" within a governance structure and is a "fundamental problem of politics."[19] It is a measure of the distribution of power that "concerns first and foremost the right to govern."[20] The right to govern is defined through a network of social values, laws, and founding principles that together define the critical "division that separates those individuals who command from those who obey."[21] In other words, legitimacy is articulated and observed at points that structure the division of power among entities that *govern* and entities that are *governed*.[22] Societies use constitutionally constructed political institutions "to settle conflicts that threaten the cohesiveness of the community."[23] These institutions are the "guarantors of the public space" in which communicative conditions foster a "network of sociability."[24] Constitutions construct a political geography by bounding "exchanges to unfold in a fixed framework and under the form of reciprocity" that "tangl[es] together ... rights and duties."[25] The constitution expresses what it means to be a member of a political space by expressing the bounds of that space in terms of rights and obligations in an "unequal distribution of power."[26] The rights and obligations themselves, often expressed through law, institutionalize shared values of the community.[27]

Legitimacy, then, is fluid across space and time,[28] but actors within a given political community will often invoke foundational or constitutional values in order to legitimate contemporary actions by framing them within the

---

[18] *See* Lessig, *Code 2.0* (2006) 6–7, 275, 314 and Martin, "Using the US Constitution to Frame the Governance of Cyberspace" (2015) 24–26.
[19] Wight, *International Theory* (1992) 99.
[20] Coicaud, *Legitimacy and Politics* (2002) 10.
[21] *Id.* at 26.
[22] *Id.* at 10.
[23] *Id.* at 21.
[24] *Id.* at 11.
[25] *Id.*
[26] *Id.* at 31
[27] *Id.* at 32; Lessig refers to these as "framing values." Lessig, *Code 2.0* (2006) 316.
[28] Coicaud, *Legitimacy and Politics* (2002) 207–08 and Power & Tobin, "Soft Law for the Internet" (2001) 39.

communicative conditions.[29] Constitutional values shape "rules of conduct [that] are indissociable from a historical context."[30] Legitimacy is not a universal norm, so each political geography must be examined in the context "of social facts ... set within the ongoing flow of history."[31] Legitimacy, as the link between the power and values, is an analytic for examining the political geography deployed by code in Cyberspace.[32]

Code is Politics

Technology as it progresses through its technical life span, from development to operations, is laden with politics.[33] Technology, often advertised as of the future, is always a product of history.[34] As a result, design decisions made in early stages of development entrench design values in a technology, and such decisions are often influenced by politics.[35] Cyberspace is no different, and this section will use the history of its development as a tool to reveal foundational values embedded in its architecture that shape its political geography.[36]

This historical inquiry focuses on the source of code: coders. As with any discussion of values, the ability to articulate them with specificity that also applies with generality is limited.[37] This section will examine the political values that the coders designed into Cyberspace. In the same way that an American constitutional lawyer might consult the *Federalist Papers* to discern the values of the constitutional designers, this section will examine how these coders articulated the values they held into the code they designed.

Making Space

Cyberspace is a globally distributed phenomenon,[38] but this is a relatively new

29   Coicaud, *Legitimacy and Politics* (2002) 23 and Clark, *Legitimacy in International Society* (2005) 2.
30   Coicaud, *Legitimacy and Politics* (2002) 83.
31   *Id.* at 192; Clark, *Legitimacy in International Society* (2005) 13.
32   Tambini *et al.*, *Codifying Cyberspace* (2008) 13 and Clark, *Legitimacy in International Society* (2005) 3.
33   *See* Lessig, *Code 2.0* (2006) 24.
34   Coicaud, *Legitimacy and Politics* (2002) 199.
35   Fleischmann *et al.*, "Thematic Analysis of Words That Invoke Values in the Net Neutrality Debate" (2015) 1.
36   Walzer, "The Moral Standing of States" (1980) 211. *See also* Lipschutz, "Environmental History, Political Economy and Change" (2001) 73.
37   Coicaud, *Legitimacy and Politics* (2002) 138.
38   Castells, "Communication, Power and Counter-Power in the Network Society"

development in its history. Though the Internet went "public" in the mid 1990s, its first vestiges were established in 1965 when the TX-2 computer in Massachusetts was connected to the Q-32 in California creating the first "wide area computer network."[39] This was followed in 1969 by the establishment of the ARPANET, a US Department of Defense funded project to establish networked computer communications that eventually "grew into the Internet."[40] The first public demonstration of Internet technology was by Bob Kahn, one of the designers of the TCP/IP, in 1972, and that same year, email was developed.[41]

Early Cyberspace was inhabited by the people that were constructing it, meaning that "networking research incorporated both work on the underlying network and work on how to utilize the network."[42] In other words, the first individuals to set foot in Cyberspace were neither natives or explorers, they were architects. Cyberspace was not territory to be claimed in an imperial sense; it was a territory springing from a community. These individuals were forming the very rules that would bind them as they interacted in Cyberspace, and they were developing these rules as a community as was seen with the IETF and the W3C in the previous chapter.

The Internet that they created "embodies a key underlying technical idea, namely that of open architecture networks."[43] As discussed in Chapter 2, this means that the overall network itself is not hindered by design choices of specific network operators as interoperability is facilitated through packet switching technologies. Packet switching is a design choice that results in there being "generally no constraints on the types of network that can be included or on their geographic scope."[44] Interoperability becomes a core communicative condition through the establishment of a common standard-ized language, the use of which is the only prerequisite for membership in the network of networks.

Bob Kahn articulated "four ground rules" for open architecture networking.[45] First, each network connecting to the Internet "would have to stand on its own" and there could be no requirement of "internal changes" to such a network for connection.[46] Second, the transmission of data packets would be

---

(2007) 247.

[39] Leiner *et al.*, "A Brief History of the Internet" (2002).

[40] *Id.*

[41] *Id.*

[42] *Id.*

[43] *Id.*

[44] *Id.*

[45] *Id.*

[46] *Id.*

on a "best efforts basis," meaning that if a node failed to transmit a packet it would have to be retransmitted from the source.[47] Third, the gateways and routers (i.e. the physical layer) would serve transmission purposes only and retain no information about the packets being transmitted.[48] And finally, "there would be no global control at the operations level."[49] These four principles, and especially the fourth principle, construct the limits of the public space through articulation of core values. They also reveal an interesting aspect of the Internet, namely that it is not a singular entity, but instead is an assemblage of technologies working together based on common rules or protocols. This technical design stood in contrast to the traditional telecommunication monopolies that were the norm during its development. The values that were entrenched can be observed in two distinct traditions in Cyberspace: in the egalitarian code that structures the logical layer and in libertarian code developed at the applications layers.

Rights Space

Open architecture networking is more than just a set of technical specifications. It is code that embodies a set of political values embedded by its designers and reflects their specific historical situation.[50] These designers were generally Americans working at research universities during the Cold War and the American Civil Rights Movement, among other historic events.[51] Their efforts established a particular type of network design that reflects the liberal values that pervaded the coding community at that time. In particular, the Internet's Cold War origins shape this design in a uniquely American way – especially since it was funded by US Department of Defense at its inception.[52]

As a result, the Internet is the product of a particular historical milieu that led its designers to seek to accompany the technology with "social conscience."[53] The designers saw that "we have the free will to either place human rights and virtues – better distribution of wealth, free speech, human rights – in lockstep with technological advances or else suffer the consequences."[54]

---

[47] *Id.*

[48] *Id.* and Post, *In Search of Jefferson's Moose* (2012) 40.

[49] Leiner *et al*, "A Brief History of the Internet" (2012).

[50] Betz & Stevens, *Cyberspace and the State* (2011) 33.

[51] Brate, *Technomanifestos* (2002) 85.

[52] *For example see* Clinton, "Internet Rights and Wrongs" (2011). *See also* U. S. Department of Defense, "Department of Defense Strategy for Operating in Cyberspace" (2011); Martin, "Using the US Constitution to Frame the Governance of Cyberspace" (2015) 24–26; and Mattelart, *Networking the World* (2000) 1, 4.

[53] Brate, *Technomanifestos* (2002) 26–27.

[54] *Id.*

These coders therefore incorporated a "rights culture" into the developing Internet. Information theorists, like Norbert Wiener, argued that distributed flows of information would lead to open discourse "unbounded by geography or politics."[55] Such flows would be made manifest as computer scientists began to design the Internet. Early Internet pioneer Douglas Engelbart focused his work on empowering the individual user of computing systems to help the collective good.[56] Engelbart was a leader in the field of human computer interaction, and invented the computer mouse. Brate connects Engelbart's ideology specifically to American politics at the time, including the Civil Rights Movement, and goes on to say that "Engelbart's values and ethics would remain hardwired into the future of the technology."[57]

Wiener, Engelbart, and others like them sought technological development that "intersected with efforts to promote and protect many human rights."[58] The open architecture reflects these values as "technologies are imperfect and incomplete physical manifestations of the current political order."[59] As Americans, these designers would be acutely influenced by the First Amendment to the American Constitution and the public space that it formulates by delegitimizing government involvement in information exchanges. The five freedoms embodied in the First Amendment are all freedoms directly related to information transfer among non-governmental individuals and entities.[60] Broadly, this can be referred to as the "freedom of expression." It should be noted that the freedoms enumerated in the First Amendment are constructs:

When the claim to freedom of expression emerged, this presupposed that an originally small but critical mass shared their desire to express their views and receive information without censorship. This desire and need were conceived and felt as something due, which in the emerging rights culture became a matter of strong expectation. This expectation grew stronger, to the point where any disregard of the expectation triggers a sense of injustice.[61]

As a construct, this freedom developed along with historical processes, and the rights culture embedded in Cyberspace reflects this historical context.[62] The design itself embeds a historically contextualized freedom of expression

---

[55] *Id.* at 25.

[56] *Id.* at 114–141.

[57] *Id.* at 136.

[58] Fidler, "The Internet, Human Rights, and U.S. Foreign Policy" (2012).

[59] Banks, "The Politics of Communications Technology" (2013).

[60] U.S. Constitution, Amend. I.

[61] Sajo, *Constitutional Sentiments* (2011) 27.

[62] *See generally*, Rychlak, "Compassion, Hatred, and Free Expression" (2007) 407.

that the designers would characterize as "free information."[63] The political geography of Cyberspace is one that places minimal restriction on the transfer of information and the autonomy of the individual user.[64] The early Internet community maintained a "dominant ethos ... [of] altruism" with a "spirit of mutual aid."[65] The code was engineered to be "vehemently public sphere."[66]

The value placed on free information would be heightened by the Internet's historical links to higher education.[67] Its use spread initially on college campuses and early Internet policy spread the Internet to all University users.[68] In the United States, higher education holds freedom of expression – in terms of information sharing and inquiry – as a core egalitarian value. The majority of the population of Cyberspace for close to half of its technical life would be primarily found in higher education.[69] The connection of the Internet to research is important, because "the network's first role was sharing the information about its own design and operation."[70] This means that the information sharing values of the academic communities became part and parcel of the values being embedded in the political geography.

The historical context in which the Internet was being designed sheds light on how the values of open architecture networking emerged. The designers were working in the midst of the Cold War threat of the USSR from abroad and the upheaval of the Civil Rights Movement domestically. These events give context to the communicative conditions that were developed to support the right of free information. First, as a product of a specific time and place – and funded by the US DoD – Cyberspace reflects values shaped by the ideological conflict in the Cold War.[71] The United States at that time emphasized openness as a way of counteracting the closed, centralized Soviet model,[72] and as a result Cyberspace is designed as a "highly decentralized" network that stands in contrast to the Soviet model.[73] The "iron curtain" was a

---

[63]   Brate, *Technomanifestos* (2002) 29 and Betz & Stevens, *Cyberspace and the State* (2011) 18.

[64]   See Held, *Democracy and the Global Order* (1995) 145–156 and Habermas, *The Postnational Constellation* (2001) 118.

[65]   Resnick, "Politics on the Internet" (1998) 51.

[66]   Tambini *et al*, *Codifying Cyberspace* (2008) 11.

[67]   Brate, *Technomanifestos* (2002) 98.

[68]   Lessig, *Code 2.0* (2006) 2.

[69]   Leiner *et al*., "A Brief History of the Internet" (2012).

[70]   *Id*.

[71]   Brate, *Technomanifestos* (2002) 89–90.

[72]   *For instance see* Bush, *Modern Arms and Free Men* (1968) 201, 223–4. *See also* Brate, *Technomanifestos* (2002) 48.

[73]   Spar, "The Public Face of Cyberspace" (1999) 345.

descriptive term of a political geography that was locked and therefore not free.[74] Vannevar Bush, head of the US Office for Scientific Research and Development during World War II – which oversaw the Manhattan Project, argued that freeing information would be a tool against totalitarianism.[75] We see this reflected in the open network architecture's underlying principle of "no global control at the operations level." The decentralized and nonhierarchical network counters the Soviet model by moving power over information to the individuals using the network.

At the same time, deep questions about political membership within the United States were being raised by the Civil Rights Movement. Images of the era show African Americans claiming space in the political geography by invading the white-only spaces of the legal and spatial geography with marches and sit-ins. The Civil Rights Movement was pushing for identity within the political community for minorities. The severe inequalities that were revealed became part of a broader narrative of liberal activism throughout the 1960s and the 1970s.[76] Open network architecture through its emphasis on interoperability had the potential to "[enhance] the equal rights of participation for all members of society" by opening access to its political geography.[77] The interoperability envisioned in the network reflects a concern of the coders for equality of access.[78] This coding was "motivated by the drive to create a greater good through empowerment of the people."[79] The Internet is designed specifically not to discriminate among different types of information or users.

The coders working on the design of the open network architecture implemented a version of the freedom of expression that is consistent with the egalitarian leanings of their particular historical context. These early designers were primarily concerned with the logical layer of the Internet, and their design was built to extend rights to users by constructing a space to facilitate interoperable communities. The notions underlying this structure rest in the ideal that the "more information is shared, the freer society is, the greater the potential is for cooperation."[80] It is the transfer of information for the public good that underlies their project, and as we will see below, transfers power to the applications layer as a result. The network was designed to create an interoperable citizenry.

---

[74] Bush, *Modern Arms and Free Men* (1968) 168.
[75] Brate, *Technomanifestos* (2002) 48, 33.
[76] Brate, *Technomanifestos* (2002) 192–93.
[77] Rawls, *A Theory of Justice* (1971) 224; Betz & Stevens, *Cyberspace and the State* (2011) 103; and Brate, *Technomanifestos* (2002) 104.
[78] Brate, *Technomanifestos* (2002) 185–87.
[79] *Id.* at 132–133.
[80] *Id.* at 208.

Liberation Space

The egalitarian bent of the open network architecture pushes power to the edges of the network as a way to incorporate individual power into the political geography. This has an interesting effect of not only facilitating communication, but giving users the ability to define the terms of their communication. The political geography extended by the logical layer allows for the development of political geography at the applications layer. This means that diverse political groups are able to create their own spaces through the use of applications. Quite possibly the best example of this is the libertarian ideals that began to drive cryptographic code as a means of individual liberation.[81] The logical layer created an opening in political space that promised "freedom without anarchy, control without government, consensus without power."[82] Libertarians saw the Internet as a place where individual rights would triumph over state control.

This libertarian turn in the design and culture of Cyberspace was a powerful one and has a strong and lasting pedigree, and libertarian philosophy to some extent is responsible for many of the applications that redefine borders.[83] The word hacker, today, is often used to describe criminals that wreak havoc in Cyberspace by stealing valuable information or defacing websites. Media accounts refer to hackers as the bad guys in Cyberspace that compromise networks and systems for fun and for profit.[84] However, this use is a far cry from its origins in the tech community, wherein hackers are individuals "who enjoy exploring the details of programmable systems and how to stretch their capabilities."[85] Hackers maintained an "ethical code [that] was driven by the progress of computer code – it was wrong, almost *evil*, to keep code or programming resources to yourself."[86] Hackers, in the original sense, believe that "information sharing is a powerful-positive good," which echoes the value of free information.[87] Though hackers often resist political categorization,[88] the hacker ethic of understanding how things work "is in one sense essentially apolitical and technically focused, while in another sense it

---

[81]   *Id.* at 226, 227 and Lessig, *Code 2.0* (2006) 2.

[82]   Lessig, *Code 2.0* (2006) 2 and Brate, *Technomanifestos* (2002) 224. *See also* Betz & Stevens, *Cyberspace and the State* (2011) 56.

[83]   *For example* Elwell, Murphy, & Seitzinger, "Bitcoin" 1 (2013) (Bitcoin); DeNardis, *Global War for Internet Governance* (2014) 8 (Bitorrent); and Bearman, "The Untold Story of Silk Road" (2015) (The Silk Road).

[84]   Betz & Stevens, *Cyberspace and the State* (2011) 16.

[85]   Raymond, *The New Hacker's Dictionary* (1996) 233.

[86]   Brate, *Technomanifestos* (2002) 243.

[87]   Raymond, *The New Hacker's Dictionary* (1996) 234.

[88]   "A Tale of Many Hackers" (2015) 5.

is subversive and profoundly ideological."[89] Hacking is a "way of knowing things"[90] that emphasizes empowerment through knowledge of technical architecture. It easily adapts itself to libertarian rhetoric characterizing mainstream society as "being led" and "being fed."[91]

The hacking ideology was extremely influential in Internet culture and groups such as the cypherpunks.[92] A cypherpunk is an individual "interested in the uses of encryption via electronic ciphers for enhancing personal privacy and guarding against tyranny by centralized, authoritarian power structures, especially government."[93] Their political views are best described as anarcho-libertarian.[94] Using the motto "privacy for the weak, transparency for the powerful," they recognized that the applications layer could give substantive meaning to their construction of freedom of expression.[95]

The central issue to the cryptographic community is that information flows unfettered by state interference, including chilling effects of extensive surveillance.[96] Cypherpunks cast communicative conditions in terms of "what is public, and what is private."[97] Freedom of expression in this political geography rests on freedom of speech as emphasized in Western liberal democracies.[98] So for instance, while giving a speech on WikiLeaks, Tor activist Jacob Appelbaum informs federal agents attending the speech that the only thing in his pockets is the Bill of Rights.[99] The freedom of speech is linked to the freedom of expression found in international human rights regimes, but Cypherpunks redeploy the anti-totalitarianism sentiment from the

---

[89] Betz & Stevens, *Cyberspace and the State* (2011) 18 and Brate, *Technomanifestos* (2011) 243.

[90] Kracht, "The Hacker Perspective" (2014) 26 and Brate, *Technomanifestos* (2002) 251–252.

[91] Kracht, "The Hacker Perspective" (2014) 26 and Prisoner #6, "The 21st Century Hacker Manifesto" (2014–2015) 50–51.

[92] Greenberg, *This Machine Kills Secrets* (2012) 94–134 and Assange *et al.*, *Cypherpunks* (2012) 21–22. *See also* Domscheit-Berg, *Inside WikiLeaks* (2011) 174–75.

[93] Raymond, *The New Hacker's Dictionary* (1996) 140

[94] Greenberg, *This Machine Kills Secrets* (2012). For other examples *see Id.* at 89–91, 122, 148, 150, 192–193, 227, 255; Domscheit-Berg, *Inside WikiLeaks* (2011) 4; Assange *et al.*, *Cypherpunks* (2012) 29, 70–1, 76; and Tambini *et al.*, *Codifying Cyberspace* (2008) 11.

[95] Assange *et al.*, *Cypherpunks* (2012) 7 and McIntosh & Cates, "Hard Travelin'" (1998) 86.

[96] *For instance*, Snowden, "Testimony before the Parliament of the European Union" (2014) 1.

[97] Domscheit-Berg, *Inside WikiLeaks* (2011) 50.

[98] Rawls, *A Theory of Justice* (1971) 197 and US Constitution, Amend. 1.

[99] Greenberg, *This Machine Kills Secrets* (2012) 167, 150.

Cold War against all power structures.

As a result, these coders deploy code that hides the individual from power structures, including the state. Cryptographic code facilitates a political geography with equal distribution of power over information as a way to reallocate power and wealth. Cypherpunks work to reclaim information technology from being "the privileged technology of neoliberalism."[100] As an example, Appelbaum endorses the dispersion of power "to people who are not simply the ones who make the decisions" through what Barlow would call a "renegotiation of power."[101] Similarly, Domscheit-Berg describes WikiLeaks as a project to shift political geography:

> In the world we dreamed of there would be no more bosses or
> hierarchies, and no one could achieve power by withholding
> from the others the knowledge needed to act as an equal
> player. That was the idea for which we fought.[102]

To anarcho-libertarians, Cyberspace's open architecture reflects their own value in individual liberty through rights, which explains the pervasive libertarian tone in the tech world.[103] Libertarian code uses digital cryptography to recode communicative conditions imposed on the individual and to rewrite political geography. They use their code "to prove that technology not pretension would define the nature of identity on the Internet."[104]

Interoperability

Cyberspace contains lots of values. Any visit to a social networking website, such as Facebook, will quickly display numerous different value sets. These value sets are not the values of Cyberspace, but the variety and scope of them are indicative of the political geography of Cyberspace. As Lessig observes, the space that is constructed "depends entirely on the values that guide development of that place."[105] As discussed above, the principles of open network architecture are constitutional, and these principles create a political geography built around interoperability. The abundance of divergent

---

[100] Harvey, *A Brief History of Neoliberalism* (2009) 159; Assange *et al.*, *Cypherpunks* (2012) 27; and Bearman, "The Untold Story of Silk Road" (2015).

[101] Greenberg, *This Machine Kills Secrets* (2012) 176, 255.

[102] Domscheit-Berg, *Inside WikiLeaks* (2011) 4.

[103] Spar, "The Public Face of Cyberspace" (1999) 347. *See also* Tambini *et al.*, *Codifying Cyberspace* (2008) 11; Sunstein, *Republic. Com 2.0* (2007) 111–12; and Bearman, "The Untold Story of Silk Road" (2015).

[104] Greenberg, *This Machine Kills Secrets* (2012) 115.

[105] Lessig, *Code 2.0* (2006) 70.

views that are expressed in Cyberspace is a result of the interoperability value.

Interoperability pervades Cyberspace and organizes its geography. More than just technical design, interoperability can be seen as the value given constitutional force in the code. It addresses concerns about closed political space and opens up the possibility of the expansion of political space through the applications layer. Interoperability is the operationalization of "information wants to be free." It recognizes that information freedom rests in the ability for information to be communicated among as many individuals as possible.

As the core value in Cyberspace, interoperability facilitates direct communication by devices, and therefore it can be seen as facilitating interoperability among individuals as well. Interoperability uses three mechanisms to shape political geography. First, it decentralizes communications. Second, it creates free access through openness. Third, it creates equality on the network through peering. Critically these mechanisms shift the division between ruler and ruled and fosters participation by opening up political membership. Interoperability means that participation is no longer subject to specific central authority; instead, participation is self-authenticating through the adoption of a standard protocol.

The networkification of the world pushes this principle to world-scale and makes geography interoperable. Networked geography is no longer bounded in terms of exclusion. Instead, its limits are understood in terms of inclusion and accessibility. This means that the bounds of the political geography of Cyberspace are not territorial, rather the bounds are the digital divide between those with access and those without.

The layered model is a conceptual stack that serves as a framework for understanding the complex technical architecture of Cyberspace. By delineating different functions, the layers model allows for the categorization of technologies to understand their discrete functions and features. The layered model, though, sometimes obscures the fact that these technologies are not always discrete, and that Cyberspace is an assemblage of these layers.

Similarly, thus far the geography of Cyberspace has been described as layered: a spatial geography layered with a legal geography that is layered with a political geography. The problem is that all these geographies happen at once. When an individual looks at the state of their nationality on a map, they do not see the drawn borders and deconstruct the state into spatial, legal, and political units. Instead, the borders represent a compression of those concepts into a single understandable geography. While one cannot see Cyberspace in terms of borders, Cyberspace functions such that individuals experience the same compression of concepts, possibly more so. In real space it is much easier to disaggregate physical geography, such as a mountain, from the other geographies of the state. In the geography of the state, the mountain stays the same while the legal and political geographies that encompass it can change, sometimes literally, at the stroke of midnight. In Cyberspace the geography can change at a keystroke.

The geographic compression in code is an extension of Lessig's principle: code is geography. Cyberspace does not have nature; it only has code and as such code is central to its organization. Part I has described Cyberspace in insular terms. This is a view of Cyberspace from within Cyberspace, which is not without its limitations. This exercise will prove essential in examining how Cyberspace as an alternative geography interacts with international space.

Interlude

"Obviously, when an old world sees a new world arise beside it, it is challenged dialectically and is no longer old in the same sense."

David Berlinski

5

The Nomos of Cyberspace

In 1543 Copernicus first published his theory of a heliocentric universe, a theologically controversial idea that would play out in the early 1600s when the Catholic Church placed Galileo on trial for supporting such views. The Church, in 1616, banned books that supported a Copernican map of the solar system and only recently recanted its position in the Galileo matter.[1] Scientifically, the work of these two scholars cannot be overstated as the heliocentric model is fundamental to human understanding of the solar system, but it is the Church's reaction to the Copernican map that shows the true impact of Copernican thinking. The Catholic Church at the time was trying to maintain dominance in Western Europe, and its claim to legitimacy and power was rooted in the space of Christendom. This sphere of Christ, oriented towards the central divine authority of the Pope, was experiencing growing pains as kings and princes made claims to similar authority. In the wake of the English Reformation and on the eve of Westphalia, the Copernican map literally changed Western human orientation within the geography of the universe.[2] The map presented by the Catholic Church was one that depended on the Church being at the center of the Universe making it the natural focal point for the heavenly gaze. The legitimating principle of divine right depended on the centralization of that right to a single point importance.[3] Copernican thinking destroyed "a world in which the spatial structure embodied a hierarchy of values" and replaced it with "a universe of indefinite proportions."[4] This fragmented the map of Christendom by diminishing the importance of its chief spatial indicators: Rome was no longer the literal center of the Universe. Indeed, the human society was displaced to the periphery.

Now, move the clock forward 400 years to 2016 and transport to a New York City street (or any street in any big city or medium sized city or, quite possibly,

---

[1]   Cowell, "After 350 Years, Vatican Says Galileo Was Right" (1992).
[2]   Schmitt, *The Nomos of the Earth* (2003) 86.
[3]   *Id.* at 112.
[4]   Coicaud, *Legitimacy and Politics* (2002) 98.

any street, anywhere). If you look around you will likely see someone looking at a map on a digital device. A map that conveniently centers on that individual's location at the touch of a button. The power in Copernicus' idea, has in a sense been lost. Humans have found their way back to the center of the map. More precisely, the digital device has found its way to the center of the map, which reveals the user's location, and the gap between device and user is shrinking.[5] These maps choose their centers dynamically, imparting importance on the device and the user as both move through space and time, and as a result the user experience is such that they become part of the map as space extends out from them both virtually and physically.

This idea that humans are at the center of the map again, is more than just a quippy metaphor. Maps, at their most basic, display the relative location of various geographic epistemic units. As a representation of the world, maps are human constructions of orientation, and as such maps construct how humans experience the world.[6] The lesson from Galileo is that the choice of where to center a map is a choice of relative importance.[7] As a result, a world map made for a U.S. middle school social studies class during the Cold War might center on the United States thereby dividing the Soviet Union into two parts. Even the seemingly neutral choice to place the Prime Meridian at the center of some world maps embeds Western primacy by entrenching the Atlantic Worldview. A further example is Buckminster Fuller's Dymaxion map, which projects the world on an icosahedron that can be unfolded in multiple ways to reveal the connections and disconnections in the world. Fuller's projection was intended as a counter narrative to politically conceived maps by challenging the boilerplate nature of the traditional world map by diminishing the importance of its center and taking away conceived notions of up and down produced by cardinal directions. [8] Fuller's map embraces the idea that geographic understandings can and do change, and these understandings change how individuals and societies understand the world.

Since maps signify space, then control of maps is linked to control of space. As a result, many states have strict mapping laws. For example, China's State Secrets Law places geographic information under the control of the Central Government.[9] Such control of space by the state is not without its complications. The Google Maps tool has repeatedly been at the center of

---

[5]   *For example see* Lessig, *Code 2.0.* (2006); Riley v. California, No. 13–132 (2014) 18; and Streck, "Pulling the Plug on Electronic Town Meetings" (1996) 25. *See also*, the literature on transhumanism, e.g. Robinson, "Addressing the Legal Status of Evolving 'Envoys of Mankind'" (2011) 470–475.

[6]   Schmitt, *The Nomos of the Earth* (2003) 86.

[7]   *See Id.* at 51.

[8]   Buckminster Fuller Institute, "The Dymaxion Map" (n.d.).

[9]   Hille, "China Cracks Down on Online Maps" (2010).

controversies on how borders are drawn in its mapping software.[10] Borders are important because they set limits: spatial, legal, and political. The center of the map, chosen for importance, is limited by borders, which show the limits of the central power. In terms of the state, for instance, the map shows a star as the central capital, and solid dividing lines as the borders of both the values and law that flows from the star.

Chapters 2–4 describe the geography of Cyberspace from within Cyberspace. This choice of perspective purposely centers Cyberspace in terms of importance and diminishes territory in terms of borders.[11] It would of course be disingenuous to argue that Cyberspace is not linked to territory, as the physical layer clearly reveals the territorial links. Thus, Goldsmith's claim still rings true, Cyberspace only exists as a result of human enterprise in a physical world, therefore Cyberspace cannot be separated from the physical world in any real sense. Virtual reality is, after all, still virtual.[12] This chapter takes the presented geography of Cyberspace and argues that it presents social actors with an alternative geography that "detach[es] social and political reality from the world of sovereign states."[13] The alternate geography is not a separate place as envisaged by Barlow, instead it is a way of knowing and conceptualizing space that rewires the way we experience the primary geography of the world. It follows then that Cyberspace changes the way in which individuals experience and approach the space they inhabit. This shift in geography does not nullify borders, but it changes their content and meaning, which in turn causes shifts in the underlying governance structures that support such borders. In essence, the argument here is that Cyberspace transforms geography and governance from the international into the interoperable global. The first section will explore the concept of borders and their changing meanings. The second section will argue that Cyberspace re-codes borders and changes their geographic content. The final section will use the concept of *nomos* to argue that the re-coding of borders is changing world order.

Borderless Worlds

The spatial narrative introduced in Chapter 2 is based on clichés that have taken root in the descriptions of Cyberspace. One of the most popular of

---

[10]   *See generally* Fenlon, "Did Google Maps Cause an International Border Dispute?" (2011); "India Google Maps Controversy Is Modern Drama" (2014); and Taylor, "The Simple Way Google Maps Could Side-Step Its Crimea Controversy" (2014).

[11]   *See* Kulesza, *International Internet Law* (2013) xii.

[12]   *But see* Ferguson & Mansbach, *Globalization* (2012) 136.

[13]   Kulesza, *International Internet Law* (2013) xi–xii and Bowman, "Thinking Outside the Border" (2007) 221–22.

these clichés references the Internet and Cyberspace as "borderless" in scope.[14] As part of the spatial narrative, borderlessness is associated with the free transfer of information across national frontiers. Designating a space without containment or limits, "borderless" is used specifically to invoke a counter narrative to international space in terms of spatial, legal, and political geography.[15]

A realist response to assertions of borderlessness is obvious: each physical component and user has location within territory and is subject to the lex loci of that place.[16] There is ample evidence to support such claims. China controls the Internet at nine locations that house physical international telecommunications links.[17] North Korea also keeps tight control over physical entry points for the Internet, and sharply controls individuals' access within its physical geography.[18] Iran has plans to create a "halal Internet" that exists exclusively within its borders.[19] The US and UK's ability to engage in mass surveillance is based on the physical location of infrastructure in the United States and the United Kingdom.[20] Egypt turned the Internet off during the Arab Spring.[21] Realists, both legal and political, have a plethora of evidence to support the claim that the Internet exists within state borders, and that states pursue their national interests in that arena just as they did when railroads were the transformative technology. To some extent, the realist is correct: borders remain an important feature of our experience of the world and they remain important in the organization of law and politics at a global level.

Both the "borderless" rhetoric and the realist argument have a central flaw. They both attempt to describe Cyberspace in terms of the state. The rhetoric miscalculates the level of integration of Cyberspace into the fiber of the state, and the realist miscalculates the lack of control that the state has over that integration. The realist view tends to react to the narrative of Cyberspace as

---

[14]   *See generally* Lessig, *Code 2.0* (2006) 71 and Martin, "Using the US Constitution to Frame the Governance of Cyberspace" (2015) 24.

[15]   Kulesza, *International Internet Law* (2013) 2. *See also,* Schmitt, *The Nomos of the Earth* (2003) 96.

[16]   Goldsmith, "Against Cyberanarchy" (2014) 7. *See also* Sofaer *et al.*, "Cyber Security and International Agreements" (2010) 190 and Yannakogeorgos & Lowther, "The Prospects for Cyber Deterrence" (2013) 50.

[17]   Kulesza, *International Internet Law* (2013) 109–10.

[18]   Sparkes, "Internet in North Korea: Everything You Need to Know" (2014).

[19]   Bernard, "Iran's Next Step in Building a 'Halal' Internet" (2015).

[20]   Greenwald & MacAskill, "NSA PRISM Program Taps in to User Data of Apple, Google and Others" (2013) and Gellman & Poitras, "U.S., British Intelligence Mining Data from Nine U.S. Internet Companies in Broad Secret Program" (2013).

[21]   Richtel, "Egypt Cuts Off Most Internet and Cellphone Service" (2011).

counterfactual to the state system by focusing on discrete layers of functionality. In the realist critique, Cyberspace is a thing, and things are the subject of territorial authority. This externalization of Cyberspace is natural for a variety of reasons, but it insufficiently theorizes Cyberspace and ignores the endogenous nature of Cyberspace that shapes the space in which law and politics unfold.

Cyberspace is not a counterfactual to the state. Cyberspace is a part of everyday human life in almost every aspect: leisure, business, commercial, political, even romantic.[22] It is no longer exogenous to social interaction, it has become an "endogenous and political"[23] factor "embedded in the material condition" of the world.[24] Geographically speaking, Cyberspace is more river than highway. It is a part of the landscape, and it is difficult to control. Maybe one of the best examples of this can be found in one of the central realist institutions: the military. Militaries around the globe now include Cyberspace as one of the domains in which they operate.[25] By joining Cyberspace with land, sea, air, and space, there is an explicit spatial recognition of Cyberspace as a space in which military operations can take place. This is more than just rhetorical, it is acknowledgement that Cyberspace constitutes a new locus for borders.[26] National defense is an act of protecting borders and Cyberspace as a domain of military operations spatializes Cyberspace as another place that intersects and influences the space of the state.[27] Military doctrine adopts Cyberspace not as a thing to be controlled, but instead as an endogenous medium with a geography that shapes the most realist of activities.

What then is to be made of the maps still inscribed with the borders of international space? The borderless rhetoric seems empty in the face of a clearly depicted international system, because borderlessness asserts an anarchic counterfactual that is not experienced by the user.[28] A better term would be re-bordered which implicates not just the location of borders, but their content as well. Users still experience the borders that appear on a

---

[22]   Liu *et al.*, "Cybersecurity" (2012) 1. *See also* Council of the European Union, "EU Human Rights Guidelines on Freedom of Expression Online and Offline" (2014) I.D.33 and Kulesza, *International Internet Law* (2013) ix.

[23]   Fritsch, "Technology and Global Affairs" (2011) 28.

[24]   Luke, "The Politics of Digital Inequality" (1996) 120.

[25]   Kulesza, *International Internet Law* (2013) 67; US Department of Defense, "Department of Defense Strategy for Operating in Cyberspace" (2011); and Hayden, "The Future of Things Cyber" (2013) 3–8.

[26]   US Department of Defense, "Department of Defense Strategy for Operating in Cyberspace" (2011) 8.

[27]   *Id.* at 5.

[28]   Johnson & Post, "Law and Borders" (1996) 1389.

political map of the world. These borders represent national frontiers many of which, if visited, might even be demarcated by walls, fences, or other physical divisions. Physical borders are often, quite literally, legal lines drawn in the sand. They demarcate jurisdiction as deployed across space by political processes. National borders demarcate people into discrete political units of difference, at least in theory. Borders are then inscribed on maps, and are often inscribed physically on the Earth's surface as states build physical barriers along the lines of political demarcation.[29] These barriers "draw on the easy legitimacy of sovereign border control even as they aim to function more as prophylactics against postnational, transnational, or subnational forces that do not align neatly with nation-states or their boundaries."[30] To states, and thus to realists, borders still matter.

These physical landmarks are not fortifications against other states, but against the ideas of other space.[31] The fortifications are attempts to construct the meaning and content of national borders in the public mind, but "[s]tate borders are certainly not comparable to fortifications" despite this physical architecture.[32] This function of borders is not new and has historically been implicated with information technologies. Vannever Bush in 1949 wrote that "[i]ron curtains are not new inventions; yet they are now harder to maintain."[33] Bush's evaluation in the wake of WWII taps into a familiar logic of transparency and liberation driven by free flow of information. Bush, though, pushes this narrative further by observing that the "same technical advances that sustain in mystery the distant emperor ... also tend to penetrate the barriers to ideas that he must maintain for his continued sway."[34] This observation places technology as central to the transformation of space through social experience. Thus, while borders maintain a "physical obdurate premodern signature," the power they contain "is networked virtually" and the people they contain are "hybridized."[35] Interoperability renders standards as "non-tariff barrier[s]" which eases interaction across these fortifications.[36]

Just as Copernicus started a process of changing the way in which humans

---

29 Brown, *Walled States, Waning Sovereignty* (2010) 7–20.
30 *Id.* at 32. *See also* Habermas, *The Postnational Constellation* (2001) 80–81.
31 *See* Bigo, "The Emergence of a Consensus" (2008) 76–94. *Compare with* Domscheit-Berg, *Inside WikiLeaks* (2011) 131.
32 Habermas, *The Postnational Constellation* (2001) 66.
33 Bush, *Modern Arms & Free Men* (1968) 168.
34 *Id. See also* Greenberg, *This Machine Kills Secrets* (2012) 128 and Assange, "Conspiracy as Governance" (2006). *But see* Morozov, "Political Repression 2.0" (2011); Lessig, *Code 2.0* (2006) 53; and Wittes, "The Intelligence Legitimacy Paradox" (2014).
35 Brown, *Walled States, Waning Sovereignty* (2010) 80.
36 Jayakar, "Globalization and the Legitimacy" (1998) 716.

orient themselves to the world, the technology of Cyberspace is causing shifts in human orientation to the world. Copernicus did not change the borders of territories, he simply reoriented those territories drawing into question the content of their borders. Cyberspace does the same. As a decentralized, interoperable network, Cyberspace presents an alternate geography that is increasingly networked into the social consciousness. It is this non-Copernican conception of the world that allows for the social construction and experience of global space by "destroying notions of traditional borders."[37] Such construction and experience happens on the other side of "a legally significant border between Cyberspace and the 'real world.'"[38] The technical design of Cyberspace, the architecture itself, is reprogramming the content layer of geography by recoding borders.

Re-coding Borders

To understand this process of re-coding borders, it would be helpful to have a map of Cyberspace.[39] A map would help to uphold the claim of cyber-geography made throughout this book. There is rich work on mapping Cyberspace that reveals a variety of aspects. These maps show the world as disaggregated networks. Borders in the traditional sense are not visible despite the state's claim to the physical layer.[40] One of the reasons for this separation is that the "cost and speed of message transmission on the Net is almost entirely independent of physical location."[41] Instead, these often beautiful maps reveal network connections in the shape of a decentralized and distributed network and display the vast opportunities for inter-operability.[42] Cyberspace is depicted as the sum of its endpoints, making its true external border the digital divide.[43] Indeed, in most maps of the Internet, geographic features – the traditional features represented on maps – are the exact feature that are obscured.[44] Instead, these maps show the configuration of the network from a variety of different perspectives.

Maps of Cyberspace are not Copernican maps, with humans at the edges circling around a central power source. These maps show the connections

---

[37]   Spar, "The Public Face of Cyberspace" (1999) 347.

[38]   Johnson & Post, "Law and Borders" (1996) 1378.

[39]   Post, *Jefferson's Moose* (2012) 24.

[40]   *See generally*, Dodge & Kitchin, "Ways to Map Cyberspace" (2001) and Post, *Jefferson's Moose* (2012) 23–30.

[41]   Johnson & Post, "Law and Borders" (1996) 1370.

[42]   Post, *Jefferson's Moose* (2012) 23–28 and Leiner *et al.*, "A Brief History of the Internet" (2012).

[43]   Luke, "The Politics of Digital Inequality" (1998) 133 and Cooper, "What Is the Concept of Globalization Good For?" (2001) 190.

[44]   Post, *Jefferson's Moose* (2012) 28.

among humans on a global scale, and these connections are strikingly decentralized.[45] In fact there is often no discernible center at all, meaning that these maps are dynamically configurable to allow for understanding of the interactions they chart. Cyberspace maps reflect spatial characteristics in terms of devices and users, placing devices and users as the external boundaries of its legal and political geography and reflecting the interoperability of open architecture networking.[46] These visualizations depict an alternative geography in which the "power to control activity in Cyberspace has only the most tenuous connections to physical geography."[47] The idea of the border is unhinged from territory, which calls for reconsideration of spatial, legal, and political geography.[48]

What we are left with is a dual geography in which the conceptual separation of Cyberspace from real space becomes increasingly untenable as there is dissonance between an observed physical reality of borders and an experienced spatial reality in which these borders do not exist.[49] This can be seen in the sociological debate between "digital dualism" and "augmented reality." These two sociological concepts are used to describe the effect of the human absorption of Cyberspace. Digital dualism suggests two selves: one online and one offline. Whereas augmented reality posits a cyber-experience that augments the perception in the real world,[50] digital dualism keeps separate the "virtual" and the "real" and augmented reality argues that "the digital and the physical are increasingly meshed" as Cyberspace "implodes atoms and bits."[51] This debate centers on how the social mind reconciles two different maps of the world. Augmented reality allows such a reconciliation to be achieved through the development of new understandings of geography.

This need for reconciliation is important in broader terms as well since it requires a reconciliation of the international with the global. International governance is structured around territorial, international assumptions as opposed to global assumptions.[52] At the root of the international is the assumption of national space as a stack of spatial, legal, and political geography compressed into concurrent territorial space.[53] Changes in the

---

[45] *Id.*

[46] Leiner *et al.*, "A Brief History of the Internet" (2012).

[47] Johnson & Post, "Law and Borders" (1996) 1371.

[48] Leiner *et al.*, "A Brief History of the Internet" (2012) and Cooper, "What Is the Concept of Globalization Good For?" (2001) 191.

[49] Gourley, "Cyber Sovereignty" (2013) 277–78.

[50] Jurgenson, "Digital Dualism versus Augmented Reality" (2011).

[51] *Id.*

[52] *See* Kulesza, *International Internet Law* (2013) 30.

[53] *See* Habermas, *The Postnational Constellation* (2001) 60, 63 and Sassen, *Territory, Authority, Rights* (2006) 40. *See also* Johnson & Post, "Law and Borders" (1996) 1369

international system are generally understood in terms of changes in borders. These lines of geographic understandings that serve as focal points for scholars of world order. This is why Westphalia is a central inquiry for many scholars, as it serves as a fulcrum point for observing transitions in the variety of geographic compressions.[54] There is recognition that changes in how territory is divided are critical to understanding the structure of the international system. Territory is the threshold question of all international legal and political issues.

This link between law and spatial organization is what Schmitt refers to as *nomos*, which explicitly ties the subdivision of the Earth's land territory to the development of law.[55] *Nomos*, as used by Schmitt, naturalizes law in the sense that law flows from *terra firma* due to a human need to divide the Earth with lines ranging from furrows in a field to national frontiers.[56] He claims that "the great primeval acts of law [are] terrestrial orientations: appropriating land, founding cities, and establishing colonies."[57] International law then is the result of *how* humans draw lines on the Earth, and Schmitt's analysis focuses on transitions that reconstitute those borders and, importantly, how understandings of space change. In other words, Schmitt's account is tied to the land.[58] Schmitt's central observation that spatial conceptualization is inherently linked to governance is salient, but in a networked world it must be understood as being linked not to land but to geography as mapped by human understanding of the spatial condition.

Schmitt's analysis thus falls short in that it fails to contemplate the opening of new space with any real depth.[59] His idea that "[l]aw is bound to the land" recenters the Earth's territory in terms of legal geography with the Earth "contain[ing] law," "manifest[ing] law upon" itself, and "sustain[ing] law above itself."[60] He flirts with alternative geographies when he discusses how technology can push forward a "global image," but his analysis is always constrained by the ends of the Earth.[61] Specifically, he argues that his idea of *nomos* is not applicable to the sea, because it is not divisible in the same way that territory in the form of land is. There is, in his estimation, no *nomos* of the sea, because the seas defy subdivision, and can only be understood as an adjacency to the land. Any law applicable to the sea flows from its adjacency

---

and Sassen, *Territory, Authority, Rights* (2006) 20.

[54]   Clark, *Legitimacy in International Society* (2005) 35

[55]   Schmitt, *The Nomos of the Earth* (2003) 70.

[56]   *Id.* at 42.

[57]   *Id.* at 44.

[58]   *Id.* at 42.

[59]   *See Id.* at 351–355.

[60]   *Id.* at 42

[61]   *Id.* at 86.

to land. The sea is a global commons except in its liminal spaces where it is sufficiently attached to territory.[62] For Schmitt, non-land can only be defined through its proximity to land.

This ignores the idea that the experience of territory itself is shaped by non-land areas. The ocean can rise up and take territory, thus individuals living on an island likely understand territory differently from individuals in a land-locked area.[63] Schmitt's theoretical limitations are exposed by the contemporaneous dawning of the space age in which humans were first able to see the planet Earth as a globe.[64] Pictures from the early days of space exploration reflect a concurrent change in the spatialization of the Earth's surface. The ability to visualize the Earth not as a map but as a photographic image, literalizing Schmitt's "global image," coincided with major shifts in international governance that began with the process of reconstructing international space in the wake of World War II. This reorganization, though ultimately based on the "territorial integrity and political independence" of the state, would for the first time include human rights as part of the organizing logic for international society.[65] Images of Earth from outer space, such as the Blue Marble, allow for and necessitate reflection on assumptions about the meaning of borders.[66] The photographic medium itself can be seen as closer to experience than a map, which encodes experience and embeds design choice.

Cyberspace has a similar, arguably, stronger effect. Cyberspace architecture allows users to experience borders differently thereby reconstituting the social understanding of those borders.[67] It "cut[s] across territorial borders" and "[undermines] the feasibility – and legitimacy – of laws based on geographic boundaries."[68] While individuals may still feel physically contained by those borders, they are no longer metaphysically contained as well. They instead can import ideas and communications at will across those borders.[69] The human conscience is extended into a global domain.[70] Tied to the values embedded by the coders of Cyberspace, this means that nations are "now

---

[62] *Id.* at 183.

[63] *For example* Carrington, "The Maldives Is the Extreme Test Case for Climate Change Action" (2013).

[64] Major, "This Is the Very First Photo of Earth From Space" (2014).

[65] UN Charter (1945) Art. 1–2.

[66] NASA, "Blue Marble – Image of the Earth from Apollo 17" (2015). *See also* Featherstone, "Genealogies of the Global" (2006) 387.

[67] *See* Habermas, *The Postnational Constellation* (2001) 42.

[68] Johnson & Post, "Law and Borders" (1996) 1367.

[69] *Id.* at 1372.

[70] Habermas, *The Postnational Constellation* (2001) 39. *See also* Coicaud, *Legitimacy and Politics* (2002) 136 and Betz & Stevens, *Cyberspace and the State* (2011) 106.

wired ... with an architecture of communication that builds a far stronger First Amendment than [American] ideology ever advanced."[71] As argued in Chapter 4, this "stronger First Amendment" is really a freedom of expression as envisioned by the designers of the Internet and its applications.

Cyberspace is not like the global commons as portrayed by Schmitt. Schmitt claims that the "sea is free" and that "[o]n the open sea there were no limits, no boundaries, no consecrated sites, no sacred orientations, no law, and no property."[72] Schmitt is asserting that the governance structure of global commons excludes these spaces for their lack of geography.[73] This is why the 'borderless world' rhetoric is a poor description of Cyberspace. It deprives it of geography. Cyberspace does not lack "sacred orientations." Quite the opposite, Cyberspace is increasingly becoming a waymarker for individuals moving in real space. Such waymarkers include phrases like "Google it"; the use of Twitter as a locus for action in traditional news coverage; and, possibly most starkly, the proliferation of printed QR codes that serve as physical doors to places in Cyberspace (see Fig 5.1).

Fig. 5.3: QR codes are images that users can scan with a device such as a phone in order to gain information. Such codes can be printed and placed in real space to give users entry into Cyberspace. The QR code pictured opens a hyperlink to http://space.blountsfolly.com

---

[71] Lessig, *Code 2.0* (2006) 236.

[72] Schmitt, *Nomos of the Earth* (2003) 43.

[73] United Nations Convention on the Law of the Sea (1982) Art. 2; Antarctic Treaty (1959) Art. IV(2); and Treaty on Principles Governing the Activities of States in the Exploration and Use of Outer Space, including the Moon and Other Celestial Bodies (1967) Art. II.

Another reason to distinguish Cyberspace from the global commons is that the sea, like other global commons (namely Antarctica and Outer Space), is uninhabitable. While there is vocabulary for transient seafarers, there is no corresponding concept of a permanent seakind.[74] As was argued in Chapter 2, Cyberspace has population. It has transitory surfers, but it also has permanent netizens, many of whom are digital natives. Schmitt's thesis requires inhabitability, because spatial division is entangled with the demarcation of inhabitation. Implicit to Schmitt's theory is the idea that there is a community of inhabitants that inscribe borders onto land.[75] However, the digital native represents "a more mobile kind of legal person."[76]

Cyberspace has inhabitants and communities that exist within its borders.[77] This forces consideration of legal concepts such as self-determination and human rights, because "for there to be principles and practices of legitimacy, there needs to be a community/society."[78] The important implication of a group of "digital natives" is that the world's population will be increasingly dominated by users who have always understood space as shaped by Cyberspace. Digital natives will not experience Cyberspace as an alternative geography any more than Native Americans experienced the Americas as a "new world." Digital natives understand Cyberspace as part and parcel of their geography. The implication is that there is a shift happening in how the world is spatialized; a shift that is deeply implicated with interoperability.

Nomos

Schmitt's object is to prove that international law itself is based on the basic question of spatial division. It is "a primary criterion embodying all subsequent criteria,"[79] and '*nomos*' is the immediate form in which the political and social order of a people becomes spatially visible."[80] Schmitt compresses spatial and legal geography into a single layer.[81] In conjunction with his *Concept of the Political*, which compresses legal geography and political geography, Schmitt reads territory as an essential agent of law and politics. Here, Schmitt's analysis is chosen for critique due to this asserted essentialness, because it is the question of territory that sits at the heart of the debate on the

---

[74] A Google search returned no pages discussing any notion of seakind. There is, however, a corresponding notion of spacekind. *See generally* Robinson, "Astronauts and a Unique Jurisprudence" (1983–1984) 483.

[75] Schmitt, *Nomos of the Earth* (2003) 42.

[76] Johnson & Post, "Law and Borders" (1996) 1400.

[77] Assange *et al.*, *Cypherpunks* (2012) 155.

[78] Clark, *Legitimacy in International Society* (2005) 6, 149.

[79] Schmitt, *The Nomos of the Earth* (2003) 45.

[80] *Id.* at 70.

[81] *Id.* at 45, 70.

nature of Cyberspace. Schmitt's "terrestrial fundament" presents a fulcrum point from which to base conceptualization, because to understand Cyberspace as an alternative geography, we must first accept the enduring and historically constructed nature of our own physical boundedness.[82] The task is not necessarily one of debunking Schmitt or of supporting Schmitt, but instead seeking an understanding of Cyberspace that resolves the dissonance in the perceptions of geography and alternate geography by articulating them as a single networked geography. This requires investigation into how the *nomos* of Cyberspace shapes the *nomos* of the Earth. Or, in other words, how does Cyberspace re-inscribe borders and transform geography on a world-scale. If *nomos* is to be understood as the "form in which the political and social order of a people becomes spatially visible," then a *nomos* of Cyberspace should be visible.[83]

The analysis in *The Nomos of the Earth* is one that is concerned with change. While Schmitt ties territory to law, he recognizes that a diversity of spatial orders can orient that space. The essential link between territory and law is not to be confused with an argument that the state is the natural unit for global organization. Schmitt clearly recognizes that "new spatial phenomenon" can change the spatial order, and he notes that human extension into airspace means that "firm land and the free sea are being altered drastically, both in and of themselves and in relation to each other."[84] He observes that this technology is not just changing the "efficacy and velocity of the means of human power, transport, and information" but the "content of this *effectivity*."[85] Technology, in his account, can have a transformative effect on the organization of law, and not as an external factor. Technology becomes an endogenous factor that shapes the content of the spatial order itself.

Observing this phenomenon, however, proves more elusive as Cyberspace is complex and expansive. Its networked nature means that it is a system with no exact size or shape. Additionally, it pervades social interaction at a scale that makes generalizations about transactions in Cyberspace severely limited. A natural place to observe border re-coding is at the geographic borders: spatial, legal, and political. Those borders can reveal how Cyberspace pushes up against the international as its territorial geography thins and runs out, and it is these places of abutment and intersection that exhibit the fault lines from which global space is emerging.

The geographic categories used in Part I correlate to the components that

---

[82] *Id.* at 47.

[83]   *Id.* at 70

[84]   *Id.* at 48.

[85]   *Id.*

Sassen argues are "assembled" into governance structures. She argues that world organizing logic can be understood through the assemblage of territory, authority, and rights, and that across history global systems are constructed and reconstructed as assemblages of these three components.[86] These components serve as points of analysis from which to observe the particular conditions within a world-scale system of governance.[87] While Schmitt and Sassen would likely not see eye-to-eye in substance, their arguments both embrace an understanding that international space is capable of being reconceptualized.

International space is constructed around a myth of Copernican-esque systems: territories with centralized governments that hold authority are the building blocks of international space. States are actors and subjects within this space, and they are given rights based on an organizing logic that aligns high degrees of legitimacy with the occupation of territorial space. Pre-1945 states were the rights bearers in international law. Post Nuremberg and the Universal Declaration of Human Rights, individuals became limited rights bearers in the international order.[88] This reallocation of rights is reflected in the noble mission of the UN, but events such as the Rwandan genocide serve as grim reminders of the concentration of state power over territory despite the 1945 reallocation of rights. Scholarship in international legitimacy portrays these allocations in terms of rightful membership.[89] This scholarship has traced a growing trend in international legitimacy of placing increasing emphasis on rightful action by the state. This shifts the gaze of international governance from the border to the interior of the state by allocating international rights to citizens. Despite this re-allocation the state remains the primary arbiter of human rights within a given territory as a result of low degrees of enforcement despite strong international rhetoric.

If Cyberspace is indeed opening up global geography, then it should be observable in international space through the reallocation of territory, authority, and rights in the international assemblage. There should be observable points where the geography of the international runs out and borders Cyberspace. When the geography of Cyberspace is layered onto the geography of international space it should reveal a networked space which "[runs] in many dimensions."[90] As Habermas observes, "'[n]etwork' has

---

[86]   Sassen, *Territory, Authority, Rights* (2006) 18.

[87]   *Id.* at 32.

[88]   *See* Donnelly, "Human Rights" (1998) 14.

[89]   Coicaud, "Deconstructing International Legitimacy" (2009) 37; Donnelly, "Human Rights" (1998) 2; Clark, *Legitimacy in International Society* (2005) 2; and Menon, "Pious Words, Puny Deeds" (2009) 237.

[90]   Habermas, *The Postnational Constellation* (2001) 66.

emerged as a key term."[91] Space ordered through the network constitutes a "new spatial phenomenon," which should be observable in the key institutions of the international order. To continue the cartographic metaphor adopted in the beginning of this chapter, by layering cybergeography onto international geography, we should be able to observe the distortions in the projection of the world.

New assemblages often incorporate aspects of historical predecessors embedding these into the construction of new assemblages.[92] Cyberspace is a paradigm shift, but despite this, much of the international system remains intact and will continue to remain intact. Cyberspace, as an alternative geography, is still "filtered through local languages and meaning systems."[93] This means that the international will remain a powerful force despite the spatial shift. International space, as a geography, can also be understood to be "filtered" through the languages and meaning systems of Cyberspace.

Part II of this research will take the geography described in Part I and use it as a conceptual map that can be juxtaposed to the geography offered by the international system. These geographies will be layered together to explain observable points where Cyberspace changes the geography of international space. Using Sassen's vocabulary of territory, authority, and rights, the thematic case studies presented in the following chapters will analyze how geographies in real space are warping as they come into contact with Cyberspace. Chapter 6, will approach territory from the perspective of transnational cyber conflict, and will examine the idea of "territorial integrity" in terms of the cyber use of force. Chapter 7 will investigate how Cyberspace redistributes authority through an examination of IOs, IGCs, and corporations that make architecture decisions in Cyberspace. This chapter will show that the concept of global multistakeholder governance shifts a great deal of authority outside the borders of the international. Finally, Chapter 8 will explore how Cyberspace transforms the individual's rights in relation to the state. This chapter will use cryptography and surveillance to illustrate how rights have been reallocated in the context of Cyberspace. These three case studies taken together will show the contours of re-coded borders as they unfold in Cyberspace.

---

[91]   *Id.*

[92]   Sassen, *Territory, Authority, Rights* (2005) 3–6. *See also* Ferguson & Mansbach, *Globalization* (2012) 69 and Burbank & Cooper, *Empires* (2010) 8.

[93]   Ferguson & Mansbach, *Globalization* (2012) 205.

Part II

Encounters with the Digital

"I think I never before quite realized the place of the fence in civilization."

W.E.B. Du Bois

6

Conflicting Territories

In May of 2013, Cody Wilson printed a working gun with a 3D printer and fired it.[1] Shortly thereafter he made the computer file, that is a set of instructions for a 3D printer to print what he called the Liberator, available online for download. It was downloaded more than 100,000 times before Wilson removed the file.[2] Little did Wilson know that he was running afoul of the United States' International Traffic in Arms Regulations (ITAR). These regulations prohibit the export of "defense items" – in other words, weapons – found on the United States Munitions List (USML) without authorization from the government.[3] ITAR also, significantly, prohibits the export of "technical data" on these items, which is data that would assist the manufacturing of the prohibited item.[4] Wilson's file was in a standard language that would allow anyone with an Internet connection to download it and use a 3D printer to manufacture a gun. The file, since it was on the Internet, was downloadable anywhere in the world, and Wilson removed the file from his website when confronted by the U.S. Government.[5]

Three years later Wilson's file is still online and freely available through sources like the Pirate Bay.[6] Wilson started a company called Defense Distributed, which now manufactures a product called the Ghost Gunner.[7] This desktop CNC mill will take a block of aluminum and mill a lower

---

[1]   Silverman, "A Gun, a Printer, an Ideology" (2013).

[2]   Cadwalladr, "Meet Cody Wilson, Creator of the 3D-Gun, Anarchist, Libertarian" (2014).

[3]   22 C.F.R. 120 (2019).

[4]   22. C.F.R. 120.6 (2019).

[5]   Cadwalladr, "Meet Cody Wilson, Creator of the 3D-Gun, Anarchist, Libertarian" (2014). *See also* Feuer, "Cody Wilson, Who Posted Gun Instructions Online, Sues State Department" (2015).

[6]   Greenberg, "I Made an Untraceable AR-15 'Ghost Gun' in My Office—And It Was Easy" (2015).

[7]   *Id.*

receiver for an AR-15.[8] Wilson's product cannot be exported, and the computer file is sold only to United States citizens to keep this product from running afoul of ITAR. Yet this product still effectively digitizes a gun, which lowers barriers to access. The gun that it creates is of high quality, and is a gun that is outside of the regulatory loop; it is an untraceable "ghost gun."[9] And while Wilson is keeping tight control over the "technical data" in the .cad files that allow the machine to manufacture the part, he has open sourced the machine itself so that the plans for the hardware and the software that runs it are freely downloadable.[10] Anyone with these files can develop new design files for the Ghost Gunner, and enable it to make a variety of guns and other items. Defense has been distributed, digitally.

The Ghost Gunner is interesting because it shows the capacity of the state to lose control over violence in two ways. First, it lowers the barriers to the production of the means of violence, which weakens government control over violence. It is legal under U.S. federal law for an individual to manufacture a lower receiver, but it was a time-consuming process and required a high level of skill.[11] The Ghost Gunner makes gunsmithing a plug-and-play venture. Second, and important to the discussion below, it shows that the state no longer has control over the spread of violence at its borders. ITAR is specifically meant to help maintain international peace and security by restricting the export of munitions to countries or persons that might use them for ill. ITAR is directly related to the international project of bracketing war, by cutting off the supply of armaments, and ITAR correlates to regimes such as the Wassenaar Arrangement[12] and the Arms Trade Treaty.[13] These initiatives are mechanisms used to stop the flow of armaments across their borders, which was easy when armaments needed to be carried on trucks. Ghost guns are digitized, just as lethal, and save on the shipping cost.

This chapter investigates how Cyberspace changes the nature of territory by examining how Cyberspace changes international conflict. Schmitt's claim "that law and peace originally rested on *enclosures in the spatial sense*" is particularly salient here as it highlights the role of borders in conflict prevention.[14] In Schmitt's territory-centric conception of international law, war is "bracketed" to locations such that it does not "disturb" the spatial order.[15]

---

[8] Guns are made up of many parts. The lower receiver is the component that is regulated under the US law. *Id.*

[9] *Id.*

[10] Defense Distributed, "Downloads" (2016).

[11] Andy Greenberg, "I Made an Untraceable AR-15 'Ghost Gun' in My Office" (2015).

[12] Wassenaar Arrangement, "About Us" (2016).

[13] Arms Trade Treaty (2014).

[14] Schmitt, *Nomos of the Earth* (2003).

[15] *Id.* at 186.

This chapter will probe this bracketing of war, and illustrate the diminished importance of the border in constructing the space of conflict.

The argument here is not meant to be a "dethroning of Clausewitz," but it does argue that Cyberspace dramatically changes the context of international conflict through the subversion of territorial borders.[16] In short, it argues that armed conflict as conceived in the international system is tied to territorial geographies, and that international governance mechanisms that are meant to minimize international armed conflict are structured around this link. The chapter then shows how the concept of cyberwar dislodges conflict from these territorial linkages, which makes the application of norms meant to control international violence ineffective at bracketing it. Section one of this Chapter will use the Stuxnet attack on Iran's centrifuges to analyze how international law has traditionally dealt with war as well as some of the observable gaps in that regime. This section will show how Cyberspace dislodges territory from the governance of international armed conflict. The second section will analyze the role of the international concepts of disarmament and deterrence in limiting cyber conflicts, and it will show that these mechanisms are ill equipped for placing substantive limitations on cyberweapons. Finally, it will use the North Korean Sony hack to show how international politics becomes de-territorialized and distributed in Cyberspace, which means that international conflicts processed through Cyberspace become de-territorialized as well.

Territorial Integrity

At the heart of the post-1945 settlement is the UN charter's Article 2(4), which prohibits "the threat or use of force against the territorial integrity or political independence of any state."[17] This article sought for the first time to create a legal prohibition against interstate armed conflict.[18] Article 2(4) and the UN Charter in general were transformative for international law as it enshrined the state as "the arena within which self-determination is worked out and from which, therefore, foreign armies have to be excluded."[19] For the first time the resort to war, characterized in the Charter as the "use of force," was legally prohibited outside of a few exceptions.[20] Article 2(4) compartmentalizes violence within the borders of a state and gives the state sovereignty over

---

[16]   Betz, "Clausewitz and Connectivity" (2013). *See also* Betz & Stevens, *Cyberspace and the State* (2011) 12.

[17]   UN Charter (1945) 2(4).

[18]   *See generally*, Pompe, *Aggressive War – An International Crime* (1953) 12, 160–64.

[19]   Walzer, "The Moral Standing of States" (1980) 210.

[20]   For those exceptions *see* UN Charter (1945) Art. 42 & 51.

violence within its borders. This compartmentalization, or "bracketing" as Schmitt would call it, is not a new process. The bracketing of war is an act of delineating order from chaos, and Schmitt's project is to show how the international spatial order emerged from the externalization of war. For instance, he notes that during the age of European empires violence was pushed to the peripheries of empires by conceptualizing newly found territories as existing outside of the Western-centric international legal system.[21] Article 2(4) represents a new bracketing of war by conceptualizing every state as an inviolate territory of order. States in this new spatialization were connected to law both internally and, importantly, externally in a legal dynamic between *de facto* control and external recognition.[22]

Art. 2(4) did not change extant borders in a way that was perceptible on a map. Nonetheless, Art. 2(4) did change the content of those borders, and in a very dramatic way. By giving all states an obligation to contain violence within their borders, it also gave all states the right to be free of chaos from outside their borders. Article 2(4) underpins the entire international legal regime, which seeks to contain international armed conflict. The Art. 2(4) prohibition on force is central to *jus ad bellum*, and its goals are further advanced through the *jus in bello* and international disarmament efforts. Cyberspace by recoding borders changes international law's ability to bracket digitized war affecting the nature of international peace and security.

The best place to start to unravel this problem is Stuxnet. Stuxnet presents a clear case for the application and analysis of the law of the use of force in the cyber arena. In 2010, researchers uncovered a computer virus that was propagating itself on computers in Iran.[23] The virus, now known as Stuxnet, was a carefully developed computer program that made its way into computers in the Natanz nuclear facility in Iran. Once there, the malware attacked industrial control systems and executed a program that sped up uranium enrichment centrifuges to damage and destroy them before the end of their expected lifetime. The program itself "displayed a level of technical sophistication and integration never before seen in malware,"[24] and it has been referred to as the "world's first digital weapon."[25] The sophistication of Stuxnet was such that it incorporated four zero-day exploits, and was able to jump an air gap that separated Natanz from the Internet.[26] The program was reportedly developed and released by the United States and Israel as a way

---

[21] Schmitt, *The Nomos of the Earth* (2003) 101–125.

[22] *See generally* Coicaud, "Deconstructing International Legitimacy" (2009) 29–86.

[23] *See generally,* Zetter, *Countdown to Zero Day* (2014) Chap. 1.

[24] Oliver, "Stuxnet" (2013) 129.

[25] Zetter, *Countdown to Zero Day* (2014) 3.

[26] Oliver, "Stuxnet" (2013) 143.

to slow the Iranian nuclear program.[27] For the purposes of the discussion below, it is assumed that this is a state on state act, placing it firmly within the realm of the international system, making international law the controlling governance mechanism. This raises the "principle intellectual challenge in the law of information conflict ... deciding which areas can be covered by a mere extension of conventional legal principles to cyberspace by analogy, and which require whole new methodologies."[28]

The first question to be asked is whether there has been a violation of Article 2(4). If the United States or Israel had flown a plane across the border and bombed the plant, as Israel did to a Syrian facility in 2007, then there would clearly be a violation of Article 2(4).[29] In this case there was no physical violence in a ballistic sense, however, violence was achieved in a kinetic sense in that the centrifuges themselves were physically manipulated in order to destroy them. The centrifuges were attacked, but it is unclear whether this amounts to a use of force under Article 2(4).[30] *The Tallinn Manual on the International Law Applicable to Cyber Warfare,* Rule 11, states that "[a] cyber operation constitutes a use of force when its scale and effects are comparable to non-cyber operations rising to the level of a use of force."[31] *The Tallinn Manual* is an attempt by a NATO group of experts to identify "the law currently governing cyber conflict,"[32] but it notes that "the lack of agreed-upon definitions, criteria, and thresholds for application creates uncertainty when applying the *jus ad bellum*."[33] When compared to a statement by a U.S. defense official on the United States Cyber Strategy, who stated "If you shut down our power grid, maybe we will put a missile down one of your smokestacks," it seems as if at least one of the parties has characterized attacks such as Stuxnet as a use of force.[34] *The Tallinn Manual* experts themselves agreed unanimously that Stuxnet was a use of force that violated international law, but they "split ... on whether it constituted an armed attack."[35] This split illustrates the disjuncture that occurs when international law is de-territorialized. The separation of "use of force" from "armed attack,"

---

[27]   Broad, Markoff, & Sanger, "Stuxnet Worm Used Against Iran Was Tested in Israel" (2011).

[28]   Wingfield, "Legal Aspects of Offensive Information Operations in Space" (1998) 1.

[29]   Zetter, *Countdown to Zero Day* (2014) 192, 215–216.

[30]   *See* Kallberg & Burk, "Cyberdefense as Environmental Protection" (2013) 265–75.

[31]   Schmitt, ed., *Tallinn Manual* (2013) 45.

[32]   *Id.* at 5.

[33]   *Id.* at 42. *See also* Libicki, "Two Maybe Three Cheers for Ambiguity" (2013) 30 and Dipert, "The Essential Features of an Ontology for Cyberwarfare" (2013) 35–48.

[34]   Gorman & Barnes, "Cyber Combat" (2011). *See also* Sanger & Bumiller, "Pentagon to Consider Cyberattacks Acts of War" (2011) and Friedman & Preble, "A Military Response to Cyberattacks Is Preposterous" (2011).

[35]   Zetter, *Countdown to Zero Day* (2014) 402.

categories that were previously substantially concurrent due to the nature of violence, is indicative of the encounter between international and cyber geographies.

Interestingly, Iran never made any complaint to the relevant UN bodies, and instead opted to maintain a high degree of silence on the matter. Iran's silence is related to its own interests in keeping its nuclear program secret, but it also points to one of the key lessons from Natanz: everyone knows that the United States and Israel were responsible for Stuxnet, but no one can prove it definitively. This is dissimilar from, for instance, U.S. covert involvement in Nicaragua, which the ICJ deemed a use of force.[36] In that case, there were physical border crossings by the U.S. and its warfighting capacity that were observed by witnesses to physical attacks.[37] In the case of Stuxnet, no one saw the attack, yet there is ample evidence pointing the finger at the United States and Israel, e.g. the complexity of programming, the target of the attack, the use of high value zero-day vulnerabilities, and anonymous sources informing journalists. There is, however, no definitive evidence of that fact, and the United States has officially made no statement confirming its involvement resting on the plausible deniability that Cyberspace provides.[38]

Digital computing enables the ability to encrypt communications and to hide the source of cyberattacks. Even if a cyberattack were to be traced to an IP address within a state, that state can claim that it is the victim of a hacker using it as a digital hiding spot or that one of its own citizens is the malefactor for which there is limited responsibility. US DoD acknowledges this potential by noting that "low barriers of entry … means that an individual or small groups of determined cyber actors can potentially cause significant damage."[39] In the case of Stuxnet, the virus was feeding information back to servers located around the world.[40] Attribution is a core concept in international law, and for there to be an internationally wrongful act the act must be attributable to a state.[41] The Draft Articles on State Responsibility state that "conduct directed or controlled" by a state is attributable to it, but this requires the establishment of a definitive link that proves such. In Cyberspace such links are hidden by veils of government secrecy, including

---

[36]   Military and Paramilitary Activities in and against Nicaragua (Nicaragua v. United States of America) (1986) 14.

[37]   *Id.* at para. 22.

[38]   McDermott, "Decision Making Under Uncertainty" (2010) 234 and Edward Snowden, "Testimony before the Parliament of the European Union" (2014) 4.

[39]   US DoD, "Department of Defense Strategy for Operating in Cyberspace" (2011) 3.

[40]   Zetter, *Countdown to Zero Day* (2014) 27.

[41]   Draft Articles on the Responsibility of States for Internationally Wrongful Acts (2001) Art. 2.

secrecy classification systems and digital veils of encryption making it difficult to attribute an act to the territory of a state and to the state itself.[42] Attribution is a necessary precondition in international law, but attribution "is an enduring problem" in Cyberspace.[43] The attack, though initiated from some specific geographic point, is experienced as coming from Cyberspace. Cyberspace as an origin for an attack is supported by the military adoption of Cyberspace as a fifth domain.[44]

This fifth domain remains outside of international space, and it obscures the geographic links to the use of force.[45] This creates an obvious problem for stability built around the centrality of a sovereign's territorial integrity in the international system, since international borders no longer separate order from chaos when anonymized weapons can pierce borders and affect physical infrastructure. The plausible deniability enabled by Cyberspace means that states are, in part, relying on the prevalence of non-state actors dispersed around the globe to create noise that covers their tracks. National defense is distributed among a network of indistinguishable actors.

Before moving on from Stuxnet, it is worth noting how this incident reflects on the *jus ad bellum's* counterpart – *jus in bello*. *Jus in bello*, or international humanitarian law (IHL), is not without problems of application, but it does seem that it is more adaptable to cyber conflicts.[46] This is primarily because IHL is not centered on questions of territory. Instead, IHL focuses on humanitarian concerns such as the limitation of pain and suffering for civilians and combatants. It is a *lex specialis* that only applies within the space and time of an international armed conflict.[47] As such, IHL principles are a bit more adaptable to Cyberspace, but they are not without gaps.

For instance, in the case of Stuxnet, it is unclear whether there was an ongoing state of armed conflict that would trigger IHL. Though the attacks occurred over the course of several months, Iran was unaware, and when it became aware it did not respond with force nor through any official channels. Despite the lack of clarity as to whether the rules had been triggered, there is evidence that the programmers of Stuxnet worked hard to make sure that it

---

[42]   *See generally* Clark & Landau, "Untangling Attribution" (2010).

[43]   Zetter, *Countdown to Zero Day* (2014) 64. *See generally* Allan, "Attribution Issues in Cyberspace" (2013) 55–201.

[44]   US DoD, "Department of Defense Strategy for Operating in Cyberspace" (2011) 5.

[45]   *Id.* at 8 and Department of the Army, "FM 3-38: Cyber Electromagnetic Activities" (2014) 1–4.

[46]   Dunlap, "Perspectives for Cyberstrategists on Cyberlaw for Cyberwar" (2013) 212. *See also* Department of the Army, "FM 3-38: Cyber Electromagnetic Activities" (2014).

[47]   Dinstein, *The Conduct of Hostilities Under the Law of International Armed Conflict* (2004) 1–16.

fell within the legal limits of a weapon. States when developing new weapons technologies are required to give the weapon a legal review to ensure that it is a weapon that can be used lawfully.[48] This review must assess whether the weapon is capable of being targeted at a specific target such that its effects, in terms of collateral damage to civilians, are limited in proportion with the military advantage gained[49] and whether the weapon causes unnecessary suffering.[50] The first thing to note is that this review cannot be done in terms of "cyber-weapons" as a class any more than it can be done of "ballistic weapons" as a class. Instead, the analysis is capability by capability, which is confirmed by a US Air Force Instruction on the legal review of cyber capabilities.[51] What Stuxnet's code revealed is that the programmers went to great lengths to infect only specific computers. Stuxnet was equipped with a kill switch that deleted it if the computer did not match very specific conditions.[52] The "missile" portion of the program replicated itself across computers, but was designed to only release its payload, which targeted industrial control boxes, in the Natanz facility.[53] Though the weapon was released through attacks on networks of private Iranian companies, the damage caused minimal threat to human life or civilian property.[54] The weapon itself was designed to work with precision, but it must be remembered that generally "[c]ollateral damage in Cyberspace has a longer reach than in the physical realm."[55] There are other complications with the application of IHL, many of these are simply that: complications. They change the context of humanitarian principles and make the issues more complicated, but IHL would have means of filling the gaps since the regulatory focus is on human lives. For instance, the issue of who constitutes a combatant becomes more complicated but is a problem that is solvable within the imagination of the IHL framework.

Other rifts are deeper. A critical concern for IHL is the military use of civilian objects. All Cyberspace attacks will depend on the use of civilian infrastructure, but Stuxnet illustrates that state cyberattacks will often do more

---

[48]   Protocol Additional to the Geneva Conventions of 12 August 1949, and relating to the Protection of Victims of International Armed Conflicts (Protocol I) (1977) Art. 36. *See also* Blount, "The Preoperational Legal Review of Cyber Capabilities: Ensuring the Legality of Cyber Weapons" (2012) 11–20.

[49]   Gompert & Saunders, *Paradox of Power* (2012) 126

[50]   *See generally* Dinstein, *The Conduct of Hostilities Under the Law of International Armed Conflict* (2004) 80–82.

[51]   United States Air Force, Legal Reviews of Weapons and Cyber Capabilities, A.F. Instruction 51–402 (2011).

[52]   Kim Zetter, *Countdown to Zero Day* (2014) 59.

[53]   *Id.* at 52.

[54]   *Id.* at 388.

[55]   *Id.* at 382. 352. On targeting in cyberspace see Department of the Army, "FM 3-38: Cyber Electromagnetic Activities" (2014) 3–12.

than just transit commercial networks. In order for Stuxnet to work, it had to take advantage of zero-days. These are vulnerabilities in software that are unknown to the programmer and as a result are not patched.[56] When an individual discovers a zero-day, he or she has a few choices of what to do with that information. Some companies have a bounty system in place to buy zero-days; there is a healthy black market for zero-days; and governments will also buy them.[57] Stuxnet had an unprecedented number of zero-days in its programming.[58] This means that a government left open vulnerabilities in commercial software with the potential to put a multitude of devices at risk. Stuxnet also used fake security certificates that marked it as genuine, so the software would be accepted by the systems on which it installed itself.[59] These digital certificates are issued by companies that rely on strong encryption in order to verify that a piece of software is from a trusted source. Stuxnet exploited these mechanisms damaging the trust system used to verify software across the Internet.[60] This means that these weapons rely on the maintenance and exploitation of vulnerabilities in the commercial infrastructure that underpins Cyberspace at a global level.[61] While Stuxnet limited the effects of its attack, another state or entity using similar vulnerabilities might not limit such an attack, a point sharpened when it is recognized that computers similar to those found in Natanz are used to run a great deal of critical infrastructure such as power grids and dams.[62]

Stuxnet is a powerful portent for the international system,[63] and, though some authors wisely note the limitations of cyberwar,[64] Stuxnet is a well-documented example of a computer attack that was used to manipulate and destroy a physical object from afar. What is striking about Stuxnet is the difficulty of placing it squarely within the international legal system. This is because weapons like Stuxnet defy the spatial geography of states. These weapons instead allow states to project force through the alternate geography of Cyberspace, allowing them to skirt around borders as well as the legal regime that supports those borders.

Stuxnet displays vulnerabilities in the Cyberspace infrastructure that

---

[56] Zetter, *Countdown to Zero Day* (2014) 6.

[57] *Id.* at 13.

[58] Oliver, "Stuxnet" (2013) 129.

[59] Zetter, *Countdown to Zero Day* (2014) 13.

[60] *Id.* and DeNardis, *The Global War for Internet Governance* (2014) 95.

[61] Gompert & Saunders, *Paradox of Power* (2012) 142; Taylor & Carter, "Cyberspace Superiority Considerations" (2013) 14.

[62] Zetter, *Countdown to Zero Day* (2014) 61–62

[63] Oliver, "Stuxnet" (2013) 128. *See also* Zetter, "Everything We Know About Ukraine's Power Plant Hack" (2016).

[64] Lee & Rid, "OMG Cyber!" (2014) 4–12.

individuals rely on globally. With other weapons of this sort (i.e. those that are legal but have global implications such as strategic nuclear weapons) states have turned to methods of disarmament and deterrence as a way to manage international peace and security. These mechanisms, which are meant to lower the risk of an Article 2(4) violation, are the subject of the next section.

Ghost Guns

The atomic bomb dropped on Hiroshima near the end of WWII ushered in a new age of warfare driven by technological advances that far outpaced previous innovation blooms. Nuclear weapons, intercontinental ballistic missile delivery systems, long-range stealth bombers, and military satellite systems all widened the ability of states to project force into the territory of other states. States found themselves in a classic security paradox in which the only way to be more secure is to have more and better weapons than one's adversary leading both parties to actively incentivize their own insecurity.[65] To decrease the risk caused by such paradoxes, states turned to disarmament and deterrence mechanisms in order to implement systems of "reciprocal restraint."[66] As discussed above, ITAR is a domestic implementation of such measures.

Disarmament mechanisms usually come in the form of international agreements that ban the development and use of certain weapons, or limit the number of a particular type of weapon that a state may have.[67] Disarmament mechanisms are underpinned by verification. Verification is the act of verifying whether or not a party is complying with an agreement. The importance of verification to disarmament can be seen in Reagan's signature quip: "trust, but verify."[68] Without verification, disarmament agreements tend to be weak and difficult to negotiate. States have traditionally relied on national technical means (NTM) in these agreements as a form of verification, which consist of satellite observation in addition to other types of remote sensing.[69] NTM was an excellent way to verify nuclear disarmament agreements, and the US and USSR were able to rely on satellite observation as a mechanism for verification since nuclear armaments were by their nature quite large. As a

---

[65] Gompert & Saunders, *Paradox of Power* (2012) 1–12.

[66] *Id.* at 115.

[67] Disarmament mechanisms are not always necessarily "legal" documents. Transparency and confidence building measures (TCBMs) that facilitate information sharing among states, such as the Hague Code of Conduct on Ballistic Missile Activities, also serve the project of disarmament. *See generally* Hague Code of Conduct against Ballistic Missile Proliferation (2002).

[68] Harrison, *Space and Verification, Volume I* (2007).

[69] Morgan, "Deterrence and First-Strike Stability in Space" (2010) 9–11.

result, NTM worked well in forging compromises between the two states as they sought to securely reduce their nuclear stockpiles. It should be noted that "[b]ecause disarmament treaties go to the heart of national and international security, states are wary of frivolously embarking on new ones that might constrain their options."[70]

Deterrence is a companion to disarmament. Whereas disarmament seeks to reduce the munitions through reciprocal restraint, deterrence is a method of reducing the risk that a state might use those weapons. [71] It is a policy designed to "discourag[e] an adversary from doing something it might otherwise choose to do by manipulating its calculation of cost and benefit."[72] For example, China's current policy of no first use of nuclear weapons is coupled with a stockpile of weapons that would not assure success in a nuclear conflict, but would be able to survive first strike and inflict unacceptable losses on an adversary thereby deterring an attack.[73] Deterrence can also be attained through international agreements. The Anti-ballistic Missile Treaty (ABM Treaty) was an example of such an agreement.[74] The US and the USSR, unable to compromise on the reduction of strategic offensive nuclear weapons agreed on a disarmament treaty that reduced the deployment of defensive systems. The ABM Treaty ensured mutually assured destruction (MAD), a concept that restrains states from engaging in an attack because any such attack will result in their own demise. Thus, the ABM Treaty is an agreement that imposes disarmament in order to achieve mutual deterrence.

Traditionally, disarmament and deterrence have been the primary mechanisms for stemming armed conflict before it happens by placing limits on a state's recourse to force. Unsurprisingly, numerous commentators have turned to these concepts as a way to reduce the threat posed by cyber-attacks and cyber-weapons. Gompert and Saunders argue that there are lessons from nuclear deterrence that could be deployed to foster "mutual restraint" in Cyberspace.[75] Yannakogeorgos and Lowther argue that US policy "suffers from a misperception that cyberspace is a virtual environment and as such, eliminates discussion of territory and sovereignty."[76] They argue that international norms can be developed to solve the attribution problem by holding states culpable for cyberattacks "originating in or transiting

---

[70]   Findlay, "Why Treaties Work, Don't Work and What to Do About It?" (2006).

[71]   Morgan, "Deterrence and First-Strike Stability in Space" (2010) 23.

[72]   *Id.* at 24.

[73]   Gompert & Saunders, *Paradox of Power* (2012) 39–67.

[74]   Treaty Between The United States of America and The Union of Soviet Socialist Republics on The Limitation of Anti-Ballistic Missile Systems (ABM Treaty) (1972).

[75]   Gompert & Saunders, *Paradox of Power* (2012) 115–150.

[76]   Yannakogeorgos & Lowther, "The Prospects for Cyber Deterrence" (2013) 50

information systems within their borders," but they give no indication of why states would agree to such an extraordinary norm.[77]

The problem with these approaches is that they ignore the inherently ambiguous nature of Cyberspace in which weapons are "in essence an algorithm."[78] As an anonymous hacker put it: "The new global arms race is no longer about who controls the most atomic bombs. It is about who controls/owns the most hackers, botnets, and exploits."[79] Zetter claims that just such a "digital arms race" was launched by Stuxnet.[80] Modern disarmament and deterrence were developed by states to deal with weapons of great magnitude, which have traditionally been rather large. NTM, thus, was an acceptable form of verification, because it gave states a tool through which they could peer into the borders of another state and literally see what that state was doing.[81]

NTM was an effective tool when addressing physical weapons, because it allowed states to maintain their borders, but it is useless in Cyberspace arms control.[82] Cyberspace diminishes "the horrors and costs of war ... tempting" countries to resort to the anonymity of a Cyberattack.[83] The weapons, if designed properly, are meant to be invisible and non-detectable so that "the origins of the attack is almost always unclear."[84] In the case of Stuxnet, discussed above, the programmers went to great lengths to make the program hide itself from the users of the targeted systems. This undermines verification, which is a reason for treaty failure."[85] The immaterial nature of cyberweapons means that states can avoid having an attack attributed to them, which is a significant reason that states would resort to cyberweapons. The attribution problem is further complicated by the trend of "privatised intelligence and information warfare."[86] As former Director of the NSA, Michael Hayden notes, "applying well-known concepts of physical space like deterrence, where attribution is assumed, to cyberspace where attribution is frequently the problem, is recipe for failure."[87]

[77] *Id.* at 51.
[78] Dipert, "The Essential Features of an Ontology for Cyberwarfare" (2013) 36. *See also* Rowe *et al.*, "Challenges in Monitoring Cyberarms Compliance" (2013) 81.
[79] Prisoner #6, "The 21st Century Hacker Manifesto" (2014–2015) 50. *See also* Department of the Army, "FM 3-38: Cyber Electromagnetic Activities" (2014) 3–11
[80] Zetter, *Countdown to Zero Day* (2014) 370.
[81] Sanger & Bumiller, "Pentagon to Consider Cyberattacks Acts of War" (2011).
[82] Zetter, *Countdown to Zero Day* (2014) 400.
[83] *Id.* at 375.
[84] Sanger & Bumiller, "Pentagon to Consider Cyberattacks Acts of War" (2011).
[85] Findlay, "Why Treaties Work, Don't Work and What to Do About It?" (2006) 4.
[86] Singer, *Corporate Warriors,* 99 (2011) 101. *See also* Scahill, *Blackwater* (2007) 415.
[87] Hayden, "The Future of Things Cyber" (2013) 4. *But see* Chen, "An Assessment of

Cyber-weapons are by nature covert. They are designed to take advantage of unknown vulnerabilities in computer software and are meant to be deniable by the country that uses them. Stuxnet used security certificates from Taiwanese companies, and the virus reported the data it collected to servers located in a variety of global locations.[88] In fact, it may not have been discovered except for the fact that it caused a malfunction in some non-targeted computers in Iran.[89] As a result, the U.S. and Israel have never acknowledged their involvement in the attack. For all useful purposes, Iran was struck by a ghost gun – an untraceable weapon that lacks materiality.

The problem with these digital ghost guns is that they defy location, and as a result they defy control. For example, cyber-weapons make use of botnets, which are a geographically distributed network of infected computers known as bots that are under the control of a single "bot master."[90] Botnets are employed in a variety of nefarious undertakings in Cyberspace as they give the bot master distributed computing power and relative anonymity. Botnets cannot be understood to exist within the bounds of a single state, despite the fact that they act as a unitary whole. International governance, a system structured around the national border, is ill equipped to develop disarmament and deterrence mechanisms to control weapons and activities that ignore these borders. Because Cyberspace is everywhere, cyber-weapons "transform [...] a limited physical battlefield to a global battlefield."[91] Disarmament and deterrence, as mechanisms are meant to create less ambiguity in international security by creating information about armaments that states can act on. As Gompert and Saunders note, "the complexity of computer networks, their myriad uses, and the many ways of interfering with them could make reciprocal restraint in cyberspace markedly more difficult than in the nuclear and space domain."[92] Cyber-weapons simply do not fit into these mechanisms for a number of reasons.

First, these weapons are immaterial, making any sort of verification system difficult and any sort of deterrence ineffective. These weapons can fit on a thumb drive and can spread through the Internet with the same ease as a viral meme. This makes verification virtually impossible as the weapon itself is not tied to any sort of infrastructure and is freely portable. Deterrence, on the other hand, which often works on the availability of data about a state's weapons systems, is also precluded. Cyber-weapons rely on vulnerabilities in systems that have not been patched. While disclosing the number and

---

the Department of Defense Strategy for Operating in Cyberspace" (2013) 6.

[88]   Zetter, *Countdown to Zero Day* (2014) 28.

[89]   *Id.* at 7–8.

[90]   *See generally* Maurushat, "Zombie Botnets" (2010) 370–83.

[91]   Department of the Army, "FM 3-38: Cyber Electromagnetic Activities" (2014) 1–5.

[92]   Gompert & Saunders, *Paradox of Power* (2012) 115.

nature of nuclear munitions can have an effect on the strategic maneuvers of other states, the disclosure of a cyber-weapon would lead to a software patch that could render the weapon useless. States developing these weapons are incentivized to keep them covert due to the nature of the technology, and this means that international disarmament and deterrence are not capable of encompassing such technologies.

Second, the plausible deniability that accompanies cyber-attacks is an important limitation on a state's ability to comply with disarmament agreements. The nature of the technology that underlies previous disarmament and deterrence mechanisms is such that the state could effectively maintain control over those technologies. While history is not without examples of individuals attempting to build nuclear reactors in their garages,[93] the technology was of such complexity and scope that states were able to detect such operations and maintain control over the development and deployment of these technologies. Cyberspace is a technological space that is built around fostering innovation. As a result, this means that "lone hackers" are empowered to develop new technologies built on the logical layer making it "largely the realm of nonstate entities."[94] Innovation is not always a good thing; it has made the "network attack ... literally a cottage industry."[95] The same innovative open door that has pushed numerous startups, boosts "the power potential of non-state actors."[96] Indeed, one might argue that the only difference between a computer virus and a cyber-weapon is the intent of the user. While commentators have argued that states should be responsible for curbing the activities of their own citizens, this gives little answer to the plausible deniability problem.[97]

Last and certainly not least, cyber-weapons are weapons that subvert territory in a way that other weapons do not. Other weapons must physically cross an international border and exert force or violence after having crossed that border. Cyber-weapons can enter from anywhere and attack physical infrastructure far outside the territory of the attacking state. States lack legal mechanisms for restricting armaments that are ephemeral and locationless, and as a result disarmament and deterrence as mechanisms for slowing the spread of armaments are ineffectual because they are dependent on the assumption that states have control over their borders and the mechanisms of physical violence within those borders.

---

[93] *For example* Aaronson, "The DIY Engineer Who Built a Nuclear Reactor in His Basement" (2014).

[94] Gompert & Saunders, *Paradox of Power* (2014) 131, 117.

[95] *Id.* at 133.

[96] Betz & Stevens, *Cyberspace and the State* (2011) 11.

[97] *See for example* Gompert & Saunders, *Paradox of Power* (2014) 117 and Sofaer *et al.*, "Cyber Security and International Agreements" (2010) 190.

Cyber-weapons create uncertainty, and uncertainty stands in contrast to verification. Indeed, as seen above with Stuxnet, "the very point of a cyberattack, at least in part, is to increase uncertainty."[98] These weapons render the border ineffectual as a geographic indicator both in their control, as seen here, and their use, as seen with Stuxnet. This means that states are able to exceed their own geography through Cyberspace, giving them more options through which to pursue politics and conflict. The final section of this chapter will address how cyber conflict functions to dislodge international politics from their terrestrial bonds.

Conflict in Black

In May of 2014, the U.S Department of Justice (USDoJ) filed an indictment against what it alleged were five cybercriminals. This in and of itself was not a necessarily novel event, but the individuals charged were novel.   The indictment was against five members of the Chinese People's Liberation Army (PLA) who notably operated and resided in China.[99] The USDoJ asserted that these individuals were guilty of economic espionage in Cyberspace. The indictment itself marked a fever pitch in the bickering between the U.S. and China over the limits of online espionage. In this diplomatic impasse, the U.S. argued that China was violating international law by spying on companies for economic advantage and stealing intellectual property.[100]   While the U.S. was pressing its concerns, though, Edward Snowden leaked a multitude of documents that revealed the United States' own espionage efforts.[101]   When China cried foul, the U.S. drew a line between diplomatic espionage and economic espionage.[102] The indictment from USDoJ was meant to reinforce the international norm that the U.S. was endorsing.

Contrary to the intentions of the U.S., the indictment served to reinforce the vast uncertainties about state action in the Cyberspace. The criminal sanctions, first and foremost, show the inability of the U.S. to stop such actions. While meant more as a diplomatic exclamation point, it must be noted that unless one of the indicted individuals sets foot into the U.S., it is powerless to enforce the law it is invoking. Indeed, the indictment, far from emphasizing a point, seems to reveal the anxiety of the U.S. over its inability

---

[98] McDermott, "Decision Making Under Uncertainty" (2010) 229.

[99] U.S. v. Wang *et al. – Indictment* (W.D. Penn. 2014).

[100] *See also*, Brenner, "Gray Matter" (2013) and U.S. v. Wang (2014) para. 5.

[101] *See* Carroll, "Barack Obama and Xi Jinping Meet as Cyber-Scandals Swirl" (2013); White House, "PPD-20: U.S. Cyber Operations" (2013); and Zetter, *Countdown to Zero Day* (2014) 369.

[102] Spying, for national security reasons, is generally considered legal under international law. Gompert & Saunders, *Paradox of Power* (2012) 140–141. *But see* Snowden, "Testimony before the Parliament of the European Union" (2014) 8.

to ebb the flow of information to Chinese hackers. It also revealed the morphing nature of diplomacy, espionage, and conflict.[103] Were these military operations? Espionage? Or were they simply criminal acts?

The murkiness caused by state action online results from the attribution issues noted above. The ability of states to effectively conceal their cyber operations gives them great leeway to act in that realm, which is coupled with a low cost of entry.[104] This is important to contemplate because it changes the space in which international politics unfold by changing the territory of war. In simplified terms, states may pursue their goals in international fora through diplomacy (here meant to mean anything that is not war including things like sanctions) or armed conflict. International law serves as a mechanism to keep states pursuing their interests within the confines of diplomatic action, which is why Art. 2(4) strikes the balance at the heart of international law by focusing on violence that crosses internationally agreed upon boundaries. Cyberspace short-circuits that balance by removing the obstacle of the border and the corresponding risk of identification. States now have a third option of engaging through the geography of Cyberspace to achieve their goals. This third option is marked by the possibility of at once using force and refraining from armed conflict. International politics, as a result, can now be mediated through the geography of Cyberspace.

This can be seen in the hack of Sony Pictures that was first revealed in November 2014.[105] The sophisticated hack affected most of Sony Pictures internal network and the company's internal information (including items such personnel records, e-mails, and unreleased movies) began to be leaked to the public.[106] The attack was soon linked to the upcoming release of the movie *The Interview*, a comedic parody about two Americans assassinating Kim Jong-un, and the attack was assumed to have North Korean ties. When Sony was defiant about releasing *The Interview*, the hack was coupled with threats of terrorism that resulted in Sony pulling the release, though it was subsequently released online and in several theaters.[107] Two days later, on 19 December, the FBI announced that it was attributing the attack to North Korea, though there has been great speculation as to the validity of this attribution.[108] President Obama, on 2 January 2015, imposed sanctions on

---

[103] Lucas, "Can There Be an Ethical Cyber War?" (2013) 201.

[104] US DoD, "Department of Defense Strategy for Operating in Cyberspace," (2011) 3.

[105] Weisman, "A Timeline of the Crazy Events in the Sony Hacking Scandal" (2014).

[106] *Id.*

[107] Richardson, "Sony kills 'The Interview' after North Korea hack, terror threat" (2014).

[108] FBI Press Office, "Update on the Sony Investigation" (2014). *But see* Lee, "The Feds Got the Sony Hack Right, But the Way They're Framing It Is Dangerous" (2015); Schneier, "Attributing the Sony Attack" (2015); Goldsmith, "The Sony Hack" (2014); and Sexton, "Accurately Attributing the Sony Hack Is More Important than Retaliating"

North Korea, which is the first time sanctions have been used in direct response to a cyber-attack.[109] Throughout this ordeal, the nature and scope of the attack made it a multidimensional threat that challenged the accepted nature of coercive action within the realm of the international.

The initial hack was credited to The Guardians of Peace (GOP) hacker group.[110] This attack was initially seen as a cybercrime against a corporation meaning that the core security concern was the security of Sony's network.[111] As a crime, the criminal is answerable to the state, but the focus is on the private network itself. At first, the hack of Sony did look criminal in nature as the hackers attempted to extort individual employees to keep their personal information from becoming public.[112] However, soon after this, security researchers began to find hints, such as Korean language packs, that linked the hack to North Korea. In a somewhat controversial move, the U.S., and specifically the FBI, attributed the attack to North Korea thus moving the hack into the national security narrative. It also moves the act out of the spectrum of a crime and into the spectrum of international relations, and as a result the U.S. issued sanctions against the North Korean regime.

Superficially, US action in this incident may seem like business as usual in the context of international governance, but a close reading reveals a number of the uncertainties that show how borders are being recoded with new content. As noted above the FBI's attribution was hotly contested by security researchers, but a number of revelations show that even if North Korea was the master puppeteer, the cast of characters taking part in the hack was a globally distributed group of non-state actors. For instance, the Lizard Squad hacker organization may have been involved in the hack as North Korean hired cyber contractors or, possibly, mercenaries.[113] The attribution question leads into a maze where the source of international conflict can no longer be pinpointed to a single site in terms of territory. The capabilities or weapons used are distributed, digital ghost guns making response difficult when the geographic source of the attack is territorially different from the attack, in this case North Korea and Cyberspace, respectively.

A second ambiguity is the nature of the attack. The attack on its face is novel, making it an interesting touchpoint for understanding how Cyberspace

---

(2015).

[109] White House, Executive Order – Imposing Additional Sanctions with Respect to North Korea (2015).

[110] Weisman, "A Timeline of the Crazy Events in the Sony Hacking Scandal" (2014).

[111] *Id.*

[112] *Id.*

[113] Diaconescu, "Inside Job" (2014).

changes international space. North Korea bought technology that allowed it to attack a private U.S. entertainment company in an attempt to halt the release of a film within the territory of the U.S., and the attack garnered a response at the executive level in the U.S. In terms of international governance, the attack on Sony raises difficult questions of classification. If the source of the attack was indeed North Korea, it is safe to say that their military was involved, so one might think that this case would resemble the PLA case noted above. Personal information of employees and corporate information and intellectual property were stolen and released online. This has all the trappings of the economic espionage charged in the PLA indictment. The U.S., however, chose a different response, which indicates that they intended to classify this cyber incident in a different category that goes beyond that of domestic criminal law, which is the usual mechanism states use against espionage within their territorial borders. The use of a presidential order for sanctions against North Korea indicates a heightened concern for U.S. national security. Indeed, the president's order states that

> provocative, destabilizing, and repressive actions and policies of the Government of North Korea, including its destructive, coercive cyber-related actions during November and December 2014, actions in violation of UNSCRs 1718, 1874, 2087, and 2094, and commission of serious human rights abuses, constitute a continuing threat to the national security, foreign policy, and economy of the United States[114]

There are two factors that heightened the U.S. response in this incident. The first is that the North Korean actions were targeted at denying freedom of speech, a fundamental human right in the view of the U.S., and the second is the additional threats of acts of physical terrorism against theaters that show the movie.[115]

What might be an even more interesting question though, would be how the North Korean authorities envisioned their actions. The regime is notoriously opaque, so ever having a full understanding of the logic that went into these actions is unlikely. North Korea's actions do show how Cyberspace changes the content of international action. Without cyber, North Korea's options would have been to choose diplomacy or conflict. If they choose diplomacy, they have a variety of peaceful options including negotiating with the U.S., placing sanctions on the U.S., or placing sanctions on Sony the company. These options seek to coerce change in another country through indirect action that

---

[114] White House, Executive Order – Imposing Additional Sanctions with Respect to North Korea (2015).
[115] Sneed, "Sony Hack Takes Darker Turn" (2014).

stays outside of that country's territorial borders. In this case, North Korea could see that these options would be ineffectual due to its relative power in the international community. It could also see that taking action in the form of direct action, i.e. conflict, within the borders of the U.S. is also not an available option due to its relative military power.[116] Cyberspace allowed North Korea to bypass this decision, by giving it the power to take a third path through the geography of Cyberspace. The similarities to Stuxnet as a coercive action should not be ignored. The Sony hack illustrates a second situation wherein a state was able to take direct actions that interfere with a state's "political independence" without the telltale violations of its "territorial integrity."[117]

Similar to Stuxnet, the Sony hack raises questions about thresholds for self-defense under Article 51 and the application of IHL.[118] These regimes are meant to limit state action to the realm of diplomacy but are dependent on the inherent territoriality seen in past conflict. The third path of action allows states the option to exceed their territory and directly encounter the space of an adversary state without geographic movement. The Sony-North Korea hack is one of a growing number of examples that demonstrate how the spatial context in which the international unfolds is being transformed by the imposition of alternate geographies, and it highlights how the nature of Cyberspace challenges underlying assumptions that shape the international space.

This chapter has shown how the governance system built around the physical territorial space of the state is being reshaped through the introduction of Cyberspace. This argument is built on illustrating how territorial borders no longer "bracket war" as envisioned in Art. 2(4). The international system, in other words, is ill equipped to create regulatory mechanisms that inhibit and control state action in Cyberspace, much less the myriad other actors that can wield such violence.

This theme of shifting international space will be extended in the next two chapters that address legal and political space. A number of subthemes will become evident as well and are worth noting as the analysis moves forward. First, the role of U.S. action will be used as an explanatory mechanism throughout these chapters. The reason for this is twofold. First, the U.S. was where the Internet originated, and it harbors a bulk of the physical,

---

[116] *For example* Fish, "Could North Koreans Ever Really Invade America?" (2012).

[117] UN Charter (1945) Art. 2(4).

[118] *See generally* Schmitt, "Cyber Operations in International Law" (2010) 151.

application, and content layers of the Internet. As such, it is of particular value in examining norm creation, or lack thereof, in Cyberspace. Second, it is hoped that the comparison of various U.S. actions reveals a certain schizophrenia in U.S. policy that indicates an understanding of Cyberspace as something extraterritorial, but an inability to coherently develop an international policy due to its own territoriality.

A second theme is that of attribution. The ability to trace an action back to an actor will recur throughout these chapters. The technology that allows for the concealment of identity will be addressed specifically in Chapter 8's exploration of encryption technologies. Attribution or lack thereof is critical in understanding how Cyberspace allows individuals and entities to transcend their own geographies and take part in other geographies.

Finally, a theme hinted at here that will become more evident in the next two chapters is the role and variety of non-state actors and their ability to contend directly with states in the geography of Cyberspace. This chapter highlighted a state's ability to blend in with the noise of non-state actors. Moving forward this theme will be addressed in terms of the ability of non-state actors to engage globally outside the strictures of the international arena.

7

Standardizing Authority

In 1975, the United States and the USSR launched a space mission to dock an Apollo module with a Soyuz module.[119] The mission was a carefully orchestrated scientific mission that was intended to show how science for peaceful purposes could bridge ideological gaps and to further détente between the two nations. The effectiveness of the mission in political terms is a story for another day. The object here is to draw an insight from a small sidebar of the narrative surrounding the mission. The two states both had their respective docking systems. Each relied on, technically speaking, a female side which received the male side of the docking apparatus, much like a headphone jack. In the tense political atmosphere, neither side wanted to become the female side of the other's docking system. As a result, the two countries developed an androgynous docking system that was interoperable with itself.[120]

The point here is not to highlight the misogyny inherent in these terms and Cold War politics, which is a continuation of an international relations discourse that often characterizes dominance as male.[121] Instead, it is to point out that the standardized docking mechanism, which is purely a technical specification, holds a great deal of political content. The standardization creates technical interoperability, but the technical standard is the mediator of state-to-state communication. In the Apollo-Soyuz mission, it was a question of technical connection that defined the parity of the states involved as they brought their quasi-territories into proximity.

Usually, questions of standardization occur when states are already in proximity, and international telecommunication has a long history of international governance mechanisms to develop such standards.[122] The ITU

---

[119]   *See* Battaglia, "Arresting Hospitality" (2012) S76–S89.

[120]   *Id.* at S82. *See also* International Docking System Standard, Interface Definition Document, Revision D (2015).

[121]   *See generally* Charlotte Hooper, *Manly States* (2001).

[122]   *See generally* Jayakar, "Globalization and the Legitimacy" (1998) 721–722.

as the world's oldest international organization represents a legacy of international cooperation and coordination on telecommunications standards. It also charts a unique history through which international law was developed in such a way that it avoided sticky issues of content by favoring interconnection over interoperability. States' ongoing ability to negotiate and adopt law in the realm of telecommunications would arguably make the international governance regime well prepared to regulate the Internet and Cyberspace, but this has not been the case. This chapter will investigate this phenomenon and argue that the development of Cyberspace governance has served to delegitimize the state as the central governance actor within the sphere. It will also argue that an important part of this delegitimization is the undermining of consent as envisioned in international law.

To construct these arguments, this chapter will proceed first by examining the nature of the ITU's power to make law and regulation concerning international telecommunications. This section will give a historical overview of the ITU and then investigate the most recent effort by states to extend the ITU's authority over the Internet. The next section will examine the development of global multistakeholder governance through an examination of the Internet Engineering Task Force (IETF) and the Internet Corporation for Assigned Names and Numbers (ICANN). The final section will examine the trend of corporate intermediaries in Cyberspace and their capacity as governance bodies.

Harmful Interference

The need to facilitate interconnection among states through telecommunication is as old as the telegraph, and the ITU dates to this period having first been established as the International Telegraph Union.[1] The utility of telegraph technology was immediately apparent, but states wanted to ensure that they controlled the technology as it crossed their borders. As a result, the ITU began as an organization that developed standards and rules for cross-border telecommunications, which allowed for interconnection among countries. This regime gave states primary control over telecommunications at the nodes where physical infrastructure crossed their borders. Today, the mission of the ITU is "facilitating peaceful relations, international cooperation among peoples and economic and social development by means of efficient telecommunications services."[2]

This strategy worked well with lined communications such as telegraph and telephone, but broadcast brought on new challenges, because radio waves

---

[1]   Codding, "The International Telecommunications Union" (1994) 501.

[2]   *Constitution of the International Telecommunication Union* (2010) preamble.

do not conform to state borders. There was, as a result, much debate in the international community on the nature of international responsibility for content crossing borders on radio waves. This can be seen in the Soviet complaints about radio propaganda during the Cold War[3] as well as in the UN General Assembly's controversial adoption of the Direct Broadcasting Principles.[4] The ITU again avoided coming into contact with the issue of content by adopting a policy of coordinating international usage of electromagnetic frequencies by nations so as to prevent harmful interference between broadcasts.[5] More recently, there was a movement in the ITU to give developing states more access to international telecommunications development resources.[6] Of course, in the realm of international relations a state's disbursement of aid is highly attenuated by a state's political goals. The ITU again avoided questions of content by developing a division that advocated for such development, but left the legal substance to bilateral or regional agreements.[7] Held argues that technical international organizations such as the ITU "have been sharply delimited" in order to make them "politically unexceptionable."[8] In the case of the ITU, its actions have been delimited to facilitating interconnection and coordinating usage.

Two key observations need to be made here. First, the ITU is a body made up of states as the basic unit of the body politic,[9] and the ITUs legitimacy, like that of other international organizations, springs from "state sovereignty."[10] Votes in the ITU are allocated one to one, and while non-governmental actors are given access to participate in deliberations,[11] the state is the primary power holder in the ITU forum for international coordination, meaning that the rules that it adopts are manifested through the "filter of domestic structures and domestic norms."[12] The ITU is a treaty-based organization, and as such it springs from within the logic of international governance, which reifies an international conceptualization of the world.

Second, the ITU makes international law and policy. The ITU's outputs consist of a variety of law and policy documents. As the international body that

---

[3]   Eppenstein & Aisenberg, "Radio Propaganda" (1979) 154.

[4]   *See* Lyall & Larsen, *Space Law* (2009) 256–269 and UNGA, Res. 37/92 (1982).

[5]   *Constitution of the International Telecommunication Union* (2010) Art. 1.2(b), Art. 45 and Eppenstein & Aisenberg, "Radio Propaganda" (1979) 154.

[6]   Codding, "The International Telecommunications Union" (1994) 505.

[7]   *See Constitution of the International Telecommunication Union* (2010) Art. 21.

[8]   Held, *Democracy and the Global Order* (1995) 109.

[9]   *Constitution of the International Telecommunication Union* (2010) Art. 2

[10]   Jayakar, "Globalization and the Legitimacy" (1998) 717.

[11]   *Id.* at 728–729. DeNardis, *The Global War for Internet Governance* (2014) 33.

[12]   Finnemore & Sikkink, "International Norm Dynamics and Political Change" (1998) 893.

adopts the rules of international telecommunication, the ITU adopts resolutions that chart its own course in addressing the issues raised by telecommunication technologies. More importantly, the ITU meets regularly to update the rules that make up the Radio Regulations. The Radio Regulations is a treaty of technical standards that is negotiated among members and sets out the regime for coordination of international radiotelecommunication. The Radio Regulations create international obligations that apply to states, not telecommunication providers, directly. In effect, the ITU depends on the member states to make its rules operable through national regulation binding upon domestic actors. Regulation as a result relies on consent of the state parties to the adopted rules.

As an international lawmaking body with the competency and a proven record for coordinating international telecommunication activities, it would seem that the ITU would be well situated to extend its hand of governance over the Internet, which fits easily within the definition of international tele-communication, which is "[a]ny transmission, emission or reception of signs, signals, writings, images and sounds or intelligence of any nature by wire, radio, optical or other electromagnetic systems."[13] The technology involved is exactly the type of technology that the ITU was developed to coordinate across borders, but the ITU has been unable to exert direct control within the sphere of Cyberspace. It has, instead, taken on a role more akin to a stakeholder within Cyberspace governance. This is in part due to the historical conditions that led to the governance of information technologies being "dominated" by other organizations.[14]

This inability of the ITU to effectively extend its competency can be seen in the results of its Plenipotentiary Conference held in Busan, Korea in 2014 (PP-14). This meeting was preluded by media chatter warning of an ITU takeover over the Internet, which taps into an established "media narrative ... about a possible Internet governance takeover" by the UN.[15] These headlines were prompted by the position being taken by the Russian Federation and other states that the ITU should have more control over the Internet.[16] The position of this bloc of states was widely interpreted as a threat to a free and open Internet. For instance, the U.S. characterized the proposals as mechanisms "that could have provided a mandate for the ITU in surveillance or privacy issues; inhibited the free flow of data; regulated Internet content and service companies; undermined the multistakeholder process; or called

---

[13]   *Radio Regulations* (2012) Art. 1.3
[14]   Jayakar, "Globalization and the Legitimacy" (1998) 719.
[15]   DeNardis, *The Global War for Internet Governance* (2014) 33.
[16]   Dickinson, "How Will Internet Governance Change after the ITU Conference?" (2014).

on the ITU to develop international regulations on these issues."[17] There was more to this than just rote suspicion of the UN. As a product of international law, the ITU would need to extend the logic of international governance to Cyberspace to effectively regulate its mechanisms. This would mean adopting measures that allow for cross border interconnection while avoiding embroiling itself into disputes over the content of communications. This would give states the ability to adopt, through the ITU forum, technical standards that facilitate national content controls. Such standards would increase state power to censor, monitor, or treat with deference communications entering their borders.

In Busan, the moves to extend the ITU's competency were defeated through the work of the U.S., which "built a broad consensus that led to success on Internet and cybersecurity issues keeping the ITU's work focused on its current mandate."[18] These efforts served "to mitigate and remove proposed language from resolutions that would have improperly expanded the scope of ITU."[19] The results of the negotiations are a handful of nonbinding resolutions that resemble policy statements.[20] So, for instance, Resolution 2 calls for a global framework to exchange information on such technologies to "support the harmonious development of telecommunication services."[21] More strikingly, Resolution 101 gives direct recognition to IGCs by "requesting" the Standardization Sector to continue "collaborative activities on IP-based networks with ISOC/IETF and other relevant recognized organizations."[22] The ITU further adopted Resolution 102, which states that "management of the Internet is a subject of valid international interest and must flow from full international and multistakeholder cooperation."[23] This resolution seemingly cedes power to an ambiguously defined "multistakeholder" system which exists outside the bounds of international legal geography.

---

[17]   United States Department of State, "Outcomes from the International Telecommunication Union 2014 Plenipotentiary Conference" (2014).

[18]   *Id. See also* Dickinson, "How Will Internet Governance Change after the ITU Conference?" (2014).

[19]   United States Department of State, "Outcomes" (2014).

[20]   *See also* ITU, "Resolution 133 (Rev. Busan, 2014) Role of Administrations of Member States in the Management of Internationalized (Multilingual Domain Names"; ITU, "Resolution 140 (Rev. Busan, 2014) ITU's Role in Implementing the Outcomes of the World Summit on the Information Society and in the Overall Review by United Nations General Assembly of Their Implementation"; and ITU, "Resolution 180 (Rev. Busan, 2014) Facilitating the Transition from IPv4 to IPv6."

[21]   ITU, "Resolution 2 (Rev. Busan, 2014) World Telecommunication/Information and Communication Technology Policy Forum."

[22]   ITU, "Resolution 101 (Rev. Busan, 2014) Internet Protocol-Based Networks."

[23]   ITU, "Resolution 102 (Rev. Busan, 2014) ITU's Role with Regard to International Public Policy Issues Pertaining to the Internet and the Management of Internet Resources, Including Domain Names and Addresses."

Trading off coordination for content is, of course, the status quo of international telecommunications regulation, which raises the question of why Internet technology has resisted the encroachment of international law from the exact international body charged with regulating that type of technology. A simple answer would be that states simply do not want to extend international law to govern Cyberspace, and to some extent this is true. However, it seems odd that Cyberspace has such a prominent role in social life at the global level, and that international law remains largely silent on the matter. To be clear, it is not that states are disinterested in the Internet – it is clearly an item on the agenda of the international community. Yet, it is one that international governance is at a loss to comprehensively address. A more satisfying answer can be found in the geography of Cyberspace that exists outside the logic of international geography. Critically, the legal geography of Cyberspace is built around code which is both content and medium. As a result, the "sharply delimited" functions of the ITU are ill equipped to expand to control a medium that is concurrently content. The state is not deprived of jurisdiction completely, as should be obvious from existing domestic laws, but those laws can only extend to the layers of Cyberspace that intersect national space. As a result, international governance has lost significant control over transnational communication, which no longer conforms to the bordered assumptions that underlie international governance.

This does not mean that Cyberspace is without authority. It means that the state becomes one of many stakeholders in a multistakeholder legal geography. The next two sections will investigate the trend of global multistakeholder governance by first examining the technical bodies that govern the logical layer of the Internet and then through analysis of corporate and commercial interests that extend governance over the Internet. These sections together reveal a world-scale legal geography that is not dominated by the state. It is most certainly not devoid of the state, but the state is no longer the central node of authority and need not consent to these governance mechanisms. This is a critical problem for international govern-ance since it is based on a model in which the state is the primary authority.

Rejecting Kings

"We reject kings, presidents and voting" is a phrase worthy of most fringe political manifestos. Though dripping with anti-authoritarian angst, the phrase is not from *The Anarchist Cookbook*. Instead, it is found in the central document, "The Tao of the IETF," that explains the workings of the Internet Engineering Task Force (IETF).[24] This is the technical body that adopts standards that govern the logical layer of the Internet. The statement is more

---

[24]   IETF, "Tao of the IETF" (2012).

than one of personal rejection of the authority; it is a community rejection of state authority over the methods and means of communication, specifically within the geography of Cyberspace.

The rejection of kings has strong roots in the anarcho-libertarian tradition of many coders who were instrumental in developing the Internet as discussed in Chapter 4. While the rhetoric used is anarcho-libertarian, this statement is not a simple denial of state authority. It is in practice an assertion of authority beyond states, which is consistent with the ITU's inability to extend its own mandate. Multistakeholder governance structures remove the state's ability to dominate regulatory decisions by removing the state's ability to consent to governance. Consent to the law by states is a bedrock principle in the international legal system. States, however, do not have the ability to consent to new standards in Cyberspace. In the multistakeholder model "[t]here is no geographically localized set of constituents" with a claim to legitimacy to deploy power.[25] Legitimacy, as a function of consent, has been redistributed from communities defined by borders to "the participants themselves," and they could be anywhere.[26] The borders of the state do not define the political community of Cyberspace, which disaggregates the core unit of international geography.[27] The legal geography of Cyberspace is not bordered. It is coded, and code is law.[28]

The IGCs discussed briefly in Chapter 2 are representative of the multistakeholder governance that diminishes a state's power to consent to law. The IETF serves as a perfect example and its actions can be seen to push its authority over states. This multistakeholder body adopts and maintains the standards that make the Internet work, including the TCP/IP, and it has the "largest influence on the technologies used to build the Internet."[29] TCP/IP is exactly the type of code that rejects kings, and it gives the IETF "a powerful seat of authority."[30] These protocols move activity to devices at the edges of the networks, which gives the user any freedom that he or she can program into Cyberspace. The state's bordered control points become null when data can move through any connection, thereby jumping those borders. Importantly, states never consented to this, whereas they did consent to telephone lines crossing their borders and to the standards for interconnection promulgated by the ITU and to the frequency allocations

---

[25]   Johnson & Post, "Law and Borders" (1996) 1375.

[26]   *Id.*.

[27]   Walzer, "The Moral Standing of States" (1980) 211 and Clark, *Legitimacy and International Society* (2005) 6.

[28]   Power & Tobin, "Soft Law for the Internet" (2011) 41.

[29]   Alvestrand & Lie, "Development of Core Internet Standards" (2009) 126 and DeNardis, *The Global War for Internet Governance* (2014) 36.

[30]   DeNardis, *The Global War for Internet Governance* (2014) 65–66.

governing terrestrial and space-based broadcast technologies. They even agreed over how postal services will be exchanged between them. However, they never agreed on the TCP/IP, which transforms other telecommunication technologies. The natural choke point found at the border fragments when information fragments through packet switching. Even physical gaps are becoming less effective as can be seen by Stuxnet, which jumped an air gap, as well as in projects that seek to get electronic devices across the border of states like North Korea.[31]

The IETF evolved out of the historical development of the Internet in which the computer scientists using the Internet were also making decision about how that space would be constructed.[32] As a result, decision making evolved from group conversations among the coders. The IETF was born from these conversations, which were extraneous to the state, and thus states were never admitted to the decision-making process. As the Internet grew, so too did the IETF. It eventually opened its membership to anyone that wanted to join and take part in that decision-making process. It was community governance built on "rough consensus and running code."[33] This form of decision-making added decisional value to the functionality of code in addition to the value of consensus. This is important because for standards to be effective they must be widely accepted."[34] States may have agents join to represent their respective interests, but these individuals are on equal footing with a variety of others including corporate agents and civic minded netizens. This removes the state from the dominant position it holds in international governance. The IETF's open and transparent process creates inter-operability standards that shape the "modern public sphere and broader conditions of political speech."[35] This means that the IETF structures the discursive space within states and without their consent.

The IETF makes decisions on how data will travel across borders outside the scope of the state, but significantly, it "has no formal authority over anything but its own publishing process,"[36] and its status is further complicated by the fact that it has "no formal membership."[37] The decisions that it takes construct the logical layer of the Internet, and state power in that decision process is limited to the ability to send representatives. The state, in the formal sense,

[31] Halvorssen & Lloyd, "We Hacked North Korea With Balloons and USB Drives" (2014).

[32] *See* Leiner *et al.*, "A Brief History of the Internet" (2012) and Power & Tobin, "Soft Law for the Internet" (2011) 41.

[33] IETF, "Tao of the IETF" (2012).

[34] Jayakar, "Globalization and the Legitimacy" (1998) 736.

[35] DeNardis, *The Global War for Internet Governance* (2014) 77.

[36] Alvestrand & Lie, "Development of Core Internet Standards" (2009) 126.

[37] DeNardis, *The Global War for Internet Governance* (2014) 69.

is never consulted on IETF decisions, which erodes the state's ability to consent to rules governing transnational communications. This is a significant development in governance at a world-scale and should not be downplayed. The spatial settlement premised on sovereign equality is, in essence, challenged by a set of rules that recode borders in such a way that states lose significant control over the flow of information across them. This is further confirmed by the IETF's lack of legal personality.[38] This feature means the IETF exists outside of the jurisdiction of any state. The IETF's organizational nebulousness resists clear classification within the space of international legal geography.

The IETF is not the only entity that exerts this type of multistakeholder control. Both the Internet Society (ISOC) and the W3C (see Chapter 3) as Internet governance communities share attributes with the IETF, though the IETF is the most extreme in its extra-stateness. While these are both interesting cases, the warping of international legal geography is observed better in a case with different attributes. Such a case can be found in the Internet Corporation for Assigned Names and Numbers (ICANN), which currently exists as a non-profit corporation under the laws of the U.S.

ICANN was also a product of the ad hoc historical processes through which computer scientists pieced together Internet governance. In the 1970s, Jon Postel began the work that would later be known as the Internet Assigned Names and Numbers Authority (IANA). Postel's work would eventually develop into a regime for managing the DNS, described above in Chapter 2. At this point in time, the Internet was largely made up of U.S. government and University networks. The U.S. National Science Foundation (NSF) was the lead government agency, and it left governance of Internet architecture up to the coders and engineers that were making the technical decisions on how to best foster interoperability on the network. Postel emerged as a one-man show at the University of Southern California, and he managed the root file of the DNS through an NSF contract.[39] The U.S. government's policy during the 1990s was to leave the development of the Internet to "private sector leadership" in hopes of privatizing the network of networks.[40] The U.S. federal government, though, soon stepped in as a reaction to various proposals for privatization of the IANA function that began to arise in 1994.[41] This action resulted in ICANN "[a]s an alternative to government."[42] ICANN was created by Postel to take over the IANA function, and it signed its first Memorandum

---

[38]   Alvestrand & Lie, "Development of Core Internet Standards" (2009) 126.

[39]   Mueller & Thompson, "ICANN and INTELSAT" (2004) 66–67.

[40]   *Id.* at 63.

[41]   *Id.* at 67–68.

[42]   *Id.* at 63.

of Understanding with the U.S. Department of Commerce in November of 1998.[43] ICANN is "a private nonprofit corporation created to manage policy and technical features" of the DNS.[44] The corporation itself functioned with oversight by the National Telecommunications and Information Administration (NTIA),[45] which maintained a "back door authority"[46] that it used to "very rarely reject" ICANN action.[47] This oversight does play an "important role in ensuring that proper processes are followed."[48]

Three things of significance should be noted here. First, ICANN has personality under U.S. law making it subject to the law of the United States. Second, despite the fact that ICANN extends from U.S. government involvement in the development of the Internet, there was never any sort of lawmaking procedure, other than a contract, that gave ICANN its authority.[49] It administers a significant governance regime that developed outside the realm of lawmaking in the domestic and international arenas.[50] Third, despite this extra legality, ICANN is subject to special government intervention through NTIA oversight function.[51] Thus on its face, ICANN fits into the state's governance structure and seems dissimilar from organizations like the IETF.

However, in 2014, the NTIA "unexpectedly" announced its intention to transfer the IANA functions of ICANN to a multistakeholder regime.[52] This serves as an interesting example of a state relinquishing control of an Internet governance body, but the relinquishment is not to the international community as might be expected. The announcement stated that the NTIA would "transition key Internet domain name functions to the global multistakeholder community."[53] Notably, the announcement employs the word 'global' as

---

[43]   *Id.* at 68.

[44]   Rosenzweig *et al.*, "Protecting Internet Freedom and American Interests" (2014) 1; Zalnieriute & Schneider, "ICANN's Procedures and Policies in the Light of Human Rights, Fundamental Freedoms and Democratic Values" (2014) 9; Partridge & Lonardo, "ICANN Can or Can It?" (2009) 24; and DeNardis, *The Global War for Internet Governance* (2014) 48–49.

[45]   *See generally* Krattenmaker, *Telecommunications Law and Policy* (1998) 21.

[46]   Mueller & Thompson, "ICANN and INTELSAT" (2004) 70.

[47]   Rosenzweig *et al.*, "Protecting Internet Freedom and American Interests" (2014) 3.

[48]   *Id.*

[49]   Mueller & Thompson, "ICANN and INTELSAT" (2004) 65, 69.

[50]   Mueller & Thompson, "ICANN and INTELSAT" (2004) 63 and DeNardis, *The Global War for Internet Governance* (2014) 46. *But see* Rosenzweig *et al.*, "Protecting Internet Freedom and American Interests" (2014) 4.

[51]   Partridge & Lonardo, "ICANN Can or Can It?" (2009) 24.

[52]   Rosenzweig *et al.*, "Protecting Internet Freedom and American Interests" (2014) 1–2.

[53]   NTIA, "NTIA Announces Intent to Transition Key Internet Domain Name Functions" (2014).

opposed to 'international.' In fact, the word 'international' only appears one time in the announcement compared to 'global's' six.[54] This indicates an intent to not turn IANA over to an international organization. Instead, the announcement posits a new form of governance body, a global multistakeholder community, that is undefined in international law. The NTIA announcement came shortly before the NETmundial conference held in Brazil in April of 2014. This civil society conference adopted a Statement on Multistakeholder Governance, which helps to shed light on the idea of a "global multistakeholder community." It states that:

> Internet governance should be built on democratic, multistakeholder processes, ensuring the meaningful and accountable participation of all stakeholders, including governments, the private sector, civil society, the technical community, the academic community and users. The respective roles and responsibilities of stakeholders should be interpreted in a flexible manner with reference to the issue under discussion.[55]

An obvious implication in this statement is that the state is just one of numerous stakeholders, and the NTIA announcement proximity to this highly publicized meeting indicates a conscious decision of the NTIA in choosing the term 'multistakeholder.'

The NTIA contract with ICANN ended on 1 October 2016. The technical and operational aspects of IANA was transferred to Public Technical Identifiers (PTI), which is an affiliate of ICANN. Though the transition can be seen as a reaction to controversies over ICANN's "legitimacy and ties to the U.S. Government,"[56] the contract between ICANN and PTI requires that PTI be located in the U.S., giving the U.S. some amount of leverage over the operational mission of PTI.[57] Despite this PTI maintains that it "aim[s] to not directly set policy by which [it] operate[s]."[58] That policy comes from ICANN supported forums meaning that "policy development for domain name operations and IP addressing is arrived at by many different stakeholders."[59] In multistakeholder governance states are just "one type of stakeholder," which removes them from their usual place of dominance in world-scale

[54] *Id.*
[55] NETmundial, NETmundial Multistakeholder Statement (2014).
[56] Partridge & Lonardo, "ICANN Can or Can It?" (2009) 24 and DeNardis, *The Global War for Internet Governance* (2014) 61–62.
[57] ICANN-PTI, IANA Naming Function Contract (2016) Sec. 4.2.
[58] IANA.org, "About Us" (n.d.).
[59] *Id.*

governance.[60]   The state as a result is functioning in a new legal geography which differs from that of international governance.

The IANA functions administered by ICANN are a "global regulatory regime."[61] The numbers they control are referred to as "critical internet resources," and these numbers define what devices are on the Internet and, thus, who is in Cyberspace.[62] ICANN also manages domain name dispute resolution administering a nonjudicial arbitration system, the Uniform Dispute Resolution Policy (UDRP), through which intellectual property disputes can be resolved.[63] ICANN manages these property rights in Cyberspace, specifically, because the state has limited ability to do so. Interoperability on the Internet necessitates a uniform root file. If two states were to resolve a domain name dispute differently, this could result in either an inability of one of these states to enforce its judgement or a fragmenting of the root file and thus the Internet. At the moment, parties can pursue domain name disputes in U.S. Federal Court, because it has jurisdiction over ICANN and PTI. This same jurisdictional authority allows U.S. law enforcement to seize domains associated with criminal activities.[64] The power of the state is still a real one, but the U.S. lacks the ability to consent on how the DNS regime and its regulatory aspects develop.

States are just one voice in multistakeholder governance, and their consent to be bound is not a necessary precursor for the adoption of a rule.[65] These Internet governance communities change the dynamic of a state's authority over transnational communications, and this is a new development in world-scale government. IGCs are not the only entities changing authority. Private corporations are also taking a seat at the multistakeholder table, and they perform a number of governance functions in Cyberspace.

Corporate Governance

As addressed in the first section of this chapter, states have traditionally maintained control over information at their borders. Their ability and right to control information at their borders was based on their ability and right to

---

[60]   Hurwitz, "A New Normal?" (2013) 239.

[61]   Mueller & Thompson, "ICANN and INTELSAT" (2004) 77.

[62]   Denardis, *The Global War for Internet Governance* (2014) 57–58 and Mueller & Thompson, "ICANN and INTELSAT" (2004) 77.

[63]   Partridge & Lonardo, "ICANN Can or Can It?" (2009) 24–29.

[64]   DeNardis, *The Global War for Internet Governance* (2014) 184–189; Gallagher, "Silk Road, Other Tor 'darknet' Sites May Have Been 'decloaked' through DDoS [Updated]" (2014); and Mueller & Thompson, "ICANN and INTELSAT" (2004) 81.

[65]   Leiner *et al.*, "A Brief History of the Internet" (2012).

control information within their borders, a right that flowed from sovereignty as recognized in the international system. This is why states may have laws that set the extent to which citizen speech is protected, as well as why states have legal controls over intellectual property. In this system, citizens rely on the state to protect their speech rights and companies must rely on states to protect their intellectual property.[66] But digitization has changed the nature of both speech and property, making both difficult for the state to regulate effectively by exponentially multiplying the sites where such interactions occur.

Digitization makes information super-portable. Media of all sorts can be digitized and sent across the Internet. This means that a song, for instance, can be encoded as an MP3, attached to an email, and sent to a friend. This is the basic concept for one of the early business ventures on the Internet: Napster. Napster allowed individuals to share files with other users of the program by enabling peer-to-peer connections. This proved to be wildly popular with college students using high bandwidth connections to share music. While this was a great boon for individuals looking for digital files of their favorite songs, record companies were predictably concerned with such technologies, because the technologies enabled the copying and distribution of their copyrighted intellectual property.

As the Napster case foretold, intellectual property would become, and still is, one of the most heated battlegrounds in Internet law and policy. Though Napster's business model was stopped by the US legal system, a number of services filled its space with different technical specifications meant to subvert the law that was used to shut down Napster.[67] Copyright is not the only area of intellectual property that has been affected by Cyberspace, though it may be the most prominent. Trademark, as noted above, has been one of the biggest issues in ICANN's management of the DNS,[68] and patent has been implicated as corporations have attempted to protect the code that they use in Cyberspace.[69]

The reason that intellectual property has become such a contentious issue in Cyberspace is twofold. First, digitization makes sharing of intellectual property easy. Intellectual property can be perfectly copied and transmitted across the Internet with ease.[70] The MP3 files that made Napster a phenomenon could be easily copied without generational degradation associated with analog

---

[66]   *For example* US Constitution, Art. 1.8.8, 1st Amend.

[67]   Lessig, *Free Culture* (2004) 73–74.

[68]   *See generally* Partridge & Lonardo, "ICANN Can or Can It?" (2009).

[69]   *See generally* Vera Ranieri, "EFFecting Digital Freedom" (2014–2015).

[70]   Lessig, *Free Culture* (2004) 62–79.

media. This means that digital files, such as a copyrighted song, can be perfectly copied and shared on massive scales when users are able to connect using peer-to-peer using technologies such as BitTorrent.[71] The means of efficient copying have been combined with the means of efficient distribution.

The second issue fueling this debate is linked to the competing business models in Cyberspace. In analog media space, while there is a black market for intellectual property, content owners are generally responsible for the production and distribution of their property. Record companies, for instance, copy the songs they own onto CDs and sell them at record stores. They control the physical copying and distribution in such a way that it diminishes the ability of others to copy and share that information. In a digital environment, intellectual property holders have the same goals: to make a profit from the sale or use of their intellectual property, but the structure of the environment in which they pursue these goals is dramatically different in Cyberspace. Users no longer enter record stores to buy music; they enter search terms. The results of that search might send them to the record company or a licensed distributor to buy the music, but it is just as likely to send the user to a third party that is distributing free copies of the file. Cyberspace creates a gap in interests between the content owner and the content distributor, the Internet Content Provider (ICP).

To see this gap in action, one merely needs to visit YouTube, an online video sharing website owned by Google. YouTube's business model is based on user generated videos spawning web traffic to the site, which nets YouTube profits through revenues from ads served to users that visit the site. In basic terms, YouTube's business interest is in having as much content as possible available through its servers. More content brings in more viewers. An ICP's business goals are often in direct conflict with intellectual property owners that want to control the dissemination of their content. This has created a clash between content owners and ICPs that has played out across a number of fora and has been the subject of domestic lawmaking, but an important trend can be traced as these intellectual property disputes have proliferated. There has been a ceding of power to commercial entities who control the content available in Cyberspace. This power is often exerted without recourse to formal legal procedures contained within the legal geography of the state.

In the case of intellectual property, this can be seen in the notice and take down procedures deployed in numerous states to balance the competing interests of content owners and ICPs who host user uploaded content. Under these regimes, content owners must give notice to the ICP that it is hosting

---

[71] DeNardis, *Global War for Internet Governance* (2014) 63–65.

protected content on its website. In return, the ICP is granted a 'safe harbor' from legal liability by promptly taking down the content. The user is then given notice that the content has been removed. In the US context this is often referred to as being 'DCMAed,' a reference to the U.S. Digital Millennium Copyright Act (DMCA), the law that enacted the US regime for notice and takedown.[72] While the equities between the content owner and the ICP seem fair here, many scholars have noted that these regimes result in a burden being shifted to the user. So, for instance, going back to YouTube, if Warner Bros. identifies a clip from one of its films, then it fills out an online form which notifies YouTube. The clip is removed, and the user is sent an email notification informing them of the takedown. The user is then given the option to send a counter notification if they think the takedown has been in error. The information page on the counter notification process informs the user that his or her personal information will be revealed and that the "claimant may use this information to file a lawsuit against you."[73] Users are left with the decision of whether they want to pursue a claim in which they are most likely out-gunned. This burden shift means that corporations can over protect their content and block potentially valid uses such as parody or fair use based on the odds stacked against the user.[74]

Notice and takedown turns corporations and the technology they deploy into mediators of speech. Such mediation also takes place in the realm of self-regulation where corporations agree amongst themselves on how to best conduct their business. Self-regulation in the sphere of content standards in the domestic context has been a feature of broadcast telecommunications that has been widely adopted in the context of Cyberspace.[75] Self-regulation of content within an interoperable arena is vastly different from broadcast and raises novel questions as to the extent that private companies should be able to control speech online. As DeNardis and Hackl note, private actors are increasingly implementing technical architectures that mediate what speech is acceptable and what speech is not.[76]

In the context of particular social media sites this seems to be just the sort of community governance contemplated by early netficianados such as Barlow. It also reveals a startling removal of the state from the regulation of the political space in which speech takes place. It shifts power away from the individual by removing the court from between the individual and those that would suppress expression. In the place of the court are corporations that are

---

[72]   Digital Millennium Copyright Act, Pub. L. 105–304 (1998). *See also* Lessig, *Free Culture* (2004) 157.

[73]   YouTube, "Copyright Counter Notification Basics" (2019).

[74]   *See* Goodman, "Media Policy and Free Speech" (2007) 1233.

[75]   *See generally* Tambini *et al.*, *Codifying Cyberspace* (2008).

[76]   DeNardis & Hackl, "Internet Governance by Social Media Platforms" (2015).

seeking to maximize profits, rather than protect user rights. Laws like the DMCA, incentivize both intellectual property owners and ICPs to over protect data. This means that on the Internet "the rules of copyright law, as interpreted by the copyright owner, get built into the technology that delivers copyright content."[77] As a result, Cyberspace has "revealed the nexus between copyright and communications law, and the impact of both on speech."[78]

While mechanisms such as user agreements are a natural way to govern speech within the "walled gardens" of user experiences, the debate over net neutrality reveals a more troubling implication of corporate governance. Net neutrality, discussed in Chapter 2, centers on whether an ISP may legally favor some data or disfavor other data.[79] So, for instance, an ISP could enter a contractual agreement with a video streaming service for its data to move faster or to block data from a competitor's server or to slow certain types of data. ISPs say that they need this capability to efficiently manage their bandwidth, but those in opposition claim that if net neutrality erodes then ISPs will effectively control the content that users receive.[80] This means that "[e]ven routine technologies of bandwidth management are value-laden."[81] Media companies now must fight for the attention of viewers amidst a din of competition, and these same media companies have converged along with the technologies on which they operate, meaning that intellectual property owners are often ISPs as well. For instance, two of the largest broadband providers in the United States, Comcast and Time Warner, also function as ICPs and intellectual property owners.

From these examples, a few key features of corporate governance can be observed. First, there is a severe lack of transparency when a corporate actor takes action against speech on the Internet, as there are no accepted procedures for such action. Second, this puts a severe burden on the individual to enforce his or her speech rights as there is a large imbalance of power between the corporate entity and the individual. Third, individuals may not even know whether their speech or access to information has been limited due to the nature of technical architecture. Finally, and most importantly, the state is passing these powers to the corporations involved to enforce directly. Notice and takedown is a statutory process, but it is one that removes the state as the central mediator of rights making it a peripheral entity in the process.

---

[77] Lawrence Lessig, *Free Culture* (2004) 148.
[78] Goodman, "Media Policy and Free Speech" (2007) 1212.
[79] DeNardis, *The Global War for Internet Governance* (2014) 131–32.
[80] Verizon v. FCC (2014) 6.
[81] DeNardis, *The Global War for Internet Governance* (2014) 8.

Other such mechanisms exist as well. The Copyright Alert System is the result of an agreement between ISPs and major copyright holders in which ISPs agree to use a tiered system to discourage copyright violators.[82] Under the agreement repeat violators can have their access to the Internet through the ISP eliminated.[83] Another example is the European 'right to be forgotten' which allows individuals to demand content about themselves to be removed from ICPs.[84] The right to be forgotten also suffers from the burden shifting that occurs with notice and takedown schemes for intellectual property.[85] Similarly, Maurushat and Shachtman both argue that ISPs are in the best position to regulate cybercrime.[86] These examples all point to a trend in which "the determination of conditions of participation in the public sphere is increasingly privatized."[87]

The governance mechanisms "delegated" to "private intermediaries" are not just economic in their effects.[88] For example, Tambini et al. note that self-governance by corporations implicates them as the mediator of the right to expression.[89] Relatedly, Sunstein notes the effects of how commercial forums can be tailored into echo chambers that restrict deliberative democracy.[90] Finally, Lessig implicates corporate governance of intellectual property with the production of culture itself.[91] This means that corporations now "play a key role in ensuring and enabling" a number of human rights, especially "when an operator is dominant."[92] As a result, a Council of Europe report argues that Internet governance should be maintained in a way that "avoids predominance of particular deep-pocketed organizations that function as gatekeepers for online content."[93]

---

[82] Center for Copyright Information, "FAQ's on The Center for Copyright Information And Copyright Alert System" (2011) and Kravets, "ISPs to Disrupt Internet Access of Copyright Scofflaws" (2011).

[83] *Id.*

[84] *See generally* Rosen, "The Right to Be Forgotten" (2012) 88.

[85] *Id.* at 91–92.

[86] Maurashat, "Zombie Botnets" (2010) 379 and Shachtman, "Pirates of the ISPs" (2011).

[87] DeNardis & Hackl, "Internet Governance by Social Media Platforms" (2015) 6.

[88] DeNardis, *The Global War for Internet Governance* (2014) 13.

[89] Tambini *et al.*, *Codifying Cyberspace* (2009) 275. *See also* DeNardis, *The Global War for Internet Governance* (2014) 157.

[90] Sunstein, *Republic.com 2.0* (2007).

[91] Lessig, *Free Culture* (2004) 28–30. *See generally* Serageldin, "Cultural Heritage as a Public Good" (1999) 240–63.

[92] Council of the EU, "EU Human Rights Guidelines on Freedom of Expression Online and Offline" (2014) I.D.34.

[93] Zalnieriute & Schneider, "ICANN's Procedures and Policies in the Light of Human Rights" (2014) 16.

This is not to say that governance by corporations is a particularly new innovation. Many European empires of the 18–19th centuries were essentially corporations licensed to go out and govern, and neoliberal processes are premised upon MNCs effectively wielding power.[94] In fact, the rise of the Internet as a global force can be traced to a U.S. preference for "private, and avowedly economically rational, mechanisms of self-regulation."[95] There is, however, something distinctive about this in the context of Cyberspace, since "[f]unctionalist and technologist concerns regarding security, encryption, and domain name allocation become increasingly difficult to separate from the individual rights concerns regarding privacy, freedom of expression and public governance of the commons."[96] MNCs in this context are mediating the rights of individuals regardless of their location. A platform like Twitter, which is often mentioned in the same sentence with phrases like "global public sphere," can implement regulations that are effective globally and without any sort of public debate over these regulatory changes. In Cyberspace code is law, and this means that those who control code have authority. While states have the ability to regulate the code that will be implemented in their borders, for instance China's Great Firewall, corporations still maintain large areas of authority over users traversing their networks – and that authority often extends non-concurrently with the jurisdictional borders of the state from which the corporation is working from.

The international governance system is designed to allocate authority in a particular legal geography, in which the sovereign territorial state is the core political unit from which authority is to flow. This authority flows in two directions: it makes the state the sole holder of authority within the bounds of its territory, and it makes the states the holders of authority to take part in international governance processes. This is why the international community has had such a difficult time dealing with mass atrocities. In order for the international community to stop such atrocities happening within the borders of a state, it must undermine its own spatial ordering.

Cyberspace presents a different legal geography that saps authority away from the state as a holder of international rights. Authority in this new legal geography is vested in those that control the development, the adoption, and the deployment of code that operates at a global level. The ITU's regime for governing telecommunications is focused on physical phenomena that clearly occur at borders. Cyber-technologies, in particular the logical layer of the

---

[94]   *See generally* Burbank & Cooper, *Empires* (2010) 149–184.

[95]   Tambini *et al.*, *Codifying Cyberspace* (2009) 15.

[96]   *Id.*

Internet, are ubiquitous, and regulation tied to the physical and legal geography of borders has proved to be ill suited for governing these technologies. Cyberspace wields its own authority, which is embedded deep within the code that architects its geography. The next and final chapter in this section will explore how this change in authority affects the rights of the individual engaging in the public sphere of Cyberspac. It will specifically engage with how changed territoriality and changed authority have reallocated the relationship between the individual and the state by introducing new ways of mediating rights.

8

Unbordered Rights

At the end of World War I, states gathered together to negotiate a structure for international governance intended to prevent conflicts like the one they had just experienced. The result of this negotiation was the Covenant of the League of Nations, an international organization that failed to live up to that promise.[97] While the League of Nations was primarily concerned with ensuring peace, there was an emerging theme in international governance endorsing the right of the self-determination of peoples. This was fueled in part by Point V of US President Woodrow Wilson's 14 Points, which called for an "adjustment of colonial claims" that weighed the "interests of the populations concerned" equally with the interests of colonial powers.[98] As the League of Nations was being formed, numerous activists courted Wilson and others in an attempt to move the role of human rights to the fore of the emerging international system.[99] Human rights, however, did not make the cut in the final covenant.

The call for self-determination would be ignored until 1945, when the world was again reeling from a world-scale conflict coupled with the horror of the Holocaust. The newly negotiated UN Charter established a new international organization, the United Nations, which would serve as the central international fora in which states could interact. The UN Charter also implemented a role for human rights in the system of international governance. While the prevention of conflict maintained priority,[100] Article 1(2) of the Charter says that states are to have "respect for the principle of equal rights and self-determination of peoples."[101] This was a sea change moment in the development of international law in that it made human rights part of the political geography of states. While the Charter has many gaps that keep the UN from directly enforcing those rights, it made human rights a valid

---

[97] *Covenant of the League of Nations* (1919).

[98] Woodrow Wilson, "Fourteen Points" (1918).

[99] Manela, *The Wilsonian Moment* (2007) 59–60.

[100] UN Charter (1945) Art 1(1).

[101] *Id.* at Art. 1(2).

inquiry for international governance. Article 1(2) was followed by a bevy of documents that supported this new international identity for the individual, such as the Universal Declaration of Human Rights, the Genocide Convention, the Covenant on Civil and Political Rights, and the Covenant on Economic and Social Rights. This expansion of political geography also included the slow development of international criminal law used to hold perpetrators of international crimes individually criminally liable for acts that violated international law.[1]

This post-WWII expansion was important, but it was soon evident that the primary place that the sovereign state holds in international governance made the state the primary entity through which rights flowed to the individual. Due to the jurisdictional "claw back provisions" in the Charter, the state was the primary provider and impediment to human rights.[2] This resulted in human rights documents, negotiated by states, defining human rights in general, non-specific terms giving states leeway in their interpretation of the content of those rights. So, for instance, while the US was actively endorsing UDHR, it was actively violating many of the rights of African Americans within its borders. This tendency of states to define rights to conform with their political geography can be seen very clearly in the universality of the acknowledgement of the freedom of speech compared to its very uneven application across the globe.[3] So, while the individual was given identity in the international legal geography, that identity is subservient to its national identity as the state remains the dominant source of rights.

Notwithstanding a few important regional human rights bodies, individuals have for the most part been unable to assert rights outside of the context of the political geography of the state in which they exist. The geography of Cyberspace is such, though, that it allows the individual to take part in a political geography that is not defined by territorial borders. Cyberspace gives the individual identity in an alternate political geography and allows individuals to be the mediator of their own rights. This chapter will investigate how Cyberspace changes international political geography by examining how Cyberspace reallocates rights through the reallocation of identity. Legal structures give "primacy to entitlements" and "release the entitled person from moral precepts and other prescriptions in a carefully circumscribed manner."[4] Such legal structures are shown here to be diminishing in importance as the "spatio-temporal location" of individuals is no longer a controlling condition for

---

[1]   *See generally* Pompe, *Aggressive War* (1953) and Cassese, *International Criminal Law* (2003).

[2]   Borgwardt, *A New Deal for the World* (2005) 191–192.

[3]   *For example compare* US Constitution, Amend. 1 *with* Korea (Democratic People's Republic of)'s Constitution of 1972 with Amendments through 1998, Art. 67.

[4]   Habermas, *The Postnational Constellation* (2001) 114.

gaining the "artificial status of bearers of individual rights."[5]

This chapter will first address how encryption technologies enable individuals to mediate their own speech and associational rights in the space of Cyberspace. This section will investigate how digitized networks diminish a state's ability to constrain individual action. Spatial changes though do not simply empower individuals against states, they often empower states against individuals. The second section will examine the use of mass surveillance technologies by states as a way of mediating the rights of individuals in extraterritorially, which causes a fissure in the usual understanding of the political space of the state. The final section will use the phenomenon of hacktivism to show how this reallocation of rights rewrites international political space and gives it global complexity.

The Encrypted Self

Modern cryptography was born in Bletchley Park, England during WWII under the hand of Alan Turing.[6] The elite group that Turing led was tasked with cracking the encrypted messages sent through the German Enigma Machine. This complex electro-mechanical machine had over 150 trillion possible combinations with which to encrypt a message, and the German military reset the combination each day. This meant that though the Allies could intercept the encrypted messages each day, it was physically impossible to manually decrypt the messages by running all possible combinations. Turing was a mathematician whose work had already described a theoretical machine, which came to be known as a Turing machine, that was foundational to the development of the modern computer.[7] At Bletchley Park, Turing worked to build a physical machine that would quickly move through the possible combinations of the Enigma Machine in search of that day's combination. His work can be credited with changing the tide of the war for the Allies.

Cryptography today is a digital game. The Enigma Machine was based on the number of combinations for encrypting a text, and this number was a result of the physical settings that could be produced by its rotors and plug board. It was strong encryption until a machine was built that worked faster. An Enigma Machine would be no match for a smart phone, much less a military grade computer, due to the comparatively massive amounts of processing power on modern devices. This same processing power can be leveraged to create

---

[5]   *Id.*

[6]   On Turing *see generally* Brate, *Technomanifestos* (2002) 53–84. For fictionalized accounts *see The Imitation Game* (Black Bear Pictures/Bristol Automotive 2014) and Stephenson, *Cryptonomicon* (1999).

[7]   *See* Berlinski, *The Advent of the Algorithm* (2000) 187.

powerful encryption that is difficult for computers to break. To crack digital encryption users must either have a key or have a computer powerful enough to do the math in reverse. Many encryption techniques are premised on the inability of contemporary computers to do such math, and it is often stated that the fastest way to decrypt some digital messages is to wait until computer technology has advanced to the point that it can do the functions necessary to decrypt the message.

Encryption may seem esoteric to the individual user, but most people use some sort of encryption technology on the Internet daily. In fact, encryption technologies form the bedrock that commerce on the Internet relies on.[8] The ability to exchange data securely is paramount to the various trust systems implemented on the Internet. As an example, if an online business such as Amazon cannot ensure that a customer's credit card information will be secure then it is likely that that business will not have any customers at all. Encryption is foundational to trust on the Internet.

Encryption, though, is not just a commercial or military technology. Individuals have long used encryption to keep their messages or identities secret, and modern computing has opened up the ability of individual users to gain access to advanced encryption technologies. The example of PGP, found in Chapter 3, is indicative of this. PGP was classified by the US as a munition, and the US sought to stop the export of the technology to foreign countries. However, the nature of the Internet was such that the US was unable to stop the spread of the program across digital networks. The result being that individuals worldwide had access to military grade digital encryption. The effect of this was to spread the freedom of expression embedded in the code (Chapter 4 above) rendering it "no local ordinance."[9]

Encryption technologies do two primary things. First, like the Enigma Machine they can encrypt the contents of a communication. Second, and unlike the Enigma they can hide the identity of the communicator by hiding the device's IP address thereby concealing the device's location.[10] As examples, PGP does the former, and the Tor web browser does the latter.[11] Encryption enables a spectrum of activities, but this section will examine two. The first of these activities is the much touted use of encryption by political

---

[8]   DeNardis, *The Global War for Internet Governance* (2014) 93.

[9]   Lessig, *Code 2.0* (2006) 236.

[10]   Greenberg, *This Machine Kills Secrets* (2012) 65 and Davis, "The Internet As a Source of Political Change in Egypt and Saudi Arabia" (2008) 35.

[11]   Tor is an "onion routing" network that conceals the IP addresses of individuals using the software. *See generally* Greenberg, *This Machine Kills Secrets* (2012) 135–168.

dissidents in oppressive regimes.[12] The Internet itself offered the benefits of "cost, speed, and ease of use" to social movements and political dissidents.[13] Encryption enhances these benefits by allowing dissidents to organize and communicate in places where such rights are not guaranteed under the local law.[14]

As discussed in Chapter 4, Encryption technologies are closely tied to the anarcho-libertarian tradition in Cyberspace and specifically the Cypherpunks. This tradition frames cryptography as anti-authoritarian and pro-democratic. Encryption is a means with which to attack dominance and power of the state.[15] Specifically they attack the dominance of the state through a technical renegotiation of identity. Cypherpunks argue that power structures maintain control on power by controlling the information that is necessary to a deliberative democracy.[16] As an example, Julian Assange, the founder of WikiLeaks, wrote a file encryption program "designed for activists in repressive regimes" and named it "Rubber Hose."[17] The name is a reference to the physical violence that the state would need to inflict in order to gain access to the contents of the encrypted files. Political dissidents are obviously criminals within their own state, but encryption allows them to remove themselves from the political geography constructed within a given territory. Greenberg casts this freedom in terms of physical geography noting that cryptography can free the individual from "governments that don't hesitate to knock down doors and haul away political enemies."[18] The individual escapes being identified by escaping their own location and thus escaping the political identity imposed on them through state mechanisms.

The criminal nature of political expression in some states leads us to a second activity that is polarized from political dissent: cybercrime. While the uses of encryption by political dissidents is important, cybercrime activities make up a substantial amount of the encrypted bandwidth used.[19] This is crime of all sorts: extortion and fraud schemes, child pornography, identity

---

[12] *See generally* Fielder, "The Internet and Dissent in Authoritarian States" (2013) 161–91 and Castells, "Communication, Power and Counter-Power in the Network Society" (2007).

[13] Fielder, "The Internet and Dissent in Authoritarian States" (2013) 162.

[14] *See, for example*, Organization for Security and Co-operation in Europe, "Freedom of Expression on the Internet" (2011).

[15] Greenberg, *This Machine Kills Secrets* (2012) 148; Domscheit-Berg, *Inside WikiLeaks* (2011) 189; and Assange, *Cypherpunks* (2012) 1.

[16] *Id.*

[17] Greenberg, *This Machine Kills Secrets* (2012) 126–27.

[18] Greenberg, *This Machine Kills Secrets* (2012) 136, 3.

[19] *For example* Moore & Rid, "Cryptopolitik and the Darknet" (2016) 21–25.

theft, and terrorism.[20]   Similar to dissidents, encryption allows criminals to step outside of their geographic strictures and escape the power of the state. However, only in the former instance can we say that the individual is expanding their rights to escape domestic political geography. Cybercriminals usually engage in activities that are criminal within both their and their victim's jurisdiction – meaning that they are only escaping their legal geography. Encryption protects both from the power of the state, but it allows dissidents to expand their political rights while it allows criminals to subvert their legal obligations.   The extension of self beyond the state and its implications for political geography may best be seen in the role of encryption in terrorism.

After the Paris and San Bernardino attacks of 2015,[21] a public debate erupted over whether the government should have a back door to commercial encryption technologies in order to combat terrorism.[22] This debate was primed by revelations in the Snowden Leaks, which will be discussed in the context of state surveillance below. Here, though, the emphasis will be on how terrorist networks are able to extend themselves beyond their territorial confines to influence "world opinion."[23] Terrorists are seemingly both political actors and criminal actors.   Indeed, it is uncontested that post 9/11 there are a number of terrorist organizations that now qualify as global political actors in an "'open source' anarchy."[24] Terrorist networks use the Internet for propaganda and recruiting as well as to communicate via encrypted networks. These technologies have allowed terrorist organizations to step beyond their territorial geography and subvert international geography through cyber-geography.

In fact, it could be argued that terrorists have organized themselves around a decentralized logic similar to the Internet's, and Bergen and Hoffman argue that the terrorist networks have a very specific strategy of diversifying the threat that they pose.[25] This means that threat innovates along with technological innovation.[26] By decentralizing, these organizations are able to

---

[20]   *See generally* National Center for Justice and the Rule of Law, *Combating Cyber Crime* (2007).

[21]   *See generally* "Paris Attacks: What Happened on the Night" (2015) and "Everything We Know about the San Bernardino Terror Attack Investigation so Far" (2015).

[22]   *For example* Gallagher, "NSA's Director Says Paris Attacks 'would Not Have Happened' without Crypto" (2016); O'Neil, "Edward Snowden and Spread of Encryption Blamed after Paris Terror Attacks" (2015); and Knight, "Controlling Encryption Will Not Stop Terrorists" (2016).

[23]   Lewis, *The Crisis of Islam* (2004) 147.

[24]   Princeton Project on National Security, "Report of the Working Group on State Security and Transnational Threats" (2008) 10–11.

[25]   Bergen & Hoffman, *Assessing the Terrorist Threat* (2010).

[26]   Stewart & Mueller, "Cost-Benefit Analysis of Advanced Imaging Technology Full

recruit operatives within the territorial geography of the target country and the digital connection to the recruit serves as a medium to wield power in that state. Cyberspace gives terrorists political identity and allows terrorist organizations to function as "quasi-states" that push subversive political ideology through violence.[27] This is not to say that encryption causes terrorism nor to say that it changes the content of the political message of terrorism. Instead, the argument is that encryption changes the political geography that surrounds the terrorist. It facilitates the strategy of allowing potentially anyone to become a global political actor by taking up the terrorist cause.

Of course, terrorism is an extreme case and there are many documented legitimate uses of encryption technology to challenge political regimes.[28] The point here is not to choose a side in the debate over encryption. It is instead to show how it extends the political reach of the individual by "shift[ing] the balance of power from those with a monopoly on violence to those who comprehend mathematics and security design."[29] Encryption extends increased autonomy to the individual to assert rights denied within territorialized political geography.[30] As noted earlier, there is a current debate over whether the government should be able to require a back door into encryption programs. The U.S. government could certainly require this through legislation, but to some extent it would be a futile move.[31] This is because, as we see from PGP, anyone can code and release an encryption program, and as we see from the Liberator 3D-printed gun in Chapter 6, it is very easy to distribute code in contravention to U.S. law. The result is that states lose exclusive control over the communicative conditions of their own political geography.[32]

Encryption enables the individual to have a "choice" in the "medium through which citizens exercise their political autonomy," where before that choice was lacking.[33] Encryption allows the individual to gain access to a political geography and participate on terms that are different from those produced by compressed territorial, legal, and political geographies. If the Internet is indeed the "public space of the 21st century," then encryption technologies

---

Body Scanners for Airline Passenger Security Screening" (2011) 2.

[27]   Clapham, "Degrees of Statehood" (1998) 150.

[28]   *See also* Clinton, "Internet Rights and Wrongs" (2011) and Dunn, "Unplugging a Nation" (2011) 15.

[29]   Greenberg, *This Machine Kills Secrets* (2012) 154

[30]   Habermas, *The Postnational Constellation* (2001) 118.

[31]   *See* Berkman Center, *Don't Panic Making Progress on the "Going Dark" Debate* (2016).

[32]   Cohen, "Privacy, Visibility, Transparency, and Exposure" (2008) 200.

[33]   Habermas, *The Postnational Constellation* (2001) 17.

can be seen as marking the limits of its political geography.[34]

Taming the Masses

Adolph Eichmann, a former Nazi leader, was kidnapped by the State of Israel from his home in Argentina to whence he escaped at the end of World War II. He was then secreted out of the country and into the jurisdiction of Israel where he stood trial for his role in the Holocaust.[35] It was generally agreed that Israel violated the sovereignty of Argentina in this extraordinary event,[36] but the two later signed an agreement settling the matter. The violation occurred because in international law territorial jurisdiction reigns supreme, or in other words, international governance favors Argentina's border over Israel's interest in justice. This is why states use extradition treaties to govern the transfer of individuals within their territorial jurisdiction to other states that may have jurisdiction over a criminal act. In the usual scenario, Israel would be forced to concede to Argentina's dominance over its own territory and request that Argentina relinquish Eichmann.

Eichmann illustrates an important feature of the 1945 spatial settlement, which is that states are generally prohibited from mediating the rights of individuals extraterritorially. The right to self-determination is expressed internationally through "political independence" of the state.[37] States depended on territorial integrity to ensure that they maintained supreme authority within a given geography. In the wake of 9/11 however, states – or at least the US – have begun to conceive of themselves as having mutable borders that can be extended at will.[38] Cyberspace is an instrumental tool in their conception of themselves in this manner. States now routinely mediate the rights of individuals in other countries through digital surveillance and other cybertechnologies.[39]

Essentially, the same features that enable individuals to extend their rights through Cyberspace, also enable governments to use Cyberspace to surveil the individual. Despite the fact that encryption technologies are freely available, the bulk of Cyberspace communications happen on commercially encrypted networks. The networks collect vast quantities of data about individuals in a phenomenon known as "big data." As Lessig notes "everything

---

[34]   Clinton, "Internet Rights and Wrongs" (2011).

[35]   *See generally* Arendt, *Eichmann in Jerusalem* (1963).

[36]   United Nations Security Council, S/RES/138 Question relating to the case of Adolf Eichmann (1960).

[37]   UN Charter (1945) Art. 1(2), 2(4).

[38]   *For example* Bowman, "Thinking Outside the Border" (2007) 189–251.

[39]   Lessig, *Code 2.0* (2006) 209.

you do on the Net produces data" that "is in aggregate extremely valuable."[40] For instance, an ISP would have a record of IP addresses connected to by a user that would reveal interests, shopping habits, and professional and private associations. Beyond IP addresses bevies more information are held on computers, and as the US Supreme Court noted the "sum of an individual's private life can be reconstructed" from the data on a cell phone.[41] A government's ability to access this information reveals much more about an individual that traditional surveillance would.[42]

This type of data is collected for commercial purposes not for a single individual but for all users. As noted in Chapter 2, Cyberspace is a ubiquitous medium, meaning that if governments can tap into the commercial entities they can gather profiles of information on individuals worldwide.[43] It is this sort of activity that Edward Snowden revealed when he leaked a large trove of documents he collected as a National Security Agency (NSA) contractor.[44] These documents revealed a hidden legal and technical infrastructure implemented by the US and its allies in the wake of 9/11 to intercept communications. The documents gave an "unparalleled first-hand look at the details of how the surveillance system actually operates."[45] Central to the public discourse on the Snowden Documents were their legality under US law in respect to US citizens, which is an important and interesting legal debate. The inquiry here though will not be into the legality of the US actions, it will instead focus on how these actions reshaped international political geography. Specifically, it argues that the Snowden leaks reveal how the US reshaped the political geography of individuals it identified as "foreign."

PRISM serves as an excellent example of this US capability for mass global surveillance. First revealed in June of 2013, PRISM is a secret program that received direct feeds of data from a number of commercial companies such as Microsoft and Google that collectively "cover the vast majority of online email, search, video and communications networks."[46] This program required

---

40   *Id.* at 216.
41   Riley v. California (2014) 18.
42   *See* US v. Jones, 132 S. Ct. 945 (Sotomayor concurring) (2012).
43   Lessig, *Free Culture* (2004) 278.
44   Greenwald, "NSA Collecting Phone Records of Millions of Verizon Customers Daily" (2013).
45   Greenwald, *No Place to Hide* (2014) 2.
46   Specific companies noted are Microsoft, Google, Facebook, Pal Talk, YouTube, Skype, AOL, and Apple. Greenwald & MacAskill, "NSA PRISM Program Taps in to User Data of Apple, Google and Others" (2013); National Security Agency, "PRISM/ US-984XN Overview of the SIGAD Used Most in NSA Reporting Overview" (2013); Gellman & Poitras, "U.S., British Intelligence Mining Data from Nine U.S. Internet Companies in Broad Secret Program" (2013); Greenwald *et al*, "Microsoft Handed the

telecommunication companies to send all communications related to a "selector," such as an email address, to the NSA. PRISM constituted 91% of the "internet communications that the NSA acquired."[47] Similarly, the NSA engaged in "upstream collection" that relied on the "compelled assistance ... of the providers that control the telecommunications backbone over which communications transit."[48] The Privacy and Civil Liberties Oversight Board (PCLOB) reports that "approximately 26.5 million Internet transactions a year" are collected through upstream collection.[49] Both of these push intelligence collection away from the locus an individual inhabits and into the Cyberspace an individual inhabits. Collected data is then retained in a database that can be queried by authorized NSA employees in order to find information on a target.[50]

The historical context of this surveillance system is important to understanding what it reveals about the changes in political geography. The overall surveillance program was authorized immediately after the 9/11 terrorist attacks via an executive order from George W. Bush.[51] The post 9/11 environment was such that "few foreign policy objectives have garnered as much support as the struggle against terrorism."[52] The Justice Department later determined that the President's Surveillance Program (PSP) needed a court approval, so it sought authorization from the classified Foreign

---

NSA Access to Encrypted Messages" (2013); and MacAskill, "NSA Paid Millions to Cover Prism Compliance Costs for Tech Companies" (2013).

[47]   Privacy and Civil Liberties Oversight Board (PCLOB), "Report on the Surveillance Program Operated Pursuant to Section 702 of the Foreign Intelligence Surveillance Act" (2014) 33–34. *See also* Greenwald & MacAskill, "NSA PRISM Program Taps in to User Data of Apple, Google and Others" (2013).

[48]   PCLOB, "Report on the Surveillance Program" (2014) 35; National Security Agency, "(TS//SI/NF) FAA Certification Renewals With Caveats" (2011).

[49]   PCLOB, "Report on the Surveillance Program" (2014) 37, 39.

[50]   Greenwald & MacAskill, "Boundless Informant" (2014) and National Security Agency, "BOUNDLESSINFORMANT – Frequently Asked Questions" (2012). *See also* Greenwald, "XKEYSCORE" (2013).

[51]   Executive Order 12333: United States Intelligence Activities (2001). *See* National Security Agency Office of Inspector General, "Working Draft Report from March 24, 2009 on Stellar Wind (PSP)" 1–3; PCLOB, "Report on the Surveillance Program" (2014) 16–18; and Gallington, "Perspectives on Collection, Retention, and Dissemination of Intelligence" (2014) 2.

[52]   Nincic & Ramos, "Torture in the Public Mind" (2011) 231–49, 233. *See also* Stewart & Mueller, "Cost-Benefit Analysis of Advanced Imaging Technology" (2011); Gallington, "Perspectives on Collection, Retention, and Dissemination of Intelligence" (2014) 10; Wittes, "The Intelligence Legitimacy Paradox" (2014); Princeton Project on National Security, "Report of the Working Group" (2008); and Greenwald, *No Place to Hide* (2014) 5.

Intelligence Surveillance Court (FISC).[53]   The program itself went through several iterations as the government struggled to meet constitutional compliance behind closed doors, and it was eventually given statutory authority, albeit in vague terms, in §702 of the Foreign Intelligence Surveillance Act (FISA).[54] At the center of the adjustments was ensuring that the surveillance methods were properly within the bounds of the search and seizure restrictions in the US Constitution's 4th Amendment.[55] Under the FISA – the same legislation that created the FISC – the US government does not need a warrant to gather "foreign intelligence" from individuals that are not US persons and are reasonably believed to be "located outside of the United States."[56] In other words, the 4th amendment does not apply to non-US citizens outside the borders of the US. As a result, the NSA's surveillance was premised on the non-territorial-ness of the target. Snowden argues that the use of "foreign" is a "rhetorical shift [that] is a tacit acknowledgement by governments that they recognize they have crossed beyond the boundaries of justifiable activities."[57]   Snowden also revealed that the foreign surveillance sometimes bled back through the borders of the US[58] "turn[ing] the U.S. into a

---

[53]   NSA OIG, "Working Draft Report from March 24, 2009" 36–37; PCLOB, "Report on the Surveillance Program" (2014) 16–18, 42; and United States Department of Justice, "Exhibit A: Procedures Used by the National Security Agency for Targeting Non-United States Persons Reasonably Believed to Be Located Outside the United States to Acquire Foreign Intelligence Information Pursuant to Section 702 of the Foreign Intelligence Surveillance Act of 1978, as Amended" (2009). *See also* Gallington, "Perspectives on Collection, Retention, and Dissemination of Intelligence" (2014) 5–6 and PCLOB, "Report on the Surveillance Program" (2014) 26–27.

[54]   Foreign Intelligence Surveillance Act of 1978, 95 Pub.L. 511; Foreign Intelligence Surveillance Act of 1978 Amendments Act of 2008, 110 Pub. L. 261; and PCLOB, "Report on the Surveillance Program" (2014) 19, 81–84. *See also* Greenwald & MacAskill, "NSA PRISM Program Taps in to User Data of Apple, Google and Others" (2013).

[55]   PCLOB, "Report on the Surveillance Program" (2014) 89–90.

[56]   PCLOB "Report on the Surveillance Program" (2014) 20–21. Foreign intelligence is "information that relates to the ability of the United States to protect against actual or potential attack by a foreign power; sabotage, international terrorism, or the proliferation of weapons of mass destruction by a foreign power; or clandestine activities by a foreign power." *Id.* at 22. *See also* Gallington, "Perspectives on Collection, Retention, and Dissemination of Intelligence" (2014) 5.

[57]   Snowden, "Testimony before the Parliament of the European Union" (2014).

[58]   Gellman & Poitras, "U.S., British Intelligence Mining Data from Nine U.S. Internet Companies in Broad Secret Program" (2013); Greenwald & Ackerman, "How the NSA Is Still Harvesting Your Online Data" (2013); Greenwald & Ball, "The Top Secret Rules That Allow NSA to Use US Data without a Warrant" (2014); Greenwald & Ackerman, "NSA Collected Americans' Email Records in Bulk for Two Years under Obama" (2013); Ball & Ackerman, "NSA Loophole Allows Warrantless Search for US Citizens' Emails and Phone Calls" (2013); Gellman, "NSA Broke Privacy Rules Thousands of Times per Year, Audit Finds" (2013); and National Security Agency, "(U//FOUO) NSAW SID

foreign nation electromagnetically."[59] The uses revealed by Snowden show that "[t]echnology is agnostic of nationality," and the US only required a "reasonable belief" that the individual was outside of US territory to fulfill the "foreignness requirement."[60] Foreignness is important, because under the international governance system, the US surveillance of its own citizens is legal as a matter of sovereignty. It is foreign surveillance of individuals in territories outside of US jurisdiction that seems to be most problematic within international political geography.

It is not exceptional that a portion of the Bill of Rights does not extend outside the borders of the US as it is a guarantee of rights in the US, and the 4th Amendment is one of the rights that is guaranteed only to citizens and to noncitizens within US borders.[61] This presents a somewhat dichotomous position for the US. On one hand, former Secretary of State Clinton argued for the extension of First Amendment rights to Cyberspace, and on the other hand the government is secretly not extending Fourth Amendment rights.[62] The dichotomy exists because the freedom of speech that the government asserts should be extended is protected by the 4th Amendment impediment to government interference in one's private life. So, the "universal" rights that Clinton offers are extended unevenly based on a political identity.

The hallmark of the activities exposed by Snowden is the replacement of individualized suspicion of criminality, critical to the U.S. Constitution 4th Amendment warrant requirement, with a permanently suspect political identity of "foreign."[63] As a result, FISC does not make determinations as to whether particular foreign individuals will be surveilled. Judicial review is instead limited to determining whether the procedures, which are adopted and authorized secretly, "are reasonably designed" to prevent surveillance of US persons or of individuals within the borders of the US.[64] What is exceptional is the US government's power to actively transform political space outside of

---

Intelligence Oversight (IO) Quarterly Report – First Quarter Calendar Year 2012 (1 January – 31 March 2012 – EXECUTIVE SUMMARY" (2012).

[59]   Greenberg, *This Machine Kills Secrets* (2012) 223. *See also* Wittes, "The Intelligence Legitimacy Paradox" (2014). *See also* PCLOB, "Report on the Surveillance Program" (2014) 23, 42, 85.

[60]   Snowden, "Testimony before the Parliament of the European Union" (2014) 5 and PCLOB, "Report on the Surveillance Program" (2014) 21, 43–52.

[61]   *Id. at* 86–7, 100–102.

[62]   Clinton, "Internet Rights and Wrongs" (2011) *See also* US DoD, "Department of Defense Strategy for Operating in Cyberspace" (2011).

[63]   PCLOB, "Report on the Surveillance Program" (2014) 18.

[64]   *For example see* United States Department of Justice, "Memorandum for the Attorney General" (2007); United States Department of Justice, "Exhibit A" (2009); and PCLOB, "Report on the Surveillance Program" (2014) 26–27.

its borders. It is able to do this because "much of the world's communications flow through the US."[65] This means that it is able to leverage its territory into the territory of other states.[66]

What Snowden revealed was not just a surveillance program, but a fundamental shift, from the state's point of view, in the extent to which a state can shape the political geography outside its own borders. It has long been understood that surveillance reshapes space, and that "[p]rivacy has a spatial dimension."[67] This is the core idea in Jeremy Bentham's Panopticon, and Cohen argues that modern rhizomatic surveillance systems dramatically change public and private space.[68] Surveillance "alters the experience of places in ways that do not depend entirely on whether anyone is actually watching."[69] Lessig terms it a "burden" that is imposed on the individual,[70] and Greenwald notes that a citizenry that is aware of always being watched quickly becomes a compliant and fearful one."[71] Transnational surveillance, then, exerts a new political geography on the individual by placing burdens on him or her that "alters the balance of powers and disabilities" within Cyberspace.[72] As a result, despite the fact that this is a government action, it is one that erodes the borders of international geography, because borders historically inhibited extraterritorial surveillance of this scale and scope. This loss of "political independence" is exhibited in Snowden's testimony before the European Parliament in which he states that "without getting out of my chair, I could have read the private communications of any member of this committee, as well as any ordinary citizen."[73] In fact, Snowden's leaks confirm that the US engaged in just this sort of surveillance,[74] which bears "implications for our assumptions of how international relations unfold."[75] The

---

[65] NSA, "PRISM/US-984XN" (2013).

[66] Lam, "EXCLUSIVE: US Hacked Pacnet, Asia Pacific Fibre-Optic Network Operator, in 2009" (2013); Lam & Chen, "EXCLUSIVE: US Spies on Chinese Mobile Phone Companies, Steals SMS Data" (2013); Poitras, Rosenbach, & Stark, "NSA Spies on 500 Million German Data Connections" (2013).

[67] Cohen, "Privacy, Visibility, Transparency, and Exposure" (2008) 181. *See also* Kirby, "Minding the Gap" (2013) 10–11.

[68] Cohen, "Privacy, Visibility, Transparency, and Exposure" (2008) 184–186

[69] *Id.* at 192

[70] Lessig, *Code 2.0* (2006) 218.

[71] Greenwald, *No Place to Hide* (2014) 3.

[72] Cohen, "Privacy, Visibility, Transparency, and Exposure" (2008) 193.

[73] Snowden, "Testimony before the Parliament of the European Union" (2014) 2.

[74] MacAskill *et al.*, "GCHQ Intercepted Foreign Politicians' Communications at G20 Summits" (2013); Poitras *et al.*, "NSA Spied on European Union Offices" (2013); MacAskill & Borger, "New NSA Leaks Show How US Is Bugging Its European Allies" (2013); "NSA Hacked UN Videocalls as Part of Surveillance Program, Claims Report" (2013).

[75] Dittmer, "Everyday Diplomacy" (2015) 604–05.

ability of the US to surveil the communications of foreign politicians indicates a change in their political geography, since "[s]paces exposed by surveillance function differently than spaces that are not so exposed."[76]

It should also be emphasized that the state's ability to transform political geography outside of its borders is based on its ceding of authority to corporate intermediaries as discussed in the previous chapter.[77] The ability of these networks to expand their reach extends the reach of the state to data, and corporations incentivize individuals to enroll in the "surveillant assemblage" using "benefits and pleasures, including price discounts, social status, and voyeuristic entertainment."[78] The state benefits from the corporate goal "to harness raw power of data."[79] Indeed, the reliance on "private intermediaries has equipped states with new forms of sometimes unaccountable and nontransparent power over information flows."[80] It should also be noted that these activities are not limited to the US, and Snowden revealed a "surveillant assemblage" that includes the UK,[81] France,[82] Australia,[83] and Germany.[84]

The state's ability to transform political geography should also be considered within the context of the ability to transform territorial geography discussed in Chapter 6. IoT allows states to control physical infrastructure in foreign domains as shown with Stuxnet. It also enables digitized violence as found in the US use of drones. The Predator drone was first developed as a surveillance tool for the Air Force, a purpose it served until the 2000s when it was fitted with munitions to carry out targeted killings in foreign countries.[85]

---

[76] Cohen, "Privacy, Visibility, Transparency, and Exposure" (2008) 194. *See also* Dittmer, "Everyday Diplomacy" (2015) 604–19.

[77] *See* Rushe, "Skype's Secret Project Chess Reportedly Helped NSA Access Customers' Data" (2013); Risen & Wingfield, "Web's Reach Binds N.S.A. and Silicon Valley Leaders" (2013); Greenwald *et al.*, "Microsoft Handed the NSA Access to Encrypted Messages" (2013); Timberg & Nakashima, "Agreements with Private Companies Protect U.S. Access to Cables' Data for Surveillance" (2013); Ball, Harding, & Garside, "BT and Vodafone among Telecoms Companies Passing Details to GCHQ" (2013); and Greenet Ltd. *et al* v. GCHQ - Statement of Grounds (2014).

[78] Cohen, "Privacy, Visibility, Transparency, and Exposure" (2008) 187.

[79] *Id.* at 186.

[80] DeNardis, *The Global War for Internet Governance* (2014) 15.

[81] Hopkins & Borger, "Exclusive: NSA Pays £100m in Secret Funding for GCHQ" (2013); Hopkins, Borger, & Harding, "GCHQ: Inside the Top Secret World of Britain's Biggest Spy Agency" (2013); and Dittmer, "Everyday Diplomacy" (2015) 604–19.

[82] Chrisafis, "France 'Runs Vast Electronic Spying Operation Using NSA-Style Methods'" (2013).

[83] Dorling, "Snowden Reveals Australia's Links to US Spy Web" (2013).

[84] "German Intelligence Agencies Used NSA Spying Program" (2013).

[85] Michel, "A History of Violence" (2015).

The Predator is connected to a user in the US via a communications link built on Internet technology and relayed by a commercial telecommunications satellite.[86] If the drone is understood as a 'thing' on the IoT, then it is the embodiment of digitized violence. The political geography ascribed to the targets of drones by the international system is transformed dramatically through Cyberspace as the state mediates the right to fair trial and the right to life.

Networked Global Politics

What has been described in the previous two sections is a cross reaching of power, and they both describe changes in the political geography at a localized perspective. A further inquiry should be made into what this does to the political geography of international space. This inquiry will reveal borders are shifted when other entities are networked in at a power level that can directly contest states. One of the implications of the previous two sections is that states have ceded authority in Internet governance, and that they rely on their ability to blend in with non-state actors online. This section will examine hacktivists as evidence of a world-scale political geography that networks in non-state actors. The term itself invokes the idea of changing technology (i.e. hacking) for political change (i.e. activism). Hacktivists "use cryptography to effect political change," as a means of giving power "to the people."[87] This section will trace a narrative of hacktivism that will illustrate this transformation in global political geography.

In November of 2010, the website WikiLeaks began to publish leaked US State Department Diplomatic cables onto the Internet, in an incident that came to be known as Cablegate. WikiLeaks is a website founded by Julian Assange that is, in its own words, a "multi-national media organization and associated library" that has a perfect record in "resistance to all censorship attempts."[88] The website "specializes in the analysis and publication of large datasets of censored or otherwise restricted official materials involving war, spying and corruption" (again in its own words).[89] Assange has gone so far as to put this in diplomatic terms, stating "WikiLeaks is a giant library of the world's most persecuted documents. We give asylum to these documents, we analyze them, we promote them and we obtain more."[90] According to Domscheit-Berg, Assange focused on the US specifically "seeking out

---

[86] *Id.*
[87] Greenberg, *This Machine Kills Secrets* (2012) 131, 168.
[88] WikiLeaks, "What is WikiLeaks" (2015).
[89] *Id.*
[90] *Id.*

the biggest possible adversary."[91]

The Cablegate releases were the catalyst for WikiLeaks' and Assange's quick rise to global prominence. This led to Assange being characterized in the rhetoric of the state as a "terrorist" and "outrageous, reckless, and despicable."[92] The releases were unprecedented in nature and caused serious embarrassment for the US as well as security concerns globally, though WikiLeaks did attempt to minimize the exposure of human life. The 251,287 documents gave an unparalleled glimpse into the international relations of the United States and exposed to the public eye government processes that in general remain closed. They were leaked by a young army soldier named Chelsea Manning, who was later prosecuted in the United States for releasing the documents.[93] The US began to mount a case against Assange, and began to apply diplomatic pressure in order to find a way to get to Assange.[94] Then in August of 2010, a warrant for Assange's arrest was issued in Sweden on the basis of rape allegations.[95] The UK placed Assange under house arrest while it determined whether or not extradition was proper with the UK Supreme Court making an affirmative decision in May of 2012.[96] Assange then fled to the Ecuadorian Embassy in London where he was granted asylum. The UN Human Rights Council's Working Group on Arbitrary Detention released an opinion in February of 2016 that ruled the detention "arbitrary."[97]

As of this writing, Assange has been expelled from the Ecuadorian Embassy as the result of an internal change in leadership in Ecuador. The leadership accused Assange of using his refuge in the embassy to meddle in internal affairs of other states and revoked his asylum status for "the trangression of international treaties."[98] He is serving a short sentence for failing to surrender to court and is facing possible extradition to either Sweden or the United States.[99]

Diplomatic pressure was not the only pressure that the United States

---

[91]   Domscheit-Berg, *Inside WikiLeaks* (2011) 189, 160.

[92]   Greenberg, *This Machine Kills Secrets* (2012) 177.

[93]   Tate, "Bradley Manning Sentenced to 35 Years in WikiLeaks Case" (2013).

[94]   Greenwald & Gallagher, "Snowden Documents Reveal Covert Surveillance and Pressure Tactics Aimed at WikiLeaks and Its Supporters" (2014).

[95]   Domscheit-Berg, *Inside WikiLeaks* (2011) 203–215.

[96]   Bowcott, "Julian Assange Loses Appeal against Extradition" (2012).

[97]   UN Human Rights Council's Working Group on Arbitrary Detention, Opinion No. 54/2015 concerning Julian Assange (2015) Para 99.

[98]   Dillet & Lomas, "Julian Assange arrested in London after Ecuador withdraws asylum" (2019).

[99]   *Id.*

mounted. It also attempted to get the corporations within their borders to put pressure on Assange by ceasing to allow their services to be used to support WikiLeaks. Several major companies, such as Amazon, PayPal, and Mastercard, succumbed to this pressure displaying their corporate authority over the Internet. There was no public legal action taken against these corporations, and the government denied such actions.[100] This cued the entrance of the hacktivist group Anonymous.

Anonymous is a hacker collective that is geographically distributed and whose identities are as secret as code can keep them. In the group's own words, "Anonymous is a loose collection of individual people around the world. [...] Anonymous is notoriously associated with hacking and hacking operations, but over the years has evolved into a majority protest/civil activist movement."[101] Significantly, Anonymous has no leader and anyone can join.[102] The "nihilistic" group has been associated with a number of high profile hacks that generally have some variety of social justice motive.[103] They have declared operations against groups like the CIA,[104] Westboro Baptist Church,[105] Mexican drug cartels,[106] the Church of Scientology,[107] the Islamic State,[108] and even Kanye West.[109] As Cablegate unfolded, Anonymous employed DDoS attacks against the corporations that they claimed were censoring WikiLeaks.[110] In addition to corporations, Anonymous also attacked governments such as Zimbabwe and Tunisia that were censoring the documents.[111] Anonymous' actions were undergirded by a philosophy that "knowledge is free," a phrase that resonates with the political geography described in Chapter 4.[112]

A third, but unlikely to be final, act in this leaking drama are the leaks of Edward Snowden. Snowden, it must be assumed, was to some extent

---

[100] Greenwald & Gallagher, "Snowden Documents Reveal Covert Surveillance" (2014) and Clinton, "Internet Rights and Wrongs" (2011).
[101] AnonHQ, "The Most Frequently Asked Questions People Have About Anonymous" (2016).
[102] *Id.*
[103] Greenberg, *This Machine Kills Secrets* (2012) 185.
[104] Albanesius, "Anonymous Takes Down CIA Web Site" (2012).
[105] Popkin, "Anonymous 'Brandjacks' Westboro Baptist Church on Facebook" (2013).
[106] Associated Press, "'Anonymous' Hackers Threaten Drug Cartel" (2011).
[107] *See* Daniel Domscheit-Berg, *Inside WikiLeaks* (2011) 35.
[108] Brooking, "Anonymous vs. the Islamic State" (2015).
[109] "Kanye West Targeted by 'Anonymous' in Searing Video" (2015).
[110] Mackey, "'Operation Payback' Attacks Target MasterCard and PayPal Sites to Avenge WikiLeaks" (2010).
[111] "Anonymous Activists Target Tunisian Government Sites" (2014).
[112] Greenberg, *This Machine Kills Secrets* (2012) 185.

inspired by this global drama over government transparency, and like Manning he released a trove of government documents to the press. Several days after the first leak, the same journalists that broke the leaks also broke the identity of the leaker by publishing an interview with Snowden. In this interview he stated that he hoped his leaks "will trigger [debate] among citizens around the globe about what kind of world we want to live in."[113] Snowden's interview was from a hotel room in Hong Kong. While the United States scrambled to put in motion the legal process for getting to Snowden, he was quietly shuttled onto a plane that took him to the international terminal of the Moscow airport before the US could cancel his passport.[114] He lived in the international zone of the airport, outside the legal and political borders of any state, for more than a month.[115] During this time, it was rumored that he was going to be given asylum in Bolivia and that he was aboard a diplomatic flight transporting the president of Bolivia.[116] The United States applied a great deal of diplomatic pressure, and as a result Portugal, France, Italy, and Spain denied access of this plane to their airspace.[117] The plane was eventually rerouted to Vienna, where it was searched and the Austrian Foreign Minister confirmed that Snowden was not aboard.[118] Snowden was granted temporary asylum for one year in Russia, which has since been renewed.[119] He was represented by WikiLeaks attorneys in the negotiations with the Russian government. In fact, WikiLeaks contributed a great deal of resources to ensure that Snowden did not fall back within the jurisdiction of the US.[120] From a legal and political enclave of Ecuador in the territory of the UK, Assange was able to wield global political power to subvert the international power of the US.

This narrative is not intended to lionize Assange, Manning, Snowden, or the members of Anonymous. The facts surrounding each require particularized ethical reflection. Instead, this narrative is used to expose a new form of global networked power that is pushing up against the territorially ordered international political system. Three observations of this narrative illustrate

---

[113] Greenwald, MacAskill, & Poitras, "Edward Snowden" (2013) and *Citizen Four* (HBO Films 2014).

[114] Branigan & Elder, "Edward Snowden Leaves Hong Kong for Moscow" (2013).

[115] Luhn, "Edward Snowden Leaves Moscow Airport after Russia Grants Asylum" (2013).

[116] Roberts, "Bolivian President's Jet Rerouted amid Suspicions Edward Snowden on Board" (2013) and Lally & Forero, "Bolivian President's Plane Forced to Land in Austria in Hunt for Snowden" (2013).

[117] *Id.*

[118] *Id.*

[119] Branigan & Elder, "Edward Snowden Leaves Hong Kong for Moscow" (2013).

[120] Kelley, "Edward Snowden's Relationship With WikiLeaks Should Concern Everyone" (2014) and Sledge, "Edward Snowden Gambles On Alliance With WikiLeaks" (2013).

aspects of the new political geography formed as cybergeography comes into proximity with international geography. The first observation is the role of encryption technologies within this narrative. Greenberg notes that "the technology that enables the spillers of secrets has been accelerating with the dawn of the computer" and that the Internet caused a "Cambrian explosion" of tools to empower the individual.[121] Encryption technologies are foundational to the WikiLeaks platform, critical to hiding the identity of Anonymous activists, and were the tool used by Snowden to transfer his leaks to the press. In the Cablegate episode, Manning may never have been caught except that she revealed herself to a fellow hacker that turned her in,[122] and Snowden revealed his own identity. Encryption allows the leaker to transform politics within the global space by transforming their own identity, a function enabled within the communicative conditions of Cyberspace.

The second observation is the role of borders within this narrative. Borders are freely deconstructed and reconstructed at will by states creating ripples in the construction of the international system. Borders themselves are recoded to hold both traditional content as well as new fluid geographies. For instance, at numerous points we see borders serving traditional functions. Assange was subject to the international process of extradition, but he claimed asylum within the diplomatic borders of Ecuador. Assange was thus protected through established international governance mechanisms, so long as Ecuador wanted to protect him (they eventually withdrew their protection and handed him over to the British police in April 2019). Similarly, Hong Kong allowed Snowden to leave for Moscow claiming that "documents filed by the US did not fully comply with legal requirements."[123] In addition, we see a display of states flexing their territorial authority in denying their airspace to a plane that potentially carried Snowden. At the same time, borders are reinscribed in different ways that reveal their imaginariness. Assange's exile reveals the legal fiction of territory, which gets highlighted when the same type of diplomatic territory is so easily violated in the case of the Austrian search of Bolivia's diplomatic flight. Similarly, Snowden's existence in the nowhere of an airport displays the fictions in territory. While Assange and Snowden are relying on international geography for protection, they at the same time reveal the imaginaries that surround the individual and hack together new spatial realities for themselves. The role of territorial, legal, and political borders across this narrative arc is indicative of geographic duality that Cyberspace enables. Individuals can exploit the geography of Cyberspace and remain unconfined in their ability to reach out and affect processes outside the territory in which they exist, so long as they have access to the network.[124]

---

[121] Greenberg, *This Machine Kills Secrets* (2012) 6.

[122] *Id.* at 31–32.

[123] Branigan & Elder, "Edward Snowden Leaves Hong Kong for Moscow" (2013).

[124] Henley, "Ecuador cuts off Julian Assange's internet access at London embassy"

Finally, the articulation of power within this narrative shows new patterns that reflect a new shape of world-scale political geography. Within this narrative, states are engaged in international politics in order to resolve the issues caused by transnational actors. This power though is often inflected through corporate power structures as can be seen in the Cablegate episode and in the programs such as PRISM that Snowden unveiled. The state's power is now part of a, pardon the pun, diversified portfolio. Power is inflected back at the state through individuals that assert themselves as adversaries on equal footing with the state and become "global political player[s]."[125] Though each has their own interesting spatial standing, each is able to leverage themselves in such a way that they challenge the political space of the state from outside its political geography. Interestingly, Assange is reported to have "adopted the language of the power mongers he claimed to be combatting," which shows how he was positioning WikiLeaks as an adversary of equal standing to the state.[126] These acts are beyond civil disobedience, which is "a public nonviolent conscientious yet political act contrary to law" with the goal of changing the status quo.[127] These technologies remove the "price" of legal consequences through the use of encryption technologies.[128] Instead, as an anonymous author stated in 2600: The Hacker Quarterly "[h]ackers are no longer anonymous independent operators or groups: We are now a known and calculated factor" in power structures.[129] While this is easily read as boastful, it is hard to ignore the attention that cybersecurity is receiving at the top levels of governments and corporations, among others. Indeed, governments, corporations, and hacktivists must be examined together to reveal "the baroque workings of power" in global politics.[130] These "baroque workings" are highlighted not just by attacks on corporations and states by groups like Anonymous, but also in cases of attacks on corporations by states such as with North Korea and Sony.

Geographic duality is maybe the best way to describe the situation in which Cyberspace exists within international space and international space exists within Cyberspace creating a unified world-scale geography in which neither is dominant. While this rings like an attempt at empty metaphysics, we find it reflected in the architecture of Cyberspace. The physical layers of Cyberspace and the users in Cyberspace exist within the borders of the state and therefore within the borders of the international. But, the logical layer of the Internet is made of algorithms, and these are ideas operationalized

---

(2018).

125   Domscheit-Berg, *Inside WikiLeaks* (2011) 270.

126   *Id.* at 200–201.

127   Rawls, *A Theory of Justice* (1971) 364.

128   *Id.* at 367.

129   Prisoner #6, "The 21st Century Hacker Manifesto" (2014–2015) 50.

130   Dittmer, "Everyday Diplomacy" (2015) 616.

through machinery.[131] This means that the logical layer is a manifestation of human consciousness. Or in simpler terms, the logical layer is ideas, and ideas are notoriously hard to control.

This chapter has shown how world-scale political geography is shifting as new actors become mediums for power within the system and serves as a capstone for Part II, which highlights encounters where cybergeographies come into proximity of international geographies. The various cases and incidents addressed in this section are meant to reveal complexity within the system by layering the spatial, legal, and political geography of Cyberspace onto the spatial, legal, and political geography of international space. This layering shows the junctures and disjunctures of these two intermingled geographies. The following final chapter will pull these various threads together and posit that Cyberspace short circuits international governance processes and allows actors to reprogram the world.

---

[131] Berlinski, *The Advent of the Algorithm* (2000) xii.

Conclusion

"The algorithm has come to occupy a central place in our imagination. It is the second great scientific idea of the West. There is no third."

David Berlinski

9

Reprogramming the World

In 1515, a live rhinoceros arrived in Portugal. It was a gift from Sultan Muzaffar II of Gujarat to King Manuel I of Portugal. The King then gifted the creature on to Pope Leo X, but the rhino died in transport. The pope instead received the taxidermied corpse, and German artist Albrecht Dürer based a drawing, titled Rhinoceron, on a sketch and secondhand description of that corpse. This drawing was then turned into a woodcut that made it reproducible on the printing press. Dürer's rhinoceros, though fairly inaccurate, was reproduced and became the dominant depiction of the rhinoceros for well over a hundred years. The medium introduced by Gutenberg, facilitated the spread of an idea that became tenaciously melded into the public understanding of what constituted the thing that was signified by "rhinoceros."[132]

The "boilerplate rhino" is a function of "Gutenberg's revolution," and it illustrates the ability of ideas to entrench themselves through reproduction.[133] The power of the image is itself a function of its reach, and Dürer's decision to make the image a woodcut shows his intent for mass market publication.[134] Similarly, Chapter 5 discussed the power of cartography in constructing imaginary cartographies. These images of the international system are the graphic conceptualization of the "Westphalian state." This term itself is one that has been entrenched through repetition and reification and is still used to describe the international system despite the dramatic differences between the contemporary nation state and the nation state that emerged from the Peace of Westphalia.[135] The resulting 'boilerplate state' is one that reifies its border through the projection of legal jurisdiction and political identity across a spatial geography denoted by solid black lines on a map. The Westphalian imaginary was repeatedly recast onto the developing international system as a descriptor and a depictor.

---

[132] Quammen, *The Boilerplate Rhino* (2000) 201–209.

[133] *Id.* at 203.

[134] *Id.* at 206.

[135] *See generally* Clark, *Legitimacy in International Society* (2005) 51–70.

This final chapter will examine how Cyberspace reprograms international governance. The first section of this chapter will use the metaphor of lawmaking as programming as an analytic lens to show how Cyberspace changes the processes of the international system. The second section will then delve into some of the theoretical implications of a reprogrammed world. Specifically, this section will examine the connection between a global cybergeography and the project of Cosmopolitanism and global governance. The final section will identify challenges and questions that a reprogrammed world presents for future research.

Rule by Algorithm

Director Terry Gilliam's film *Brazil* depicts a dystopian future governed by complexly bureaucratic government. In the film, a farcical error in a printer causes the death of an innocent civilian by putting in motion a bureaucratic process that must run to completion. The bureaucracy is such that a terrorist, played by Robert De Niro, is a renegade heating and air conditioning repairman who now fixes HVAC systems without filing the proper paperwork, much to the chagrin of the process-oriented government. The film's aesthetic is marked by the use of bizarre machines that personify the complex bureaucratic machinations of the governance system. Indeed, De Niro's character, Archibald Tuttle's crime of terror is that of short-circuiting the governance system and bypassing established processes. In the world Gilliam creates, code is not law so much as law is code.

What Gilliam portrays is a government that has become so process burdened, that its own existence and internal legitimacy are functions of its processing power – its ability to administer the state, which is distinct from governing the state. The metaphor Gilliam exploits is that of governance as a machine. The reason this metaphor has such resonance is that the modern bureaucratic state emerged alongside the industrial age. Bureaucracy is a form of government that is meant to work like a machine to some extent. Lawmakers make laws that are implemented and carried out by government officials. In this model, lawmakers define the inputs and the outputs and the administrative branch of government devises procedures (i.e. regulation) for accomplishing these tasks. While administrators make decisions, the processes they must follow confine their actions in such a way as to ensure the legislated outcomes.

If it is accepted that code is law, then programmers become lawmakers. Whether they are working to spec on a contract or working for their own personal purposes, programmers create rules by writing algorithms. Computer programs are made of algorithms, which are *"effective procedure[s* or] a way of getting something done in a finite number of discrete steps."[1] This is similar to the role of procedural legitimacy in governance systems, which seeks to set procedures that reproduce just outcomes consistently. Rawls, for instance, noted this metaphorical link between computing and governance, describing the "political process as a machine which makes social decisions when the views of representatives and their constituents are fed into it."[2] This observation points to the central metaphor employed by this section, which is understanding law as code. This metaphor will be used as an analytic tool to illustrate pragmatically how Cyberspace reprograms the world. At the outset, it should be noted that this is a limited metaphor, but it is being used at a very high level of application in order to illustrate why the model presented herein matters to scholars of international governance.

Computer code is esoteric to the average individual despite its ubiquity. It is the magic in the machine that is often depicted in movies as a dizzying stream of green 1s and 0s whizzing past coders typing at lightning speed. While computer code can be quite complex, how it functions should not be esoteric. Code can be understood as a syntax for instructions to produce different results. Code is a manifestation of formal logic in that it often occurs as if/then and x=y type statements. Code is, quite simply, a set of instructions or procedures.

Code tells the computer (i.e. the machine itself) what to do through a set of logical arguments that come in a specific order. As an example, a microcontroller is a small computer that can be programmed to manipulate physical objects. Beginners are often taught how to write code that uses the microcontroller to turn an LED light on and off with the press of a button. This code functions in a series of steps (see Fig. 9.1). It will first assign the button to an input and the LED to an output. Next, it will tell the computer to check the state of the input and store it. Then it instructs the machine that if the button is pushed, then the light should be turned on. Otherwise, the light should be off. These procedures run over and over, constantly monitoring for the state of the button and adjusting the state of the LED as necessary. Until the program is stopped these are the rules that govern the functions of the machine by instructing how to turn its inputs into outputs.

---

[1] Berlinski, *The Advent of the Algorithm* (2000) xvi.
[2] Rawls, *A Theory of Justice* (1971) 196.

```
#define LED 12        //assigns LED to output pin
#define BUTTON 7      //assigns button to input pen

int val = 0;          //val is a variable used to
                      //store the staof the input
int state = 0;        //state is a variable,
                      //0=LED on & 1 =LED on

void setup()          //portion of the program sets up
                      //microcontroller
{
  pinMode(LED, OUTPUT);   //LED is an output
  pinMode(BUTTON, INPUT); //BUTTON is an input
}

void loop()           //the procedures that will be repeated

{
  val = digitalRead(BUTTON); //read the input and store it as val

  if (val == HIGH){   //Check to see if the button is pressed
    state = 1 - state;       //Change state variable

  }
  if  (state == 1) {  //if the button is pressed
    digitalWrite(LED, HIGH); //turn on the LED
  }
  else {              //if the button is not pressed
    digitalWrite(LED, LOW);  //turn off the LED
}}
```

Fig. 9.1: Simple Arduino microcontroller program from turning an LED light on and off with a button. The portions after the "//" are comments that tell what each line of code does. Adapted from Banzi.[3]

One of the unexplored areas of Lessig's "code is law" principle is the use of it as a means to reflect back on law as code. In a modern bureaucratic state, law can be explained in terms of code.[4] In this model a state's constitution is an operating system, its legislation becomes its programs, and regulations become the procedures that are performed over and over to produce results, such as justice, until the program is changed by users. The international system is akin to a network that connects the various operating systems and mediates the interactions between these autonomous computers.

---

3   Banzi, *Getting Started With Arduino* (2011).
4   Berlinski, *The Advent of the Algorithm* (2000) xiii.

The first thing to note here is how this connects with legitimacy as discussed in Chapter 4. The legislature in this model sets outputs which include things such as practical outcomes (e.g. lowering of crime), efficiency outcomes (e.g. in procurement process), and political outcomes in terms of rights (e.g. justice). The procedure serves the purpose of maintaining consistency in these outcomes and as a verification mechanism that allows users to ensure that the system is properly programmed to produce the desired outcome. Procedures are used to compute or process outputs consistent with the requirements of substantive legitimacy within that operating system and are meant to be a limitation of choice by excluding the whims of individual government agents from the governance process.[5] This is similar to a computer program, which is a set of processes that the computer goes through in order to create an output, the major difference being that the computer, without reprogramming, is unable to violate the rules it has been given, whereas the administrative official can violate those rules.

This difference aside, at a high level we can see that the metaphor of law as code reveals something interesting about the nature of governance. Programming is a skill that requires a coder to conceptualize and set the outputs of a program through a set of instructions written in a standardized language. Importantly, different programmers accomplish tasks in different ways, and they must make decisions that balance between practical outputs, efficiency, and substantive outputs for the user of the program. The nature of the computer transforms the governance as machine metaphor into a governance as computation metaphor. The "abstract norms that obtain regularity and predictability" for programmers are written in algorithms.[6] The algorithm itself emerged well before the computer and was posited as a way in which abstract mathematical formulas could be used to describe quite literally the entire cosmos.[7] The algorithm found in the digital computer is a device that could make the algorithm's output manifest. It becomes the process through which programmers can manipulate and recreate the world. It allows for the creation of imagined spaces – and Cyberspace might best be understood as a multiverse of ideas.[8]

Law and regulation are similarly ideas that are given effect through the bureaucratic administrative machine. A simple government program for the disbursement of a government benefit functions analogously. Legislation defines the inputs and outputs and regulation then puts into place a series of

---

[5]   Coicaud, *Legitimacy and Politics* (2002) 32.

[6]   *Id.* at 20.

[7]   Berlinski, *The Advent of the Algorithm* (2002).

[8]   *For example* Tanz, "Playing for Time" (2016). *See also* Lloyd, *Programming the Universe* (2006).

procedures that government officials use to process public administration. A citizen seeking to claim a benefit would give inputs required by the program. These inputs would then be checked against a set of variables or criteria. If the individual meets those criteria the official disburses the benefit, else the government official does not disburse the benefit.

In this metaphor, the international governance system becomes a networking protocol that allows the state operating systems to communicate by instituting transaction points for the different systems to communicate, such as the ITU. The protocol though is one that facilitates interconnection and not interoperability. As a result, it requires those it connects to have certain features in order to take part in the network. This allows us to probe why Cyberspace can be said to reprogram the world. As noted in Chapter I, international governance has historically been successful at deploying international law that governs world scale technology, but it has been unable to encompass Cyberspace technologies effectively within its regime. It is submitted here that this is a direct result of the materiality of international governance. The territorial rootedness of the international system indicates a need for transnational physicality in order for it to effectively interconnect parties for solutions. As noted in Chapter 7, the ITU's ability to successfully govern international telecommunications is a function of its ability to create law that governs the physical circumstances of the technology, but not the ideational content carried on that technology. This is a constant theme in international law. A good example can be found in the Genocide Convention and the UDHR, which were both passed in December 1948. The Genocide Convention did not include a provision on racist and discriminatory speech, because the United States opposed its inclusion on grounds that it violated the right of free speech.[9] The Universal Declaration of Human Rights, on the other hand, included the right to free speech, but was not adopted as a binding treaty and the Soviet States abstained from voting.

In international governance, the state is the only device that can connect to the network and take part as a full member of the political geography. International governance is only equipped with tools that ensure "territorial integrity" against physical incursions. Ideational incursions have always been outside the realm of the international network, and states have been left free to control these incursions in a best efforts system. The international network then is not interoperable because the operating systems are able to resist certain inputs. The physical layer components of the Internet are clearly technologies that the international system is equipped to regulate fueling realist interpretations of Cyberspace. The logical layer, though, subverts the physicality of that border crossing by freeing content from its analog barriers.

---

9   Schabas, *Genocide in International Law* (2009) 320.

The protocols that function at the core of the Internet pushes code-making (i.e. regulatory) abilities to the user by making human interaction interoperable across borders. It breaks the strictures of the operating system allowing for geographic convergence and multiplying interaction points.

An example might better illustrate this. The operating system on a device limits the types of instructions that the device can run, which limits the programs it can run. In the early days of computing the operating system was a significant limitation on what programs one could run, and the operating system in use can still be very limiting. Applications like Google Docs subvert the strictures of the operating system by allowing the user to run a program through their web browser, erasing the borders set by the operating system. This is analogous to what is happening in the international system. The logical layer of the Internet is at once content and medium; the medium is literally inseparable from the message.[10] This allows interoperability not conceived of within international geography and gives entrance to hackers like Assange who are able to hack into the international network. Cyberspace is a geography that enables individuals, corporations, and states to short-circuit the international protocols and create interoperability across borders and among actors.

What this reveals is that law is code is just as important as code is law. For instance, the mass surveillance discussed in Chapter 8 allows the state to extend its law and power over individuals outside its borders in contravention of the assumed materiality found in international governance. The state is clearly circumventing the coordinating process of the international system through Cyberspace. This hack cannot be patched by international governance, because it has never been vested with the ability to regulate ideas. The technology opens the possibility of global interoperability.

A Digital Cosmopolis

Much of the juxtaposition in this research has been to pit Cyberspace in contrast to 'realist' readings that tend to imagine the state as pursuing its interests against other states using power, which is embodied by military might and economic wealth – that is: blood and treasure.[11] While a reprogrammed world does not completely diminish realism's explanatory power, it does remove the state from its dominance over a number of activities including war. For instance, while Stuxnet could be read in realist terms, such an analysis will likely gloss over some of the central problems that Cyberspace causes for realism. The primary problem is in realism's

---

10   *See* Berlinski, *The Advent of the Algorithm* (2000) 309–310.
11   Caney, "Review Article" (2001) 986–87.

conception of power. Power in terms of military might is no longer something monopolized by the state. The state still has access to and the ability to wield power in Cyberspace, but it is no longer the sole holder of that power. Power itself has been reprogrammed so as to allow others to wield power on par with the state. Similarly, power in terms of treasure has changed as well. Technologies like Bitcoin have changed the nature of currency, removing the state's ability to control the flow of funds. Digitized power is transferable outside of the zero-sum world of the realist.

This critique of realism might lead one to try and place the reprogrammed world within the context of cosmopolitan theory. Cosmopolitanism exists in various forms, but its theorists all converge on the idea of a world governance system that extends political and social rights to individuals as opposed to states.[12] These theorists argue that the development of a world-scale governance order is the only way to overcome the various global injustices by extending "[p]rinciples of distributive justice ... [to] a global scope."[13] Cosmopolitanism is different in scope from the "loose community of states" represented by the UN. It is a project that seeks ways to form a "community of world citizens, who can legitimate their political decisions ... on the basis of democratic opinion."[14] Cosmopolitan theorists extend reciprocal rights and obligations from the sphere of the state, making a universalist claim giving individuals "moral personality."[15]

At face value, cosmopolitanism seems like a theoretical outlook that could accommodate the alternative geographies of the reprogrammed world, since the Internet "has unleashed the extraordinary possibility for many to participate in the process of building and cultivating culture that reaches far beyond local boundaries."[16] Even Schmitt notes the power of a "global consciousness ... oriented to a common hope" in the shaping of world space.[17] Cosmopolitanism embraces such respatializations as it itself pushes a global rather than international perspective abandoning the "state [as] the natural container of and vehicle for politics.[18] Cosmopolitanism even shares rhetorical and discursive ties to cyber-utopians like John Perry Barlow.[19]

---

12   *See generally*, Caney, "Review Article" (2001); Craig, "The Resurgent Idea of World Government" (2008) 133–42; and Dallmayr, "Cosmopolitanism" (2003) 421–42.

13   Caney, "Review Article" (2001) 975.

14   Habermas, *The Postnational Constellation* (2001) 105–106. *See also* Held, *Democracy and Global Order* (1995) 22–23.

15   Caney, "Review Article" (2001) 977.

16   Lessig, *Free Culture* (2004) 9.

17   Schmitt, *Nomos of the Earth* (2003) 50.

18   *For instance* Goodhart, "Human Rights and Global Democracy" (2008) 401.

19   *See generally* Turner, *From Counterculture to Cyberculture* (2006).

Despite the decentralized nature of Cyberspace, its technology holds a hope for cosmopolitanism. Cyberspace displays the ability to reconceptualize global space and connect individuals without the interference of the state. Multistakeholder governance reflects core notions of cosmopolitanism in its deliberative approach that places governance in a "global context ... defined by multiple and overlapping networks."[20] Cyberspace represents "global space," and from the perspective of the cosmopolitan, it manifests the possibility of new global imaginations, and social movements using Cyberspace often employ "cosmopolitan repertoires."[21] Pragmatically, the technology could help to fill gaps in data that would be critical to any such enterprise,[22] and it holds the most promise as a technology for facilitating world-scale deliberation.

Despite the hope found in the technology, the reprogrammed world does not necessarily mesh with cosmopolitanism. Central to this is the authority structure discussed in Chapter 7. The Internet as part of its code bucks centralization. A core function of packet switching is to eliminate "global control."[23] So while cosmopolitanism seeks the "establishment of some sort of authoritative regime" to spread equality, Cyberspace only serves to unite the globe through an interoperable protocol which fragments the world into networks.[24] Cyberspace does not seek equality in its users, only interoperability. So, while Cyberspace opens global geographies, it cannot be said to have yet opened a cosmopolitan geography that could accommodate deliberative democracy of a global scale.

What this tells us is that while Cyberspace presents an unprecedented opportunity for the deployment of cosmopolitan or utopian visions, technological determinism is a mistake. Technological solutions for building world-scale community were critiqued as early as the 1930s through "skepticism about the capacity of a global community of connectivity to transmute into a global community of responsibility."[25] The technology itself may be a necessary precursor to a cosmopolitan system, but is not sufficient by itself.[26] Despite all the tools that Cyberspace presents, "society may lack the informational tools necessary to involve everyone in democratic decision-making and to foster widespread economic and social flourishing."[27] As a

---

[20] Goodhart, "Human Rights and Global Democracy" (2008) 401–402.

[21] Fielder, "The Internet and Dissent in Authoritarian States" (2013) 167.

[22] *See generally* Coicaud & Tahri, "Nationally Based Data" (2014) 135–45.

[23] Leiner et al., "A Brief History of the Internet" (2012).

[24] Craig, "The Resurgent Idea of World Government" (2008) 135.

[25] Critique by Reinhold Niebhur in Menon, "Pious Words, Puny Deeds" (2009) 236. *See also* Cooper, "What Is the Concept of Globalization Good For?" (2001) 193.

[26] Streck, "Pulling the Plug on Electronic Town Meetings" (1998) 19.

[27] Goodman & Chen, "Modeling Policy for New Public Service Media Networks" (2010)

result despite the increase in intercultural interchange "global democracy is nowhere in sight,"[28] and "programmed utopias" should likely be met with skepticism.[29] Technology is powerful, but cosmopolitanism is still at its core a problem of developing global knowledge."[30]

It is easy to view Cyberspace as a tool with which to reprogram the world into a digital cosmopolis, but the capability of the technology to restructure global affairs along cosmopolitan values will be closely related to how Cyberspace itself is governed. As Lessig reminds, the Cyberspace that currently exists is not the only Cyberspace possible.[31] Whether or not cosmopolitan geographies are possible will depend in large part on the innovative capacity that is pushed to the edges of the networks.

Defragmenting the International

This research posits that the international system developed to coordinate world scale governance in the wake of WWII is being transformed by cyber-technologies that are driving a reconceptualization of global order. The first section in this chapter used the metaphor of programming to show how Cyberspace allows borders to be hacked and recoded. The second section used cosmopolitanism as a lens to show that though Cyberspace helps to conceptualize other global geographies, it has its own logics that these structures must also contend with as they seek to build global knowledge. These two discussions both point to uncertainty in the future that Cyberspace might enable. This is because the "mental consequences of the Internet ... are still very hard to assess."[32] One thing is certain though: Cyberspace will continue to shape the space in which global affairs unfold. This calls for tracking future encounters between Cyberspace and international geography to build a proper understanding of how geography is being reprogrammed. Outside of defining the nature and scope of systemic changes, there are a number of theoretical questions that are ripe to be evaluated in light of restructured world-scale geography.

The primary question that should be raised is how we can conceptualize legitimation within dual geographies. International legitimacy and Cyberspace legitimacy are based on different principles, but they both tap into similar

---

114.

28   Rao, "Equity in A Global Public Goods Framework" (1999) 68.

29   Bearman, "The Untold Story of Silk Road" (2015).

30   Featherstone & Venn, "Problematizing Global Knowledge and the New Encyclopaedia Project" (2006) 10–11.

31   Lessig, *Code 2.0* (2006) 31–37.

32   Habermas, *The Postnational Constellation* (2001) 43.

ideas of democracy and human rights.[33] For instance, the Western liberal democratic state is premised on representative democracy in which voters are defined by territory. Cyberspace as a spatial geography is everywhere, so Internet governance communities depend on democratic voting, but are open to participation by all interested individuals. Legitimacy is closely tied to consent, which is skewed as a result of Cyberspace. The state's ability to legislate change in the Internet within its territory maintains the risk of changing the Internet in another state's territory contrary to the consent of its citizens. At the same time, a small group of elites that form IGCs can make decisions based on consent that can change how the Internet works without going through processes established within a state to ensure in part the administration of justice.[34] This raises deep questions about the nature of legitimacy within the space of multiple dynamic regulatory systems.

A second, related question is what the nature of democracy is within Cyberspace. Cyber-utopians have long called for community governance arguing that such governance is more democratic, but the suggestion that "democracy in cyberspace means democracy in the real world ... is false."[35] Democracy is not a static condition, and the democracy observed in IGCs is open and inclusive in thought, but participation is de facto limited by the high level of technical knowledge needed to meaningfully participate. This means that not only are most people unable to engage in these processes, the processes themselves are in potential danger of being co-opted by groups that flood the membership of IGCs. Corporations and states can send individual representatives to take part in the deliberations and are seemingly not limited to a single representative since membership is open. In other words, how do users reconcile their "multiple identities" and "plural affiliations," and take part in multiple governance systems.[36]

Additionally, community governance can be seen to have undemocratic tendencies, and can come in "its form of lynch-mob" sanctions.[37] Libertarian coders have even sought to use it as a marketplace for assassinations.[38] Thus, a second layer of questions on democracy in Cyberspace result from the fora of public discourse being privately owned social media platforms such as Facebook and Twitter.[39] While a private fourth estate has been considered central to liberal democracy, the lines become blurred through the

---

[33] *Id.* at 119.
[34] Alvestrand & Lie, "Development of Core Internet Standards" (2009) 129.
[35] Streck, "Pulling the Plug on Electronic Town Meetings" (1998) 18–47, 40–41.
[36] Sen, "Global Justice" (1999) 120–121.
[37] Tambini et al., *Codifying Cyberspace* (2008) 3.
[38] Greenberg, *This Machine Kills Secrets* (2012) 69–70 and Bearman, "The Untold Story of Silk Road" (2005).
[39] DeNardis & Hackl, "Internet Governance by Social Media Platforms" (2015).

phenomenon of the "citizen reporter." The WikiLeaks controversy is instructive as it shows how states can use diplomatic pressure to place burdens on expression through pressure on dominant corporations. This example shows that "the privatization of information flows offers possibilities for private monopoly and sub-optimal exclusion of social groups."[40] These technologies recode the public discursive space, and democracy under such conditions is insufficiently theorized.[41] This is especially so in light of the widespread election interference by Russia in a number of other states.[42] This interference took advantage of the way in which social media allows for echo chambers to emerge and shape public discourse.[43] By flooding these systems with #fakenews, an external state was able to influence the public discourse occurring outside its borders. While these activities certainly affect the "political independence" of other states, there was no need for a prohibited use of force.

Third, and building upon the previous two questions, is what the nature of global multistakeholder governance will be as it unfolds as a new category within world-scale governance structure.[44] This question is one of determining how such a governance structure, which removes the state from the dominant position, will interact with international government mechanisms. This new category of governance will create rules and norms that can be made effective within the territory of a state without the consent mechanisms found in traditional international organizations. Multistakeholder governance is still an emerging concept and it is still yet to be defined with much clarity.

Finally, a raft of ethical and philosophical questions arises in terms of how to best structure Cyberspace. Its design is currently foundational to the way in which it alters geography, and its architecture is highly contested in a number of fora.[45] If we accept that "we can and we should make more use of technology for participatory democracy," then there are critical issues to ensuring that Cyberspace governance maintains that possibility,[46] so that it can "promote communicative opportunities."[47] Cyberspace, like other major technological advances, has already changed the world, but there is a challenge in ensuring that it impacts the world in a positive manner. As we see with incidents like Stuxnet and cybercrime, Cyberspace also has the potential to be used in a way that causes harm to humanity as a whole. As a

---

[40]   Tambini et al., *Codifying Cyberspace* (2008) 10.

[41]   *See generally* Chadwick, "Bringing E-Democracy Back In" (2003) 443–55.

[42]   *See generally* Galante & Ee, *Defining Russian Election Interference* (2018).

[43]   *See generally* Sunstein, *Republic.com 2.0* (2007).

[44]   Leiner et al., "A Brief History of the Internet" (2012).

[45]   *See generally* DeNardis, *The Global War for Internet Governance* (2014).

[46]   Noveck, "Designing Deliberative Democracy in Cyberspace" (2003) 5.

[47]   Goodman, "Media Policy and Free Speech" (2007) 1211.

result, it should be expected that Cyberspace governance will become more contested as its uses and reach increase. Amidst policy circles there is a need for understanding the role of Cyberspace in the reprogrammed world, and the technical nature of its social imbrication. Cyberspace is an incomplete, and likely an incompletable, process. Based on the logic of the algorithm, Cyberspace grows at the rate of ideas. As a result, we can think of Cyberspace as a manifestation of the human consciousness. Cyberspace is more than just technical standards, and governance must contend with the age-old problem of constructing political space that allows freedom of ideas, but at the same time keeps the governance structure from collapsing on itself.

The questions raised here are by no means ignored in the vast literature on Cyberspace, but they are most often engaged with at the level of particular technologies. These questions are raised here in relation to Cyberspace as an alternative geography to international geography. The international system is a legal and political settlement that defines territorial space, but Cyberspace is a technology that is pushing against this order by recoding the borders that flow from the international system. As such, these questions need to be addressed as the technology continues to reshape global social life.

Computer programs are ideas that are both medium and message. International governance has been effective at regulating conduits for information, but has had limited success in extending its regulatory net to include the content of the information in these conduits. Digitization presents a unique challenge to international governance because it inseparably bonds the message and the medium. As a result, states have shown a limited ability to exert a variety of controls over Cyberspace domestically, but they have been unable to address it as a transborder phenomenon that is a "composite of the space of flows and the space of places."[48]

The convergence of medium and message creates a challenge for international governance that is premised on material territorial borders. This is not the only reason that the international will be increasingly challenged by Cyberspace. The message-medium convergence is also implicit in emerging social understandings of the space of consciousness. The networking of the world means that individuals "can change [their] geography, and anything that happens there creates a change in someone's physical geography."[49] It is

---

[48] Castells, "Communication, Power and Counter-Power in the Network Society" (2007) 249.
[49] Hayden, "The Future of Things Cyber" (2013) 4.

these innovative connections that are currently driving economics, politics, and a range of other social interactions. In much the same way that the dropping of Little Boy on Hiroshima and the first orbit of Sputnik did, Cyberspace is changing the shape of the world. The Cold War fear of distant powers raining fire from the sky has been replaced by a post 9/11 fear of the Internet radicalized neighbor. Similarly, the power and awe of strategic nuclear weapons and space exploration that has held so much sway over international politics is being replaced by the power of Cyberspace and the struggle to maintain and manage it in such a way as to enrich humanity. If the Internet and Cyberspace are to be effective tools of liberty, freedom, and justice then Cyberspace must be understood not just within domestic governance frameworks, but also within the international governance system, which defines the borders that enclose domestic systems. In Schmitt's words:

> The new nomos of our planet is growing irresistibly. [...] But what is coming is not therefore boundless or a nothingness hostile to nomos. Also in timorous rings of old and new forces, right measures and meaningful proportions can originate.[50]

---

[50]   Schmitt, *The Nomos of the Earth* (2003) 355.

Bibliography

"A Tale of Many Hackers," *2600: The Hacker Quarterly*, 2015.

"A Thing About Machines," *The Twilight Zone*, season 1, episode 40 (1960).

Aaronson, Xavier, "The DIY Engineer Who Built a Nuclear Reactor in His Basement," Motherboard, August 27, 2014, http://motherboard.vice.com/read/the-diy-engineer-who-built-a-nuclear-reactor-in-his-basement.

"About Pong," www.ponggame.org (last visited February 11, 2016).

Addis, Adeno, "The Thin State in Thick Globalism: Sovereignty in the Information Age," *Vanderbilt Journal of Transnational Law* 37, (2004): 1-107.

Agreement on the Rescue of Astronauts, the Return of Astronauts and the Return of Objects Launched into Outer Space (December 3, 1968).

Albanesius, Chloe, "Anonymous Takes Down CIA Web Site," *PC Magazine*, February 10, 2012, http://www.pcmag.com/article2/0,2817,2400140,00.asp.

American Broadcasting Company v. Aereo, 573 U.S. __ (2014).

AnonHQ, "The Most Frequently Asked Questions People Have About Anonymous," (Jan. 16, 2016), http://anonhq.com/43605-2/

"Anonymous Activists Target Tunisian Government Sites," *BBC News*, January 4, 2014, http://www.bbc.com/news/technology-12110892.

Akehurst, Michael, "Jurisdiction in International Law," *Brit. YB Int'l L.* 46 (1972): 145.

Allan, Collin S., "Attribution Issues in Cyberspace," *Chi.-Kent J. Int'l & Comp. L.* 13 (2013): 55–201.

Alvestrand, Harald and Hakon Wium Lie, "Development of Core Internet Standards: The Work of IETF and W3C," in *Internet Governance: Infrastructure and Institutions*, ed. Lee A. Bygrave and Jon Bing (Oxford: Oxford University Press, 2009), 126–46.

American Convention on Human Rights (entered into force July 18, 1978).

Antarctic Treaty (December 1, 1959).

Arendt, Hannah, *Eichmann in Jerusalem: A Report on the Banality of Evil* (New York: Penguin, 1963).

Arms Trade Treaty (entered into force Dec. 24, 2014).

Assange, Julian, "Conspiracy as Governance," *IQ. Org*, 2006, http://library.blountsfolly.com/space/items/show/172.

Assange, Julian et al., *Cypherpunks: Freedom and the Future of the Internet* (Or Books, 2012).

Associated Press, "'Anonymous' Hackers Threaten Drug Cartel," *CBS News*, October 31, 2011, http://www.cbsnews.com/news/anonymous-hackers-threaten-drug-cartel/.

Ball, James and Spencer Ackerman, "NSA Loophole Allows Warrantless Search for US Citizens' Emails and Phone Calls," *The Guardian*, August 9, 2013, http://www.theguardian.com/world/2013/aug/09/nsa-loophole-warrantless-searches-email-calls.

Ball, James, Luke Harding, and Juliette Garside, "BT and Vodafone among Telecoms Companies Passing Details to GCHQ," *The Guardian*, August 2, 2013, http://www.theguardian.com/business/2013/aug/02/telecoms-bt-vodafone-cables-gchq.

Banks, David, "The Politics of Communications Technology," Cyborgology, May 5, 2013, http://thesocietypages.org/cyborgology/2013/05/04/the-politics-of-communications-technology/.

Banzi, Massimo, *Getting Started With Arduino*, 2nd ed. (Beijing: O'Reilly 2011).

Barlow, John Perry, "The Declaration of Independance for Cyberspace," February 8, 1996, https://projects.eff.org/~barlow/Declaration-Final.html.

Battaglia, Debbora, "Arresting Hospitality: the Case of the 'Handshake in Space'," *Journal of the Royal Anthropological Institute*, v. 18/1 (June 2012) S76-S89.

Bearman, Joshua, "The Untold Story of Silk Road, Part 2: The Fall," *WIRED*, May 14, 2015, http://www.wired.com/2015/05/silk-road-2/.

Bell, Daniel, "The East Asian Challenge to Human Rights: Reflections on an East West Dialogue," *Human Rights Quarterly* 18, no. 3 (1996): 641–67.

Bellamy, Alex J., "Whither the Responsibility to Protect? Humanitarian Intervention and the 2005 World Summit," *Ethics & International Affairs* 20, no. 2 (2006): 143–69.

Bergen, Peter L. and Bruce Hoffman, *Assessing the Terrorist Threat: A Report of the Bipartisan Policy Center's National Security Preparedness Group* (Bipartisan Policy Center, 2010).

Berkman Center, *Don't Panic Making Progress on the "Going Dark" Debate* (Feb. 1, 2016) https://cyber.law.harvard.edu/pubrelease/dont-panic/Dont_Panic_Making_Progress_on_Going_Dark_Debate.pdf.

Berlinski, David, *The Advent of the Algorithm: The 300-Year Journey from an Idea to the Computer* (Houghton Mifflin Harcourt, 2000).

Bernard, Doug, "Iran's Next Step in Building a 'Halal' Internet," *Voice of America*, March 9, 2015, http://www.voanews.com/content/irans-next-step-in-building-a-halal-internet/2672948.html.

Betz, David J., "Clausewitz and Connectivity," *Infinity Journal* 3, no. 1 (March 2013), https://www.infinityjournal.com/article/84/Clausewitz_and_Connectivity/.

Betz, David J. and Tim Stevens, *Cyberspace and the State: Toward a Strategy for Cyber-Power* (London: Routledge, 2011).

Bigo, Didier, "The Emergence of a Consensus: Global Terrorism, Global Insecurity, and Global Security.," in *Immigration, Integration, and Security.*

America and Europe in Comparative Perspective, ed. Ariane Chebel d'Appollonia and Simon Reich (University of Pittsburgh Press, 2008), 76–94.

Blount, P. J., "Jurisdiction in Outer Space: Challenges of Private Individuals in Space," *J. Space L.* 33 (2007): 299.

Blount, P. J., "The Preoperational Legal Review of Cyber Capabilities: Ensuring the Legality of Cyber Weapons," *Northern Kentucky Law Review* 39, no. 2 (2012): 211–20, http://papers.ssrn.com/abstract=2380359.

Blount, P. J., "Renovating Space: The Future of International Space Law," *Denv. J. Int'l L. & Pol'y* 40 (2012): 515–686.

Borger, Julian, "NSA Files: Why The Guardian in London Destroyed Hard Drives of Leaked Files," *The Guardian*, accessed April 12, 2014, http://www.theguardian.com/world/2013/aug/20/nsa-snowden-files-drives-destroyed-london.

Borgwardt, Elizabeth, *A New Deal for the World: America's Vision for Human Rights* (Cambridge, MA: Belknap, 2005).

Bowcott, Owen, "Julian Assange Loses Appeal against Extradition," *The Guardian*, May 30, 2012, sec. Media, http://www.theguardian.com/media/2012/may/30/julian-assange-loses-appeal-extradition.

Bowman, Gregory W., "Thinking Outside the Border: Homeland Security and the Forward Deployment of the US Border," *Houston Law Review* 44, no. 2 (2007): 189–251.

Branigan, Tania and Miriam Elder, "Edward Snowden Leaves Hong Kong for Moscow," *The Guardian*, June 23, 2013, sec. US news, http://www.theguardian.com/world/2013/jun/23/edward-snowden-leaves-hong-kong-moscow.

Brate, Adam, *Technomanifestos: Visions of the Information Revolutionaries*, 1 edition (New York: Texere, 2002).

Brazil (Embassy International Productions/Brazil Productions 1985).

Brenner, Joel, "Gray Matter," *Foreign Policy*, March 8, 2013, http://www.foreignpolicy.com/articles/2013/03/08/gray_matter.

Broad, William J., John Markoff, and David E. Sanger, "Stuxnet Worm Used Against Iran Was Tested in Israel," *The New York Times*, January 15, 2011, http://www.nytimes.com/2011/01/16/world/middleeast/16stuxnet.html.

Brooking, E.T., "Anonymous vs. the Islamic State," *Foreign Policy*, November 13, 2015, https://foreignpolicy.com/2015/11/13/anonymous-hackers-islamic-state-isis-chan-online-war/.

Brown, Mark, "Pirate Bay Mirror Is Proxy-Friendly, Bypasses UK Ban," *Wired UK*, May 24, 2012, http://www.wired.co.uk/news/archive/2012-05/24/the-proxy-bay.

Brown, Wendy, *Walled States, Waning Sovereignty* (New York; Cambridge, Mass.: Zone Books ; Distributed by the MIT Press, 2010).

Buckminster Fuller Institute, "The Dymaxion Map," https://bfi.org/about-fuller/big-ideas/dymaxion-world/dymaxion-map (last visited Feb. 15, 2016).

Burbank, Jane and Frederick Cooper, *Empires in World History: Power and Politics of Difference* (Princeton: Princeton University Press, 2010).

Bush, Vannevar, *Modern Arms & Free Men* (MIT Press, 1968).

Cadwalladr, Carole, "Meet Cody Wilson, Creator of the 3D-Gun, Anarchist, Libertarian," *The Guardian*, February 10, 2014, sec. Technology, http://www.theguardian.com/technology/2014/feb/10/cody-wilson-3d-gun-anarchist.

Caney, Simon, "Review Article: International Distributive Justice," *Political Studies* 49, no. 5 (2001): 974–97.

Carey, James, "A Cultural Approach to Communication," in *McQuail's Reader in Mass Communication Theory*, ed. Denis McQuail, 2002, 36–45.

Carrington, Damian, "The Maldives Is the Extreme Test Case for Climate Change Action," *The Guardian*, September 26, 2013, sec. Environment, http://www.theguardian.com/environment/damian-carrington-blog/2013/sep/26/maldives-test-case-climate-change-action.

Carroll, Rory, "Barack Obama and Xi Jinping Meet as Cyber-Scandals Swirl," *The Guardian*, June 8, 2013, sec. US news, http://www.theguardian.com/world/2013/jun/08/obama-xi-jinping-meet-cyberscandals.

Cassese, Antonio, International Criminal Law (Oxford: Oxford University Press 2003).

Castells, Manuel, "Communication, Power and Counter-Power in the Network Society," *International Journal of Communication* 1, no. 1 (2007): 29.

Center for Copyright Information, "FAQ's on The Center for Copyright Information And Copyright Alert System," July 7, 2011, http://library.blountsfolly.com/space/items/show/183.

Chen, Thomas M., "An Assessment of the Department of Defense Strategy for Operating in Cyberspace" (DTIC Document, 2013), http://oai.dtic.m nm,. oaoai?verb=getRecord&metadataPrefix=html&identifier=ADA58643.

Chrisafis, Angelique, "France 'Runs Vast Electronic Spying Operation Using NSA-Style Methods,'" *The Guardian*, July 4, 2013, http://www.theguardian.com/world/2013/jul/04/france-electronic-spying-operation-nsa.

Citizen Four (HBO Films 2014).

Chadwick, Andrew, "Bringing E-Democracy Back In Why It Matters for Future Research on E-Governance," *Social Science Computer Review* 21, no. 4 (2003): 443–55.

Clapham, Christopher, "Degrees of Statehood," *Review of International Studies* 24, no. 02 (1998): 143–57.

Clark, Ian, *Legitimacy in International Society* (Oxford University Press, 2005).

Clark, David D. and Susan Landau, "Untangling Attribution," in *Proceedings of a Workshop on Deterring Cyberattacks: Informing Strategies and Developing Options for U.S. Policy*, 2010.

Clinton, Hillary, "Internet Rights and Wrongs: Choices & Challenges in a Networked World," remarks, *U.S. Department of State*, (February 15, 2011), http://www.state.gov/secretary/20092013clinton/rm/2011/02/156619.htm.

Codding Jr., George A., "The International Telecommunications Union: 130 Years of Telecommunications Regulation," *Denver Journal International Law & Policy* 23 (1994): 501.

Cohen, Julie E., "Privacy, Visibility, Transparency, and Exposure," *The University of Chicago Law Review*, 2008, 181–201.

Coicaud, Jean-Marc, "Deconstructing International Legitimacy," in *Fault Lines of International Legitimacy*, ed. Hilary Charlesworth and Jean-Marc Coicaud (Cambridge University Press, 2009), 29–86.

Coicaud, Jean-Marc, *Legitimacy and Politics: A Contribution to the Study of Political Right and Political Responsibility*, trans. David Ames Curtis (Cambridge: Cambridge University Press, 2002).

Coicaud, Jean-Marc and Ibrahim Tahri, "Nationally Based Data: Challenges for Global Governance (and Global Policy)," *Global Policy* 5, no. 2 (2014): 135–45.

Constitution of the International Telecommunication Union (2010).

Convention on Civil Aviation (Dec. 7, 1944).

Convention on Cybercrime (entered into force July 1, 2004).

Convention on the Prevention and Punishment of the Crime of Genocide, (Dec. 9,1948).

Cooper, Frederick, "What Is the Concept of Globalization Good For? An African Historian's Perspective," *African Affairs* 100, no. 399 (2001): 189–213.

Council of the European Union, "EU Human Rights Guidelines on Freedom of Expression Online and Offline," May 12, 2014, ec.europa.eu//digital-agenda/en/news/eu-human-rights-guidelines-freedom-expression-online-and-offline.

Covenant of the League of Nations (April 28, 1919).

Cowell, Alan, "After 350 Years, Vatican Says Galileo Was Right: It Moves," *The New York Times*, October 31, 1992, sec. World, http://www.nytimes.com/1992/10/31/world/after-350-years-vatican-says-galileo-was-right-it-moves.html.

Craig, Campbell, "The Resurgent Idea of World Government," *Ethics & International Affairs* 22, no. 2 (2008): 133–42.

Dallmayr, Fred, "Cosmopolitanism: Moral and Political," *Political Theory* 31, no. 3 (2003): 421–42.

Davis, Creighton Powell, "The Internet As a Source of Political Change in Egypt and Saudi Arabia," *Al Noor* 1, no. 1 (2008), http://alnoorjournal.org/wp-content/uploads/2012/05/Al-Noor-2008.pdf#page=33.

Defense Distributed, "Downloads," https://defdist.org/downloads/ (last visted Feb. 17, 2016).

DeNardis, Laura, *The Global War for Internet Governance* (New Haven: Yale University Press, 2014).

DeNardis, Laura and A. M. Hackl, "Internet Governance by Social Media Platforms," *Telecommunications Policy*, 2015.

Department of the Army, "FM 3-38: Cyber Electromagnetic Activities," February 12, 2014, http://library.blountsfolly.com/space/items/show/194.

Diaconescu, Adrian, "Inside Job: Lizard Squad and Ex-Sony Employees Likely Aided North Korea's Hack Attack," *Digital Trends*, December 14, 2014, http://www.digitaltrends.com/computing/lizard-squad-and-ex-sony-employees-likely-involved-in-hack/.

Dickinson, Samantha, "How Will Internet Governance Change after the ITU Conference?," *The Guardian*, November 7, 2014, sec. Technology, http://www.theguardian.com/technology/2014/nov/07/how-will-internet-governance-change-after-the-itu-conference.

Digital Millennium Copyright Act, Pub. L. 105-304 (1998).

Dinstein, Yoram, *The Conduct of Hostilities Under the Law of International Armed Conflict* (Cambridge University Press, 2004).

Dipert, Randall R., "The Essential Features of an Ontology for Cyberwarfare," in *Conflict and Cooperation in Cyberspace: The Challenge to National Security*, ed. Panayotis A. Yannakogeorgos and Adam B. Lowther (Boca Raton: Taylor & Francis, 2013), 35–48.

Dittmer, J., "Everyday Diplomacy: UKUSA Intelligence Cooperation and Geopolitical Assemblages," *Annals of the Association of American*

Geographers 105, no. 3 (04 2015): 604–19.

Dodge, Martin, "An Atlas of Cyberspace," https://personalpages.manchester.ac.uk/staff/m.dodge/cybergeography/atlas/topology.html (last visited February 15, 2016).

Dodge, Martin and Rob Kitchin, "Ways to Map Cyberspace," Directions Magazine, November 7, 2001, http://www.directionsmag.com/entry/ways-to-map-cyberspace/124119

Domscheit-Berg, Daniel, *Inside Wikileaks : My Time with Julian Assange at the World's Most Dangerous Website* (New York: Crown Publishers, 2011).

Donnelly, Jack, "Human Rights: A New Standard of Civilization?," *International Affairs* 74, no. 1 (1998): 1–23.

Dorling, Philip, "Snowden Reveals Australia's Links to US Spy Web," *The Sydney Morning Herald*, July 8, 2013, http://www.smh.com.au/world/snowden-reveals-australias-links-to-us-spy-web-20130708-2plyg.html.

Draft Articles on the Responsibility of States for Internationally Wrongful Acts, 53 UN GAOR Supp. (No. 10) at 43, U.N. Doc. A/56/10 (2001).

Du Bois, W. E. B., *The Souls of Black Folk* (New York: Pocket Books, 2005).

Dunlap Jr., Charles J. , "Perspectives for Cyberstrategists on Cyberlaw for Cyberwar," in *Conflict and Cooperation in Cyberspace: The Challenge to National Security*, ed. Panayotis A. Yannakogeorgos and Adam B. Lowther (Boca Raton: Taylor & Francis, 2013), 211–32.

Dunn, Alexandra, "Unplugging a Nation: State Media Strategy During Egypt's January 25 Uprising," *Fletcher F. World Aff.* 35 (2011): 15.

e-Estonia, "What is e-Residency?", https://e-estonia.com/e-residents/about/ (last accessed October 6, 2015).

Elwell, Craig K., M. M. Murphy, and Michael V. Seitzinger, "Bitcoin: Questions, Answers, and Analysis of Legal Issues," Report (United States: Library of Congress. Congressional Research Service., December 20, 2013), United States.

Eppenstein, Madelaine and Elizabeth J. Aisenberg, "Radio Propaganda in the Contexts of International Regulation and the Free Flow of Information as a Human Right [notes]," *Brooklyn Journal of International Law* 5 (1979): 154.

European Convention on Human Rights (entered into for June 1, 2010)

EUTELSAT, "Eutelsat condemns jamming of broadcasts from Iran and renews appeals for decisive action to international regulators," PR/62/12, Oct. 4, 2012, http://www.eutelsat.com/home/news/press-releases/Archives/2012/press-list-container/eutelsat-condemns-jamming-of-bro.html.

"Everything We Know about the San Bernardino Terror Attack Investigation so Far," *Los Angeles Times*, December 14, 2015, http://www.latimes.com/local/california/la-me-san-bernardino-shooting-terror-investigation-htmlstory.html.

Executive Order 12333: United States Intelligence Activities (2001).

FBI Press Office, "Update on the Sony Investigation," Dec. 19, 2014, http://www.fbi.gov/news/pressrel/press-releases/update-on-sony-investigation.

Featherstone, Mike, "Genealogies of the Global," *Theory, Culture & Society* 23, no. 2/3 (March 2006): 387–92.

Featherstone, Mike and Couze Venn, "Problematizing Global Knowledge and the New Encyclopaedia Project: An Introduction," *Theory, Culture & Society* 23, no. 2–3 (2006): 1–20.

Fenlon, Wesley, "Did Google Maps Cause an International Border Dispute?," *HowStuffWorks*, October 3, 2011, http://computer.howstuffworks.com/google-maps-international-border-dispute.htm.

Ferguson, James, *Global Shadows: Africa in the Neoliberal Global Order* (Durham: Duke University Press, 2006).

Ferguson, Yale H. and Richard W Mansbach, *Globalization: The Return of Borders to a Borderless World?* (New York: Routledge, 2012).

Feuer, Alan, "Cody Wilson, Who Posted Gun Instructions Online, Sues State Department," *The New York Times*, May 6, 2015, http://www.nytimes.com/2015/05/07/us/cody-wilson-who-posted-gun-instructions-online-sues-state-department.html.

Fidler, David P., "The Internet, Human Rights, and U.S. Foreign Policy: The Global Online Freedom Act of 2012," *ASIL Insights* 16, no. 18 (May 24, 2012), http://www.asil.org/insights/volume/16/issue/18/internet-human-rights-and-us-foreign-policy-global-online-freedom-act.

Fielder, James D., "The Internet and Dissent in Authoritarian States," in *Conflict and Cooperation in Cyberspace: The Challenge to National Security*, ed. Panayotis A. Yannakogeorgos and Adam B. Lowther (Boca Raton: Taylor & Francis, 2013), 161–91.

Findlay, Trevor, "Why Treaties Work, Don't Work and What to Do About It?" (Canadian Institute of International Affairs, January 25, 2006), http://carleton.ca/npsia/wp-content/uploads/ciia_present_06.pdf.

"Finland Makes Broadband a 'Legal Right,'" *BBC News*, accessed December 2, 2015, http://www.bbc.com/news/10461048.

Finnemore, Martha and Kathryn Sikkink, "International Norm Dynamics and Political Change," *International Organization* 52, no. 04 (1998): 887–917.

Fish, Isaac, "Could North Koreans Ever Really Invade America?," *Foreign Policy*, November 21, 2012, https://foreignpolicy.com/2012/11/21/could-north-koreans-ever-really-invade-america/.

Fleischmann, Kenneth R. et al., "Thematic Analysis of Words That Invoke Values in the Net Neutrality Debate," March 15, 2015, https://www.ideals.illinois.edu/handle/2142/73433.

Foreign Intelligence Surveillance Act of 1978, 95 Pub.L. 511 (1978).

Foreign Intelligence Surveillance Act of 1978 Amendments Act of 2008, 110 Pub. L. 261 (2008).

Friedman, Benjamin H. and Christopher A. Preble, "A Military Response to Cyberattacks Is Preposterous," *Cato Institute*, June 2, 2011, http://www.cato.org/publications/commentary/military-response-cyberattacks-is-preposterous.

Fritsch, Stefan, "Technology and Global Affairs," *International Studies Perspectives* 12, no. 1 (2011): 27–45.

Galante, Laura and Shaun, Ee, *Defining Russian Election Interference: An Analysis of Select 2014 to 2018 Cyber Enabled Incidents* (Atlantic Council 2018).

Gallagher, Sean, "NSA's Director Says Paris Attacks 'would Not Have Happened' without Crypto," *Ars Technica*, February 18, 2016, http:// arstechnica.com/tech-policy/2016/02/nsas-director-says-paris-attacks-would-not-have-happened-without-crypto/.

Gallagher, Sean, "Silk Road, Other Tor 'darknet' Sites May Have Been 'decloaked' through DDoS [Updated]," *Ars Technica*, November 9, 2014, http:// arstechnica.com/security/2014/11/silk-road-other-tor-darknet-sites-may-have-been-decloaked-through-ddos/.

Gallington, Daniel, "Perspectives on Collection, Retention, and Dissemination of Intelligence," Marshall Policy Outlook (United States: George C. Marshall Institute, May 2014), http://marshall.org/wp-content/uploads/2014/05/Collection-PO-May-14.pdf.

Gelernter, David, "The End of the Web, Search, and Computer as We Know It," *Wired Opinion*, February 1, 2013, http://www.wired.com/opinion/2013/02/the-end-of-the-web-computers-and-search-as-we-know-it/.

Gellman, Robert, "Civil Liberties and Privacy Implications of Policies to Prevent Cyberattacks," in *Proceedings of a Workshop on Deterring Cyberattacks: Informing Strategies and Developing Options for U.S. Policy*, by Committee on Deterring Cyberattacks: Informing Strategies and Developing Options; National Research Council (Washington, D.C.: National Academies Press, 2010), 273–309, http://www.nap.edu/openbook.php?record_id=12997&page=273.

Gellman, Barton, "NSA Broke Privacy Rules Thousands of Times per Year, Audit Finds," *The Washington Post*, August 15, 2013, http://www. washingtonpost.com/world/national-security/nsa-broke-privacy-rules-thousands-of-times-per-year-audit-finds/2013/08/15/3310e554-05ca-11e3-a07f-49ddc7417125_story.html.

Gellman, Barton and Laura Poitras, "U.S., British Intelligence Mining Data from Nine U.S. Internet Companies in Broad Secret Program," *The Washington Post*, June 7, 2013, http://www.washingtonpost.com/investigations/us-intelligence-mining-data-from-nine-us-internet-companies-in-broad-secret-program/2013/06/06/3a0c0da8-cebf-11e2-8845-d970ccb04497_story.html.

"German Intelligence Agencies Used NSA Spying Program," *Spiegel Online*, July 20, 2013, http://www.spiegel.de/international/germany/german-intelligence-agencies-used-nsa-spying-program-a-912173.html.

Geyer, Michael and Charles Bright, "World History in a Global Age," *The American Historical Review* 100, no. 4 (1995): 1034–60.

Goldsmith, Jack L., "Against Cyberanarchy," *The University of Chicago Law Review* 65, no. 4 (1998): 1199–1250.

Goldsmith, Jack L., "The Sony Hack: Attribution Problems, and the Connection to Domestic Surveillance," *Lawfare*, December 19, 2014, https://www.lawfareblog.com/sony-hack-attribution-problems-and-connection-domestic-surveillance.

Gompert, David C. and Phillip C. Saunders, *Paradox of Power: Sino-American Strategic Restraint in an Age of Vulnerability* (Washington, DC: National Defense University Press, 2012).

Goodhart, Michael, "Human Rights and Global Democracy," *Ethics & International Affairs* 22, no. 4 (2008): 395–420.

Goodman, Ellen P., "Media Policy and Free Speech: The First Amendment at War with Itself," *Hofstra Law Review* 35 (2007).

Goodman, Ellen P. and Anne H. Chen, "Modeling Policy for New Public Service Media Networks," *Harv. JL & Tech.* 24 (2010): 111.

Gorman, Siobahn and Julian E. Barnes, "Cyber Combat: Act of War," *Wall Street Journal*, May 31, 2011, sec. Tech, http://www.wsj.com/articles/SB10001424052702304563104576355623135782718.

Gourley, Stephen K., "Cyber Sovereignty," in *Conflict and Cooperation in Cyberspace: The Challenge to National Security*, ed. Panayotis A. Yannakogeorgos and Adam B. Lowther (Boca Raton: Taylor & Francis, 2013), 277–89.

Greenberg, Andy, "I Made an Untraceable AR-15 'Ghost Gun' in My Office—And It Was Easy," *WIRED*, June 3, 2015, http://www.wired.com/2015/06/i-made-an-untraceable-ar-15-ghost-gun/.

Greenberg, Andy, *This Machine Kills Secrets: How WikiLeakers, Cypherpunks and Hacktivists Aim to Free the World's Information* (New York: Dutton, 2012).

Greenet Ltd. et al v. GCHQ - Statement of Grounds (Investigatory Powers Tribunal (UK) 2014).

Greenwald, Glenn, *No Place to Hide: Edward Snowden, the NSA, and the U.S. Surveillance State* (New York: Metropolitan Books 2014).

Greenwald, Glenn, "NSA Collecting Phone Records of Millions of Verizon Customers Daily," *The Guardian*, accessed May 6, 2014, http://www.theguardian.com/world/2013/jun/06/nsa-phone-records-verizon-court-order.

Greenwald, Glenn, "XKEYSCORE: NSA Tool Collects 'Nearly Everything a User Does on the Internet,'" *The Guardian*, July 31, 2013, http://www.theguardian.com/world/2013/jul/31/nsa-top-secret-program-online-data.

Greenwald, Glenn and Spencer Ackerman, "How the NSA Is Still Harvesting Your Online Data," *The Guardian*, June 27, 2013, http://www.theguardian.com/world/2013/jun/27/nsa-online-metadata-collection.

Greenwald, Glenn and Spencer Ackerman, "NSA Collected Americans' Email Records in Bulk for Two Years under Obama," *The Guardian*, June 27, 2013, http://www.theguardian.com/world/2013/jun/27/nsa-data-mining-authorised-obama.

Greenwald, Glenn and James Ball, "The Top Secret Rules That Allow NSA to Use US Data without a Warrant," *The Guardian*, accessed May 6, 2014, http://www.theguardian.com/world/2013/jun/20/fisa-court-nsa-without-warrant

Greenwald, Glenn and Ryan Gallagher, "Snowden Documents Reveal Covert Surveillance and Pressure Tactics Aimed at WikiLeaks and Its Supporters," *The Intercept*, February 18, 2014, https://theintercept.com/2014/02/18/snowden-docs-reveal-covert-surveillance-and-pressure-tactics-aimed-at-wikileaks-and-its-supporters/.

Greenwald, Glenn and Ewen MacAskill, "Boundless Informant: The NSA's Secret Tool to Track Global Surveillance Data," *The Guardian*, accessed May 6, 2014, http://www.theguardian.com/world/2013/jun/08/nsa-boundless-informant-global-datamining.

Greenwald, Glenn and Ewen MacAskill, "NSA PRISM Program Taps in to User Data of Apple, Google and Others," *The Guardian*, June 7, 2013, http://www.theguardian.com/world/2013/jun/06/us-tech-giants-nsa-data.

Greenwald, Glenn, Ewen MacAskill, and Laura Poitras, "Edward Snowden: The Whistleblower behind the NSA Surveillance Revelations," *The Guardian*, June 11, 2013, sec. US news, http://www.theguardian.com/world/2013/jun/09/edward-snowden-nsa-whistleblower-surveillance.

Greenwald, Glenn, Ewen MacAskill, Laura Poitras, Spencer Ackerman, and Dominic Rushe. "Microsoft Handed the NSA Access to Encrypted Messages." The Guardian. July 12, 2013. http://www.theguardian.com/world/2013/jul/11/microsoft-nsa-collaboration-user-data.

Habermas, Jürgen, *The Postnational Constellation: Political Essays*, ed. and trans. Max Pensky (MIT Press, 2001).

Hague Code of Conduct Against Ballistic Missile Proliferation (November 25, 2002).

Halvorssen, Thor and Alexander Lloyd, "We Hacked North Korea With Balloons and USB Drives," *The Atlantic*, January 15, 2014, http://www.theatlantic.com/international/archive/2014/01/we-hacked-north-korea-with-balloons-and-usb-drives/283106/.

Hamill, Jasper, "Pirate Bay Is BACK - Torrent Site to Return in One Week," *The Mirror*, January 26, 2015, http://www.mirror.co.uk/news/technology-science/technology/pirate-bay-back---torrent-5045073.

Harrison, Roger, *Space and Verification, Volume I: Policy Implications* (Eisenhower Center for Space and Defence Studies 2007).

Harvey, David, *A Brief History of Neoliberalism* (Oxford: Oxford Univ. Press, 2009).

Hayden, Michael V., "The Future of Things Cyber," in *Conflict and Cooperation in Cyberspace: The Challenge to National Security*, ed. Panayotis A. Yannakogeorgos and Adam B. Lowther (Boca Raton: Taylor & Francis, 2013), 3–8.

Heddaya, Mostafa, "See A Map, Not a Territory: Apple and the End of Skeuomorphism," Hyperallergenic, June 27, 2013, http://hyperallergic. com/74308/a-map-not-a-territory-apple-and-the-end-of-skeuomorphism/.

Held, David, *Democracy and the Global Order: From the Modern State to Cosmopolitan Governance* (Stanford: Stanford University Press 1995).

Hille, Kathrin, "China Cracks Down on Online Maps," *Financial Times*, May 21,2010, http://www.ft.com/cms/s/0/9569b59e-64f3-11df-aa4d-00144feab49a. html#axzz40FUFCz8W.

Henley, Jon "Ecuador cuts off Julian Assange's internet access at London embassy," *The Guardian*, March 28, 2018, https://www.theguardian.com/ media/2018/mar/28/julian-assange-internet-connection-ecuador-embassy-cut-off-wikileaks.

Hooper, Charlotte, *Manly States: Masculinities, International Relations, and Gender Politics* (New York: Columbia University Press 2001).

Hopkins, Nick and Julian Borger, "Exclusive: NSA Pays £100m in Secret Funding for GCHQ," *The Guardian*, August 1, 2013, http://www.theguardian. com/uk-news/2013/aug/01/nsa-paid-gchq-spying-edward-snowden.

Hopkins, Nick, Julian Borger, and Luke Harding, "GCHQ: Inside the Top Secret World of Britain's Biggest Spy Agency," *The Guardian*, August 1, 2013, http://www.theguardian.com/world/2013/aug/02/gchq-spy-agency-nsa-snowden.

Hurwitz, Roger, "A New Normal? The Cultivation of Global Norms as Part of a Cybersecurity Strategy," in *Conflict and Cooperation in Cyberspace: The Challenge to National Security*, ed. Panayotis A. Yannakogeorgos and Adam B. Lowther (Boca Raton: Taylor & Francis, 2013), 233–64.

IANA.org, "About Us," https://www.iana.org/about.

ICANN-PTI, IANA Naming Function Contract, (Sept. 30, 2016), https://pti. icann.org/iana_pti_docs/151-iana-naming-function-contract-v-30sep16.

The Imitation Game (Black Bear Pictures/Bristol Automotive 2014).

"India Google Maps Controversy Is Modern Drama," Democracy Chronicles, July 29, 2014, https://democracychronicles.com/india-google-maps-controversy-modern-drama/.

International Covenant on Civil and Political Rights (entered into force Mar. 23, 1976).

International Covenant on Economic, Social and Cultural Rights (Dec. 16, 1966).

International Docking System Standard, Interface Definition Document, Revision D (April 30, 2015) http://www.internationaldockingstandard.com/download/IDSS_IDD_Revision_D_043015.pdf.

International Table Tennis Federation, "The Laws of Table Tennis," http://www.ittf.com/ittf_handbook/2016/2016_EN_HBK_CHPT_2.pdf (last visited February 11, 2016).

International Telecommunication Union, *ICT Facts and Figures 2017* (2017).

International Telecommunication Union, "Resolution 2 (Rev. Busan, 2014) World Telecommunication/Information and Communication Technology Policy Forum," 2014.

International Telecommunication Union, "Resolution 101 (Rev. Busan, 2014) Internet Protocol-Based Networks," 2014.

International Telecommunication Union, "Resolution 102 (Rev. Busan, 2014) ITU's Role with Regard to International Public Policy Issues Pertaining to the Internet and the Management of Internet Resources, Including Domain Names and Addresses," 2014.

International Telecommunication Union, "Resolution 133 (Rev. Busan, 2014) Role of Administrations of Member States in the Management of Internationalized (Multilingual Domain Names," 2014.

International Telecommunication Union, "Resolution 140 (Rev. Buan, 2014) ITU's Role in Implementing the Outcomes of the World Summit on the Information Society and in the Overall Review by United Nations General Assembly of Their Implementation," 2014.

International Telecommunication Union, "Resolution 180 (Rev. Busan, 2014) Facilitating the Transition from IPv4 to IPv6," 2014.

International Traffic in Arms Regulations, 22 C.F.R. 120-130 (2015).

Internet Engineering Task Force, "The Tao of IETF: A Novice's Guide to the Internet Engineering Task Force" (2012) at https://www.ietf.org/tao.html.

Jayakar, Krishna, "Globalization and the Legitimacy of International Telecommunications Standard-Setting Organizations," *Indiana Journal of Global Legal Studies* 5 (1998): 711–38.

Johnson, David R. and David Post, "Law and Borders: The Rise of Law in Cyberspace," *Stanford Law Review* 48, no. 5 (1996): 1367–1402.

Jentleson, Bruce W., "The Obama Administration and R2P: Progress, Problems and Prospects," *Global Responsibility to Protect* 4, no. 4 (2012): 399–423.

Jurgenson, Nathan, "Digital Dualism versus Augmented Reality," *Cyborgology*, February 24, 2011, http://thesocietypages.org/cyborgology/2011/02/24/digital-dualism-versus-augmented-reality/.

Kallberg, Jan and Rosemary A. Burk, "Cyberdefense as Environmental Protection - The Broader Potential Impact of Failed Defensive Counter Cyber Operations," in *Conflict and Cooperation in Cyberspace: The Challenge to National Security*, ed. Panayotis A. Yannakogeorgos and Adam B. Lowther (Boca Raton: Taylor & Francis, 2013), 265–75.

"Kanye West Targeted by 'Anonymous' in Searing Video," *Billboard*, March 12, 2015, http://www.billboard.com/articles/columns/the-juice/6501935/anonymous-kanye-west-video.

Kelley, Michael B., "Edward Snowden's Relationship With WikiLeaks Should Concern Everyone," *Business Insider*, January 4, 2014, http://www.businessinsider.com/edward-snowden-and-wikileaks-2014-1.

Kellner, Douglas, "Intellectuals, the New Public Sphere, and Technopolitics," in *The Politics of Cyberspace*, ed. Chris Toulouse and Timothy W. Luke (New York: Routledge, 1998), 147–86.

Kende, Michael, "The Digital Handshake: Connecting Internet Backbones" (Washington, D.C.: Federal Communications Commission, 2000).

Kennedy, Charles H. and M. Veronica Pastor, *An Introduction to International Telecommunications Law* (Boston: Artech House, 1996).

Kirby, Debra, "Minding the Gap: The Growing Divide between Privacy and Surveillance Technology" (Thesis, Naval Postgraduate School, 2013), http:// oai.dtic.mil/oai/oai?verb=getRecord &metadataPrefix=html&identifier=ADA585523.

kliq, "Xfinite Absurdity: True Confessions of a Former Comcast Tech Support Agent," *2600: The Hacker Quarterly*, 2014.

Knight, Will, "Controlling Encryption Will Not Stop Terrorists," *New Scientist*, accessed February 19, 2016, https://www.newscientist.com/article/dn1309-controlling-encryption-will-not-stop-terrorists/.

Korea (Democratic People's Republic of)'s Constitution of 1972 with Amendments through 1998, https://www.constituteproject.org/constitution/ Peoples_Republic_of_Korea_1998.pdf.

Kracht, James, "The Hacker Perspective," *2600: The Hacker Quarterly*, 2014.

Krattenmaker, Thomas G., *Telecommunications Law and Policy*, 2nd ed. (Durham, NC: Carolina Academic Press, 1998).

Kravets, David, "ISPs to Disrupt Internet Access of Copyright Scofflaws," *Wired*, July 7, 2011, http://www.wired.com/2011/07/disrupting-internet-access/.

Kulesza, Joanna, *International Internet Law*, trans. Magdalena Arent and Wojciech Wotoszyk (Routledge, 2013).

Lally, Kathy and Juan Forero, "Bolivian President's Plane Forced to Land in Austria in Hunt for Snowden," *The Washington Post*, July 3, 2013, https:// www.washingtonpost.com/world/bolivian-presidents-plane-forced-to-land-in-austria-in-hunt-for-snowden/2013/07/03/c281c2f4-e3eb-11e2-a11e-c2ea876a8f30_story.html.

Lam, Lana, "EXCLUSIVE: US Hacked Pacnet, Asia Pacific Fibre-Optic Network Operator, in 2009," *South China Morning Post*, June 22, 2013, http://www.scmp.com/news/hong-kong/article/1266875/exclusive-us-hacked-pacnet-asia-pacific-fibre-optic-network-operator.

Lam, Lana and Stephen Chen, "EXCLUSIVE: US Spies on Chinese Mobile Phone Companies, Steals SMS Data: Edward Snowden," *South China Morning Post*, June 22, 2013, http://www.scmp.com/news/china/article/1266821/us-hacks-chinese-mobile-phone-companies-steals-sms-data-edward-snowden?page=all.

Lee, Robert M., "The Feds Got the Sony Hack Right, But the Way They're Framing It Is Dangerous," *Wired*, January 10, 2015, http://www.wired.com/2015/01/feds-got-sony-hack-right-way-theyre-framing-dangerous.

Lee, Robert M. and Thomas Rid, "OMG Cyber! Thirteen Reasons Why Hype Makes for Bad Policy," *The RUSI Journal* 159, no. 5 (2014): 4–12.

Leiner, Barry M. et al., "A Brief History of the Internet" (The Internet Society, October 15, 2012), http://www.internetsociety.org/internet/what-internet/history-internet/brief-history-internet.

Lessig, Lawrence, *Code 2.0* (Basic Books, 2006).

Lessig, Lawrence, *Free Culture : The Nature and Future of Creativity* (New York: New York : Penguin Books., 2004).

Lewis, Bernard, *The Crisis of Islam: Holy War and Unholy Terror* (Random House LLC, 2004).

Libicki, Martin C., "Two Maybe Three Cheers for Ambiguity," in *Conflict and Cooperation in Cyberspace: The Challenge to National Security*, ed. Panayotis A. Yannakogeorgos and Adam B. Lowther (Boca Raton: Taylor & Francis, 2013), 27–34.

Lipschutz, Ronnie D., "Environmental History, Political Economy and Change: Frameworks and Tools for Research and Analysis," *Global Environmental Politics* 1, no. 3 (2001): 72–91.

Liste, Philip. "Transnational Human Rights Litigation and Territorialised Knowledge: Kiobel and the 'Politics of Space.'" *Transnational Legal Theory* 5, no. 1 (2014): 1–19.

Liu, Edward C. et al., "Cybersecurity: Selected Legal Issues," Report (Congressional Research Service, Library of Congress, April 20, 2012).

Lloyd, Seth, *Programming the Universe: A Quantum Computer Scientist Takes on the Cosmos*, 2006.

Lucas Jr., George R. , "Can There Be an Ethical Cyber War?," in *Conflict and Cooperation in Cyberspace: The Challenge to National Security*, ed. Panayotis A. Yannakogeorgos and Adam B. Lowther (Boca Raton: Taylor & Francis, 2013), 195–209.

Luhn, Alec, "Edward Snowden Leaves Moscow Airport after Russia Grants Asylum," *The Guardian*, August 1, 2013, sec. US news, http://www.theguardian. com/world/2013/aug/01/edward-snowden-grant-temporary-asylum-russia.

Luke, Timothy W., "The Politics of Digital Inequality: Access, Capability and Distribution in Cyberspace," in *The Politics of Cyberspace*, ed. Chris Toulouse and Timothy W. Luke (New York: Routledge, 1998), 120–43.

Lyall, Francis, "Reaction of International Law to Technical Developments," in *Innovation in Outer Space: International and African Legal Perspectives*, ed. Mahulena Hofmann and P.J. Blount (Nomos 2018).

Lyall, Francis and Paul B. Larsen, Space Law: A Treatise (Ashgate 2009).

MacAskill, Ewen, "NSA Paid Millions to Cover Prism Compliance Costs for Tech Companies," *The Guardian*, August 23, 2013, sec. US news, http://www. theguardian.com/world/2013/aug/23/nsa-prism-costs-tech-companies-paid.

MacAskill, Ewen and Julian Borger, "New NSA Leaks Show How US Is Bugging Its European Allies," *The Guardian*, June 30, 2013, http://www.theguardian.com/ world/2013/jun/30/nsa-leaks-us-bugging-european-allies.

MacAskill, Ewen, Nick Davies, Nick Hopkins, Julian Borger, and James Ball. "GCHQ Intercepted Foreign Politicians' Communications at G20 Summits." The Guardian. June 17, 2013. http://www.theguardian.com/uk/2013/jun/16/gchq-intercepted-communications-g20-summits.

Macklem, Patrick, "Humanitarian Intervention and the Distribution of Sovereignty in International Law," *Ethics & International Affairs* 22, no. 4 (2008): 369–93.

Mackey, Robert, "'Operation Payback' Attacks Target MasterCard and PayPal Sites to Avenge WikiLeaks," *The Lede*, 1291819254, http://thelede.blogs. nytimes.com/2010/12/08/operation-payback-targets-mastercard-and-paypal-sites-to-avenge-wikileaks/.

Major, Jason, "This Is the Very First Photo of Earth From Space," *Universe Today*, October 24, 2014, http://www.universetoday.com/115641/this-is-the-very-first-photo-of-earth-from-space/.

Manela, Erez, *The Wilsonian Moment: Self-Determination and the International Origins of Anticolonial Nationalism* (Oxford: Oxford University Press 2007) 59-60.

Martin, C. Dianne, "Using the US Constitution to Frame the Governance of Cyberspace," *ACM Inroads* 6, no. 1 (2015): 24–26.

Mattelart, Armand, *Networking the World, 1794-2000* (University of Minnesota Press, 2000).

Mattice, Lynn, "Taming the '21st Century's Wild West' of Cyberspace?," in *Conflict and Cooperation in Cyberspace: The Challenge to National Security*, ed. Panayotis A. Yannakogeorgos and Adam B. Lowther (Boca Raton: Taylor & Francis, 2013), 9–12.

Maurashat, Alana, "Zombie Botnets," *SCRIPTed* 7, no. 2 (2010): 370–83, http://www2.law.ed.ac.uk/ahrc/script-ed/vol7-2/maurushat.asp.

McDermott, Rose, "Decision Making Under Uncertainty," in *Proceedings of a Workshop on Deterring Cyberattacks: Informing Strategies and Developing Options for U.S. Policy*, by Committee on Deterring Cyberattacks: Informing Strategies and Developing Options; National Research Council (Washington, D.C.: National Academies Press, 2010), 227–41, http://www.nap.edu/openbook.php?record_id=12997&page=273.

McIntosh, Wayne and Cynthia Cates, "Hard Travelin': Free Speech in the Age of the Information Super Highway," in *The Politics of Cyberspace*, ed. Chris Toulouse and Timothy W. Luke (New York: Routledge, 1998), 84–118.

McTaggart, Craig, "A Layered Approach to Internet Legal Analysis," *McGill LJ* 48 (2003): 571.

Menon, Rajan, "Pious Words, Puny Deeds: The 'International Community' and Mass Atrocities," *Ethics & International Affairs* 23, no. 3 (September 1, 2009): 235–46.

Merges, Robert P., Peter S. Menell, and Mark A. Lemley, *Intellectual Property in the New Technological Age, Sixth Edition*, 6th edition (New York: Aspen Publishers, 2012).

Michel, Arthur Holland, "A History of Violence: How Rogue Techies Armed the Predator, Almost Stopped 9/11, and Accidentally Invented Remote War," *WIRED*, January 2016, http://www.wired.com/2015/12/how-rogue-techies-armed-the-predator-almost-stopped-911-and-accidentally-invented-remote-war/.

Microsoft, "HoloLens," https://www.microsoft.com/microsoft-hololens/en-us (last accessed October 6, 2015).

Military and Paramilitary Activities in and against Nicaragua (Nicaragua v. United States of America). Merits, Judgment. I.C.J. Reports 1986, p. 14.

Mlot, Stephanie, "The Pirate Bay Is Back Online (Sort Of)," *PCMAG*, December 15, 2014, http://www.pcmag.com/article2/0,2817,2473661,00.asp.

Moore, Daniel and Thomas Rid, "Cryptopolitik and the Darknet," *Survival*, 58:1 (2016) 7–38.

"Moore's Law," http://www.mooreslaw.org (last visited Feb. 18, 2016).

Morgan, Forrest E., "Deterrence and First-Strike Stability in Space: A Preliminary Assessment" (DTIC Document, 2010).

Morozov, Evgeny, "Political Repression 2.0," *The New York Times*, September 1, 2011, sec. Opinion, http://www.nytimes.com/2011/09/02/opinion/political-repression-2-0.html.

Mueller, Milton, and Dale Thompson. "ICANN and INTELSAT: Global Communication Technologies and Their Incorporation into International Regimes." In *The Emergent Global Information Policy Regime*, edited by Sandra Braman, 62–85. Palgrave Macmillan, 2004.

National Aeronautics and Space Administration, "Blue Marble - Image of the Earth from Apollo 17," NASA, (July 31, 2015), http://www.nasa.gov/content/blue-marble-image-of-the-earth-from-apollo-17.

National Center for Justice and the Rule of Law, *Combating Cyber Crime: Essential Tools and Effective Organizational Structures* (Univ. of Mississippi 2007).

National Security Agency, "BOUNDLESSINFORMANT - Frequently Asked Questions," September 6, 2012.

National Security Agency, "(TS//SI/NF) FAA Certification Renewals With Caveats," October 12, 2011.

National Security Agency, "(U//FOUO) NSAW SID Intelligence Oversight (IO) Quarterly Report - First Quarter Calendar Year 2012 (1 January - 31 March 2012 - EXECUTIVE SUMMARY," May 3, 2012.

National Security Agency, "PRISM/US-984XN Overview of the SIGAD Used Most in NSA Reporting Overview," 2013.

National Security Agency Office of Inspector General, "Working Draft Report from March 24, 2009 on Stellar Wind (PSP)," March 24, 2009.

National Telecommunications & Information Administration, "NTIA Announces Intent to Transition Key Internet Domain Name Functions," March 14, 2014, http://www.ntia.doc.gov/press-release/2014/ntia-announces-intent-transition-key-internet-domain-name-functions.

NetMudial, *NETmundial Multistakeholder Statement* (April 24, 2014) http://netmundial.br/wp-content/uploads/2014/04/NETmundial-Multistakeholder-Document.pdf.

Nincic, Miroslav and Jennifer Ramos, "Torture in the Public Mind," *International Studies Perspectives* 12, no. 3 (2011): 231–49.

Noveck, Beth Simone, "Designing Deliberative Democracy in Cyberspace: The Role of the Cyber-Lawyer," *BUJ Sci. & Tech. L.* 9 (2003): 1.

"NSA Hacked UN Videocalls as Part of Surveillance Program, Claims Report," *Al Jazeera America*, August 25, 2013, http://america.aljazeera.com/articles/2013/8/25/nsa-bugged-u-n-headquarters.html.

O'Meara, Richard M., "Jus Post Bellum: War Closure in the 21st Century," in *Routledge Handbook of Ethics and War: Just War Theory in the 21st Century*, ed. Fritz Allhoff, Nicholas G. Evans, and Adam Henschke (Routledge, 2013), 105–19.

O'Neil, Patrick Howell, "Edward Snowden and Spread of Encryption Blamed after Paris Terror Attacks," *The Daily Dot*, December 9, 2015, http://www.dailydot.com/politics/paris-attack-encryption-snowden/.

Oliver, Eric P., "Stuxnet: A Case Study in Cyber Warfare," in *Conflict and Cooperation in Cyberspace: The Challenge to National Security*, ed. Panayotis A. Yannakogeorgos and Adam B. Lowther (Boca Raton: Taylor & Francis, 2013), 127–59.

Olmstead v. United States, 277 U.S. 438, 466 (1928).

Organization for Security and Co-operation in Europe, "Freedom of Expression on the Internet: A Study of Legal Provisions and Practices Related to Freedom of Expression, the Free Flow of Information and Media Pluralism on the Internet in OSCE Participating States," 2011.

Orwell, George, *1984* (London: Secker & Warburg 1949).

Osgood, Rick, "Net Neutrality and the FCC Hack," in *Hackaday Omnibus 2014*, ed. Mike Szczys, 2014.

"Paris Attacks: What Happened on the Night," *BBC News*, December 9, 2015, http://www.bbc.com/news/world-europe-34818994.

Partridge, Mark V.B. and Scott T. Lonardo, "ICANN Can or Can It?: Recent Developments in Internet Governance Involving Cybersquatting, Online Infringement, and Registration Practices," *Landslide* 1, no. 5 (2009): 24–29.

Poitras, Laura, Marcel Rosenbach, Fidelius Schmid, and Holger Stark. "NSA Spied on European Union Offices." Spiegel Online. June 29, 2013. http://www.spiegel.de/international/europe/nsa-spied-on-european-union-offices-a-908590.html.

Poitras, Laura, Marcel Rosenbach, and Holger Stark, "NSA Spies on 500 Million German Data Connections," *Spiegel Online*, June 30, 2013, http://www.spiegel.de/international/germany/nsa-spies-on-500-million-german-data-connections-a-908648.html.

Pompe, Cornelis Arnold, *Aggressive War - An International Crime* (Martinus Nijhoff, 1953).

Post, David G., "Against 'Against Cyberanarchy,'" *Berkeley Technology Law Journal* 17 (2002): 1365.

Post, David G., *In Search of Jefferson's Moose: Notes on the State of Cyberspace* (Oxford; New York: Oxford University Press, 2012).

Post, David, "It's 'the Internet.' Please.," *The Volokh Conspiracy*, August 11, 2011, http://volokh.com/2011/08/11/its-the-internet-please/.

Popkin, Helen A. S., "Anonymous 'Brandjacks' Westboro Baptist Church on Facebook," *NBC News*, April 17, 2013, http://www.nbcnews.com/technology/anonymous-brandjacks-westboro-baptist-church-facebook-1C9395459.

Power, Andrew and Oisín Tobin, "Soft Law for the Internet, Lessons from International Law," *SCRIPTed* 8, no. 1 (2011): 31–45, http://www2.law.ed.ac.uk/ahrc/script-ed/vol8-1/power.pdf.

Princeton Project on National Security, "Report of the Working Group on State Security and Transnational Threats" (Princeton, NJ, 2008), https://www.princeton.edu/~ppns/conferences/reports/fall/SSTT.pdf.

Prisoner #6, "The 21st Century Hacker Manifesto," *2600: The Hacker Quarterly*, 2014-2015.

Privacy and Civil Liberties Oversight Board, "Report on the Surveillance Program Operated Pursuant to Section 702 of the Foreign Intelligence Surveillance Act," July 2, 2014, http://library.blountsfolly.com/space/items/show/185.

Protocol Additional to the Geneva Conventions of 12 August 1949, and relating to the Protection of Victims of International Armed Conflicts (Protocol I) (June 8, 1977)

Quammen, David, *The Boilerplate Rhino: Nature in the Eye of the Beholder* (New York: Scribner, 2000).

Radio Regulations (2012) http://www.itu.int/dms_pub/itu-s/oth/02/02/S02020000244501PDFE.PDF.

Ramey, Christopher H., "When AT&T Asked Us to 'Reach out and Touch Someone', Did They Mean That Literally?," *Psychology Today*, July 7, 2008, http://www.psychologytoday.com/blog/the-metaphorical-mind/200807/when-att-asked-us-reach-out-and-touch-someone-did-they-mean.

Ranieri, Vera, "EFFecting Digital Freedom," *2600: The Hacker Quarterly*, v. 31/3 (2014).

Ranieri, Vera, "EFFecting Digital Freedom," *2600: The Hacker Quarterly*, v. 31/4, (2014-2015).

Rao, J. Mohan, "Equity in A Global Public Goods Framework," in *Global Public Goods: International Cooperation in the 21st Century*, ed. Inge Kaul, Isabelle Grunberg, and Marc Stern (New York, Oxford: Oxford University Press, 1999), 68–87.

Rawls, John, *A Theory of Justice* (Cambridge, Mass.: Belknap Press, 1971).

Raymond, Eric S., *The New Hacker's Dictionary*, 3d ed. (Cambridge, MA: MIT Press 1996).

Reed, David P., "Critiquing the Layered Regulatory Model," *J. on Telecomm. & High Tech. L.* 4 (2005): 281.

Reisman, W. Michael, "International Incidents: Introduction to a New Genre in the Study of International Law," *Yale J. Int'l L.* 10 (1984): 1.

Resnick, David, "Politics on the Internet: The Normalization of Cyberspace," in *The Politics of Cyberspace*, ed. Chris Toulouse and Timothy W. Luke (New York: Routledge, 1998), 48–68.

Richardson, Valerie, "Sony kills 'The Interview' after North Korea hack, terror threat," The Washington Times, Dec. 17, 2014, http://www.washingtontimes.com/news/2014/dec/17/sony-kills-the-interview-after-north-korea-hack-te/?page=all.

Richtel, Matt, "Egypt Cuts Off Most Internet and Cellphone Service," *The New York Times*, January 28, 2011, http://www.nytimes.com/2011/01/29/technology/internet/29cutoff.html.

Riley v. California, No. 13-132 (Supreme Court 2014).

Risen, James and Nick Wingfield, "Web's Reach Binds N.S.A. and Silicon Valley Leaders," *The New York Times*, June 19, 2013, sec. Technology, http:// www.nytimes.com/2013/06/20/technology/silicon-valley-and-spy-agency-bound-by-strengthening-web.html.

Roberts, Dan, "Bolivian President's Jet Rerouted amid Suspicions Edward Snowden on Board," *The Guardian*, July 3, 2013, sec. World news, http:// www.theguardian.com/world/2013/jul/03/edward-snowden-bolivia-plane-vienna.

Robertson, Horace B., "The Suppression of Pirate Radio Broadcasting: A Test Case of the International System for Control of Activities Outside National Territory," *Law and Contemporary Problems*, 1982, 71–101.

Robinson, George S., "Addressing the Legal Status of Evolving 'Envoys of Mankind,'" *Annals of Air and Space Law* 36 (2011): 447–512.

Robinson, George, "Astronauts and a Unique Jurisprudence: A Treaty for Spacekind," 7 *Hastings Int'l & Comp. L. Rev.* 483 (1983-1984).

Roht-Arriaza, Naomi, "The Pinochet Precedent and Universal Jurisdiction," *New England Law Jour*nal 35, no. 2 (2001): 311–19.

Rosen, Jeffrey, "The Right to Be Forgotten," *Stanford Law Review Online* 64 (February 13, 2012): 88, http://www.stanfordlawreview.org/online/privacy-paradox/right-to-be-forgotten.

Rosenzweig, Paul et al., "Protecting Internet Freedom and American Interests: Required Reforms and Standards for ICANN Transition," Heritage Foundation Backgrounder (Washington, D.C.: The Heritage Foundation, June 16, 2014), http://www.heritage.org/research/reports/2014/06/protecting-internet-freedom-and-american-interests-required-reforms-and-standards-for-icann-transition.

Rowe, Neil C. et al., "Challenges in Monitoring Cyberarms Compliance," in *Conflict and Cooperation in Cyberspace: The Challenge to National Security*, ed. Panayotis A. Yannakogeorgos and Adam B. Lowther (Boca Raton: Taylor & Francis, 2013), 81–99.

Rushdie, Salman, *Midnight's Children* (New York: Random House 2006).

Rushe, Dominic, "Skype's Secret Project Chess Reportedly Helped NSA Access Customers' Data," *The Guardian*, June 20, 2013, http://www.theguardian.com/technology/2013/jun/20/skype-nsa-access-user-data.

Rychlak, Ronald J., "Compassion, Hatred, and Free Expression," *Miss. CL Rev.* 27 (2007): 407.

Sadiq, Kamal, *Paper Citizens: How Illegal Immigrants Acquire Citizenship in Developing Countries* (Oxford: Oxford University Press 2010).

Sanger, David E. and Elisabeth Bumiller, "Pentagon to Consider Cyberattacks Acts of War," *The New York Times*, May 31, 2011, http://www.nytimes.com/2011/06/01/us/politics/01cyber.html.

Sajó, András, *Constitutional Sentiments* (New Haven [Conn.]: Yale University Press, 2011).

Saro-Wiwa, Ken, "On Environmental Rights of the Ogoni People in Nigeria (1995)" in Micheline Ishay, The Human Rights Reader: Major Political Writings, Essays, Speeches, and Documents from the Bible to the Present (Routledge, 2007) 360-363.

Sassen, Saskia, *Territory, Authority, Rights: From Medieval to Global Assemblages* (Princeton University Press 2006).

Scahill, Jeremy, *Blackwater: The Rise of the World's Most Powerful Mercenary Army* (New York: Nation Books, 2007).

Schabas, William A., *Genocide in International Law: The Crime of Crimes*, 2d ed. (Cambridge: Cambridge University Press 2009).

Schmitt, Carl, *The Nomos of the Earth in the International Law of the Jus Publicum Europaeum*, trans. G.L. Ulmen (New York: Telos Press, 2003).

Schmitt, David D., "Cyber Operations in International Law: The Use of Force, Collective Security, Self-Defense, and Armed Conflict," in *Proceedings of a Workshop on Deterring Cyberattacks: Informing Strategies and Developing Options for U.S. Policy*, 2010, 151.

Schmitt, Michael N., ed., *Tallinn Manual on the International Law Applicable to Cyber Warfare* (Cambridge: Cambridge University Press, 2013).

Schneier, Bruce, "Attributing the Sony Attack," Schneier on Security, Jan. 7, 2015, https://www.schneier.com/blog/archives/2015/01/attributing_the.html.

Seife, Charles, *Decoding the Universe: How the New Science of Information Is Explaining Everything in* the Cosmos, from Our Brains to Black Holes, 2007.

Sen, Amartya, "Global Justice: Beyond International Equity," in *Global Public Goods: International Cooperation in the 21st Century*, ed. Inge Kaul, Isabelle Grunberg, and Marc Stern (New York, Oxford: Oxford University Press, 1999), 116–25.

Serageldin, Ismail, "Cultural Heritage as a Public Good: Economic Analysis Applied to Historic Cities," in *Global Public Goods: International Cooperation in the 21st Century*, ed. Inge Kaul, Isabelle Grunberg, and Marc Stern (New York, Oxford: Oxford University Press, 1999), 240–63, http://econpapers.repec.org/RePEc:oxp:obooks:9780195130522.

Sexton, Michael, "Accurately Attributing the Sony Hack Is More Important than Retaliating," *Georgetown Security Studies Review*, January 13, 2015, http://georgetownsecuritystudiesreview.org/2015/01/13/accurately-attributing-the-sony-hack-is-more-important-than-retaliating/.

Shachtman, Noah, "Pirates of the ISPs: Tactics for Turning Online Crooks Into International Pariahs," *Brookings Cybersecurity Paper*, June 2011, http://www.brookings.edu/~/media/Files/rc/papers/2011/0725_cybersecurity_shachtman/0725_cybersecurity_shachtman.pdf.

Shaw, Malcolm, *International Law*, 4th ed. (Cambridge: Cambridge University Press 1997).

Silverman, Jacob, "A Gun, a Printer, an Ideology," *The New Yorker*, May 7, 2013, http://www.newyorker.com/tech/elements/a-gun-a-printer-an-ideology.

Singer, Peter Warren, *Corporate Warriors: The Rise of the Privatized Military Industry* (Ithaca, NY: Cornell University Press, 2011).

Sledge, Matt, "Edward Snowden Gambles On Alliance With WikiLeaks," *The Huffington Post*, June 27, 2013, http://www.huffingtonpost.com/2013/06/27/edward-snowden-wikileaks_n_3506232.html.

Sneed, Tierney, "Sony Hack Takes Darker Turn," *US News & World Report*, December 17, 2014, http://www.usnews.com/news/articles/2014/12/17/sony-hack-takes-darker-turn-with-interview-terror-threat.

Snowden, Edward, "Testimony before the Parliament of the European Union," March 7, 2014, http://library.blountsfolly.com/space/items/show/171.

Sofner, Abraham, David Clark, and Whitfield Diffie, "Cyber Security and International Agreements," in *Proceedings of a Workshop on Deterring Cyberattacks: Informing Strategies and Developing Options for U.S. Policy*, ed. Committee on Deterring Cyberattacks: Informing Strategies and Developing Options; National Research Council (Washington, DC; [s.l.]: National Academies Press, 2010), http://www.nap.edu/catalog.php?record_id=12997.

Solum, Lawrence B. and Minn Chung, "The Layers Principle: Internet Architecture and the Law," *Notre Dame L. Rev.* 79 (2003): 815.

Spar, Debora L., "The Public Face of Cyberspace," in *Global Public Goods: International Cooperation in the 21st Century*, ed. Inge Kaul, Isabelle Grunberg, and Marc Stern (New York, Oxford: Oxford University Press, 1999), 344–62.

Sparkes, Matthew, "Internet in North Korea: Everything You Need to Know," December 23, 2014, sec. Technology, http://www.telegraph.co.uk/technology/11309882/Internet-in-North-Korea-everything-you-need-to-know.html.

Stadtmiller, Mandy, "Virtual Reality Sex Is Coming — and the Toys Are Already Here," *Mashable*, May 29, 2015, http://mashable.com/2015/05/29/virtual-reality-sex/.

"Static," *The Twilight Zone*, season 2, episode 20 (1961).

Stephenson, Neal, *Cryptonomicon* (New York: Avon Books 1999).

Stewart, Mark G. and John Mueller, "Cost-Benefit Analysis of Advanced Imaging Technology Full Body Scanners for Airline Passenger Security Screening," *Journal of Homeland Security and Emergency Management* 8, no. 1 (2011), http://politicalscience.osu.edu/faculty/jmueller/ait2.pdf.

Stiglitz, Joseph E., "Knowledge as a Global Public Good," in *Global Public Goods: International Cooperation in the 21st Century*, ed. Inge Kaul, Isabelle Grunberg, and Marc Stern (New York, Oxford: Oxford University Press, 1999), 308–25.

Stout, Hilary, "Comcast-Time Warner Cable Deal's Collapse Leaves Frustrated Customers Out in the Cold," *The New York Times*, April 26, 2015, http://www.nytimes.com/2015/04/27/business/media/mergers-collapse-leaves-frustrated-cable-customers-out-in-the-cold.html.

Streck, John, "Pulling the Plug on Electronic Town Meetings: Participatory Democracy and the Reality of Usenet," in *The Politics of Cyberspace*, ed. Chris Toulouse and Timothy W. Luke (New York: Routledge, 1998), 18–47.

Sunstein, Cass R., *Republic.com 2.0* (Princeton, NJ: Princeton University Press, 2007).

Sy, J. Habib, "Global Communications for a More Equitable World," in *Global Public Goods: International Cooperation in the 21st Century*, ed. Inge Kaul, Isabelle Grunberg, and Marc Stern (New York, Oxford: Oxford University Press, 1999), 326–43.

Tambini, Damian, Danilo Leonardi, and Christopher T. Marsden, *Codifying Cyberspace: Communications Self-Regulation in the Age of Internet Convergence* (Routledge, 2008).

Tanz, Jason, "Playing for Time: A Father, a Dying Son, and the Quest to Make the Most Profound Videogame Ever," *Wired*, January 2016, http://www.wired.com/2016/01/that-dragon-cancer/.

Tate, Julie, "Bradley Manning Sentenced to 35 Years in WikiLeaks Case," *The Washington Post*, August 20, 2013, https://www.washingtonpost.com/world/national-security/judge-to-sentence-bradley-manning-today/2013/08/20/85bee184-09d0-11e3-b87c-476db8ac34cd_story.html.

Taylor, Adam, "The Simple Way Google Maps Could Side-Step Its Crimea Controversy," *The Washington Post*, April 1, 2014, https://www.washingtonpost.com/news/worldviews/wp/2014/04/01/the-simple-way-google-maps-could-side-step-its-crimea-controversy/.

Taylor, Jr., Fred and Jerry Carter, "Cyberspace Superiority Considerations," in *Conflict and Cooperation in Cyberspace: The Challenge to National Security*, ed. Panayotis A. Yannakogeorgos and Adam B. Lowther (Boca Raton: Taylor & Francis, 2013), 13–25.

Thingiverse, https://www.thingiverse.com/ (last accessed September 30, 2015).

Timberg, Craig and Ellen Nakashima, "Agreements with Private Companies Protect U.S. Access to Cables' Data for Surveillance," *The Washington Post*, July 6, 2013, http://www.washingtonpost.com/business/technology/agreements-with-private-companies-protect-us-access-to-cables-data-for-surveillance/2013/07/06/aa5d017a-df77-11e2-b2d4-ea6d8f477a01_story.html.

Toulouse, Chris, "Introduction," in *The Politics of Cyberspace*, ed. Chris Toulouse and Timothy W. Luke (New York: Routledge, 1998), 1–16.

Treaty Banning Nuclear Weapon Tests in the Atmosphere, in Outer Space and Under Water, (entered into force October 10, 1963).

Treaty Between The United States of America and The Union of Soviet Socialist Republics on The Limitation of Anti-Ballistic Missile Systems (ABM Treaty) (May 26, 1972).

Treaty on Principles Governing the Activities of States in the Exploration and Use of Outer Space, Including the Moon and Other Celestial Bodies, (entered into force October 10, 1967).

Treaty on the Non-Proliferation of Nuclear Weapons, 729 UNTS 161 (entered into force March 5, 1970).

Turner, Fred, *From Counterculture to Cyberculture: Stewart Brand, the Whole Earth Network and the Rise of Digital Utopianism* (Chicago: University of Chicago Press 2006).

UN Charter (1945).

United Nations Convention on the Law of the Sea (December 10, 1982).

United Nations General Assembly, Res. 217 A(III). Universal Declaration of Human Rights, (December 10, 1948).

United Nations General Assembly, "Res. 37/92: Principles Governing the Use by States of Artificial Earth Satellites for International Direct Television Broadcasting," December 10, 1982.

United Nations Human Rights Council's Working Group on Arbitrary Detention, Opinion No. 54/2015 concerning Julian Assange (Sweden and the United Kingdom of Great Britain and Northern Ireland).

United Nations Security Council, S/RES/138 Question relating to the case of Adolf Eichmann (1960).

United States Air Force, *Legal Reviews of Weapons and Cyber Capabilities, A.F. Instruction 51-402* (July 27, 2011).

United States Constitution.

United States Department of Defense, "Department of Defense Strategy for Operating in Cyberspace," July 2011, http://library.blountsfolly.com/space/items/show/184.

United States Department of Justice, "Exhibit A: Procedures Used by the National Security Agency for Targeting Non-United States Persons Reasonably Believed to Be Located Outside the United States to Acquire Foreign Intelligence Information Pursuant to Section 702 of the Foreign Intelligence Surveillance Act of 1978, as Amended," (July 28, 2009).

United States Department of Justice, "Memorandum for the Attorney General: Proposed Amendment to the Department of Defense Procedures to Permit the National Security Agency to Conduct Analysis of Communications Metadata Associated with Persons in the United States," (November 20, 2007.)

United States Department Of State, "Outcomes from the International Telecommunication Union 2014 Plenipotentiary Conference in Busan, Republic of Korea," Press Release/Media Note, *U.S. Department of State*, (November 11, 2014), http://www.state.gov/r/pa/prs/ps/2014/11/233914.htm.

United States v. Jones, 132 S. Ct. 945 (2012).

United States v. Wang et al. - Indictment (W.D. Penn. 2014).

Verizon v. FCC, No. 11-1355, 740 F. 3d 623 (Court of Appeals, Dist. of Columbia Circuit 2014)

Wakefield, Jane, "Smart LED Light Bulbs Leak Wi-Fi Passwords," *BBC News*, July 8, 2014, http://www.bbc.com/news/technology-28208905.

Walzer, Michael, "The Moral Standing of States: A Response to Four Critics," *Philosophy & Public Affairs*, 1980, 209–29.

Wassenaar Arrangement, "About Us," http://www.wassenaar.org/about-us/ (last visited Feb. 17. 2016).

Weisman, Aly, "A Timeline of the Crazy Events in the Sony Hacking Scandal," *Business Insider*, December 9, 2014, http://www.businessinsider.com/sony-cyber-hack-timeline-2014-12.

Werbach, Kevin, "A Layered Model for Internet Policy," *J. on Telecomm. & High Tech. L.* 1 (2002): 37.

Werbach, Kevin, "Breaking the Ice: Rethinking Telecommunications Law for the Digital Age," *J.* on Telecomm. & High Tech. L. 4 (2005): 59.

White House, Executive Order -- Imposing Additional Sanctions with Respect to North Korea (Jan. 2, 2015), http://www.whitehouse.gov/the-press-office/2015/01/02/executive-order-imposing-additional-sanctions-respect-north-korea

White House, "PPD-20: U.S. Cyber Operations," January 2013,

Alfred North Whitehead, *Science and the Modern World* (Simon and Schuster, 1967).

Wight, Martin, *International Theory: The Three Traditions* (Holmes & Meier for the Royal Institute of International Affairs, 1992).

Wikileaks, "What is Wikileaks" (Nov. 3, 2015) https://wikileaks.org/What-is-Wikileaks.html.

Wilson, Woodrow, "Fourteen Points" (Jan. 8, 1918) http://avalon.law.yale.edu/20th_century/wilson14.asp.

Wingfield, Thomas C., "Legal Aspects of Offensive Information Operations in Space," 1998, http://www.au.af.mil/au/awc/awcgate/dod-io-legal/wingfield.pdf.

Wittes, Benjamin, "The Intelligence Legitimacy Paradox," blog, *Lawfare*, (May 15, 2014), http://www.lawfareblog.com/2014/05/the-intelligence-legitimacy-paradox/.

World Wide Web Consortium, "About W3C," https://www.w3.org/Consortium/ (last visited Feb. 11, 2016).

Yahoo! Inc. v. La Ligue Contre Le Racisme, 433 F. 3d 1199 (9th Cir. 2006).

Yannakogeorgos, Panayotis A. and Adam B. Lowther, "The Prospects for Cyber Deterrence: American Sponsorship of Global Norms," in *Conflict and Cooperation in Cyberspace: The Challenge to National Security*, ed. Panayotis A. Yannakogeorgos and Adam B. Lowther (Boca Raton: Taylor & Francis, 2013), 49–77.

Zaid, Mark S., "Military Might versus Sovereign Right: The Kidnapping of Dr. Humberto Alvarez-Machain and the Resulting Fallout," *Hous. J. Int'l L.* 19 (1996): 829.

Zalnieriute, Monika, "An International Constitutional Moment for Data Privacy in the Times of Mass-Surveillance," *International Journal of Law and Information Technology* 23, no. 2 (2015): 99–133.

Zalnieriute, Monika and Thomas Schneider, "ICANN's Procedures and Policies in the Light of Human Rights, Fundamental Freedoms and Democratic Values" (Council of Europe, June 16, 2014).

Zetter, Kim, *Countdown to Zero Day : Stuxnet and the Launch of the World's First Digital Weapon* (New York: Crown Publishers, 2014).

Zetter, Kim, "Everything We Know About Ukraine's Power Plant Hack," *WIRED*, January 20, 2016, http://www.wired.com/2016/01/everything-we-know-about-ukraines-power-plant-hack/.

Note on Indexing

E-IR's publications do not feature indexes. If you are reading this book in paperback and want to find a particular word or phrase you can do so by downloading a free PDF version of this book from the E-IR website.

View the e-book in any standard PDF reader such as Adobe Acrobat Reader (pc) or Preview (mac) and enter your search terms in the search box. You can then navigate through the search results and find what you are looking for. In practice, this method can prove much more targeted and effective than consulting an index.

If you are using apps (or devices) to read our e-books, you should also find word search functionality in those.

You can find all of our e-books at: http://www.e-ir.info/publications